The Monon

American Science

M000272053

CRITICAL EXPLORATIONS IN SCIENCE FICTION AND FANTASY
(a series edited by Donald E. Palumbo and C.W. Sullivan III)

The Monomyth in American Science Fiction Films

28 Visions of the Hero's Journey

Donald E. Palumbo

CRITICAL EXPLORATIONS IN SCIENCE FICTION AND FANTASY, 48
Series Editors Donald E. Palumbo *and* C.W. Sullivan III

McFarland & Company, Inc., Publishers
Jefferson, North Carolina

The author and the publisher gratefully acknowledge permission to reprint excerpts from the following: "The Monomyth in James Cameron's *The Terminator*: Sarah as Monomythic Heroine" by Donald C. Palumbo. *The Journal of Popular Culture* 41:3 (2008): 413–27. Used by permission of *The Journal of Popular Culture*. "The Monomyth in *Star Trek* (2009): Kirk and Spock Together Again for the First Time" by Donald C. Palumbo. *The Journal of Popular Culture* 46:1 (2013): 143–72. Used by permission of *The Journal of Popular Culture*. "The Monomyth in *Back to the Future*: Science Fiction Film Comedy as Adolescent Wish Fulfillment Fantasy" by Donald C. Palumbo. *The Journal of the Fantastic in the Arts* 17:1 (Spring 2006): 60–76. Used by permission of *The Journal of the Fantastic in the Arts*. "The Monomyth in *Star Trek* Films" by Donald C. Palumbo. From *The Influence of* Star Trek *on Television, Film and Culture* © 2008. Edited by Lincoln Geraghty. Series Editors Donald E. Palumbo and C. W. Sullivan III. Used by permission of McFarland & Company, Inc., Box 611, Jefferson NC 28640. www.mcfarlandpub.com. "*Star Wars*: A Myth for Our Time" by Andrew Gordon. *Literature/Film Quarterly* 6:4 (Fall 1978): 314–26. Used by permission of *Literature/ Film Quarterly* @ Salisbury University, Salisbury, MD 21801.

LIBRARY OF CONGRESS CATALOGUING-IN-PUBLICATION DATA

Palumbo, Donald, 1949–
    The monomyth in American science fiction films : 28 visions of the hero's journey / Donald E. Palumbo.
        p.   cm. — (Critical explorations in science fiction and fantasy ; 48)
    [Donald E. Palumbo and C.W. Sullivan III, series editors]
    Includes bibliographical references and index.
    Includes filmography.

    ISBN 978-0-7864-7911-5 (softcover : acid free paper) ⬳
    ISBN 978-1-4766-1851-7 (ebook)

    1. Heroes in motion pictures.   2. Science fiction films—United States—History and criticism.   3. Heroes on television.   4. Superhero television programs—United States—History and criticism.   5. Campbell, Joseph, 1904–1987—Criticism and interpretation.   I. Title.
PN1995.9.H44P36 2014
791.43'652—dc23   2014037043

BRITISH LIBRARY CATALOGUING DATA ARE AVAILABLE

On the cover: Keanu Reeves in *The Matrix*, 1999 (Photofest)

Printed in the United States of America

McFarland & Company, Inc., Publishers
    Box 611, Jefferson, North Carolina 28640
    www.mcfarlandpub.com

Table of Contents

Introduction—On Joseph Campbell's Monomyth and *The Hero with a Thousand Faces*

Already abstracted from numerous mythological, religious, and fantastic sources, the monomyth has also been repeatedly replicated since (as well as prior to) Joseph Campbell's compelling and spiritually insightful explication in 1949's *The Hero with a Thousand Faces*. In addition to serving as the underlying plot structure in the initial *Star Wars* trilogy, for which it is most widely known, Campbell's interpretation likewise occurs in meticulous detail in some of the most highly regarded, artistically successful science fiction novels from the second half of the twentieth century—such as Alfred Bester's *The Stars My Destination*, Daniel Keyes' *Flowers for Algernon*, each of the six volumes in Frank Herbert's *Dune* series, and Gene Wolfe's four-volume *The Book of the New Sun* and its sequel, *The Urth of the New Sun*—as well as in numerous science-fiction films from this period and the beginning of the twenty-first century.[1] In addition to the initial *Star Wars* trilogy—*Star Wars Episode IV: A New Hope* (1977), *Star Wars Episode V: The Empire Strikes Back* (1980), and *Star Wars Episode VI: Return of the Jedi* (1983)—these films include *The Time Machine* (1960), *Logan's Run* (1976), *Time After Time* (1979), *Escape from New York* (1981), *Tron* (1982), *Dreamscape* (1984), *The Last Starfighter* (1984), *Dune* (1984), *The Terminator* (1984), *Back to the Future* (1985), *Total Recall* (1990), *The Matrix* (1999), and each of the first eleven *Star Trek* films (1980 through 2009). Moreover, as well as informing both Herbert's and David Lynch's *Dune*, the monomyth plot structure also underlies the subsequent SciFi channel miniseries *Dune* (2000) and *Children of Dune* (2003). While these films and miniseries span half a century, they are concentrated in the eight-year period between 1977 and 1985, the second great American science-fiction film boom inaugurated by *Star Wars* and culminating in *Back to the Future*. Thus, it is tempting to surmise that the phenomenal success of *Star Wars Episode IV* inspired a large number of filmmakers

1

to try to emulate that success by employing the same complex but versatile plot structure in their various projects. Yet the monomyth is a mythological or fantasy, and not a science-fiction, plot structure; so its use in science fiction films, miniseries, and novels is somewhat counterintuitive. This volume will examine these twenty-six such films and two miniseries to demonstrate to what extent they all use the monomyth as their underlying plot structure and to what extent, in doing so, they collectively ring a wide variety of innovative changes on this archetypal narrative pattern.

Although it does contain a most elaborate articulation of the monomyth— a term coined by James Joyce in *Finnegans Wake* (Campbell 30 n, citing *Finnegans Wake* 581)[2]—*The Hero with a Thousand Faces* is far more than the mere explication of a literary formula passed down to the present day from the prehistory of the oldest myths, legends, and folk tales. *The Hero with a Thousand Faces* is arguably one of the many great intellectual achievements of the twentieth century, and in it Campbell derives the monomyth from the lives of Christ, Mohamed, and the Buddha, from dream analysis, and from the mythologies, fairy tales, legends, and fables of Judeo-Christianity, Islam, Buddhism, Hinduism, the Aztecs, the Mayans, the Native Americans of the plains, the Eskimos, the Pacific Islanders, the Chinese, the Greeks, the Egyptians, the Scandinavians, the Irish, the Persians, the Babylonians, the Sumerians, and the peoples of Iceland, Africa, Siberia, and Peru. Campbell focuses on the common elements in these many and varied myths, fairy tales, fables, and dreams—which he feels demonstrate the commonality of the human experience—in the hope that his study might contribute to the world's unification (Campbell viii). Yet the underlying subject matter of *The Hero with a Thousand Faces* is spiritual enlightenment.

That the monomyth is derived in part from the lives of religious leaders is not a coincidence, as it deals with deeply spiritual issues; and *The Hero with a Thousand Faces* is not only an extended essay on enlightenment, it is also in itself a way to enlightenment. The monomyth *per se* is so deeply engaging because it deals essentially with the process, and difficulty, of negotiating life's many transitions; it does this through imitating the overall structure of the primitive rites of passage: separation or departure, initiation, and return. (These rituals serve to protect us from two truths—that change is unavoidable and that the individual is insignificant in the cosmic scheme of things—by implying that the ritual itself causes and controls change and by focusing on the individual who is to be transformed by the ritual.) Thus, the monomyth's innate theme is transcendence, getting past what you are in order to become what you are becoming. And its underlying message is the message of mythology: that all of life's many metamorphoses, and the challenges they engender, happen to everyone. The monomyth is the story of negotiating these transitions in the self and in one's station in life via rituals of transformation and renewal; thus, it is about everybody's inevitable and recurring transformations and renewals, about the continuous rebirth and rediscovery of the self. The hero's physical journey symbolizes everyone's psychological journey of rebirth and rediscovery. And in the monomyth these life transitions are represented by the symbolic or literal death and rebirth of the hero, being swallowed in the belly of the whale, the final episode of the Departure Stage. Moreover, the monomyth's innate theme of transcendence is represented in the penultimate episode of the Initiation Stage, Apotheosis, which in itself symbolizes attaining spiritual enlightenment. Finally, as the monomyth *per se* exhibits a thoroughly like-things-within/beside-like-things or fractal structure, the structure of real systems as they exist in the real world, it can be seen to be an organic or naturally occurring narrative pattern; it is the lucid dream, rather than the premeditated invention, of all humankind.

Campbell asserts that the hero is each of us (365). The monomyth is deeply compelling as a plot structure because it symbolizes everyone's continuous rediscovery of the self as each of us evolves from one stage of life to the next, as each of us transcends continuously what-we-are to become what-we-are-becoming; that is, the outward, physical journey of the hero represents everybody's inward, psychological journey of continuous re-creation and self-discovery (29, 259, 321). Campbell defines the monomyth as that single "consciously controlled" pattern most widely exhibited in the world's folk tales, myths, and religious fables (255–56). Its morphology is, in broad outline, that of the quest. The hero is called to an adventure, crosses the threshold to an unknown world to endure tests and trials, and usually returns with a boon that benefits his fellows (36–38). Although agreeing with Carl Jung that the many variations on the monomyth "defy description," Campbell's analysis fills in this outline with an anatomy of the archetypal hero and descriptions of those specific incidents likely to occur at each stage of his adventure (246).

Sometimes the product of a virgin or special birth (297–314), the hero may have been exiled or orphaned, may be seeking his father, and may triumph over pretenders as the true son (318–34). His mother may be assumed into heaven or crowned a queen (119–20). He possesses exceptional gifts, and the world he inhabits may suffer symbolic deficiencies (37). He does not fear death, and he may be destined to make the world spiritually significant or humankind comprehensible to itself (356, 388). If a warrior, he will change the status quo (334–41). If a lover, his triumph may be symbolized by a woman and accomplishing the impossible task may lead him to the bridal bed (342–45). If a tyrant or ruler, his search for the father will lead him to the invisible unknown from which he will return as a lawgiver (345–49). If a world-redeemer, he will learn that he and the father are one (349–54). If a saint or mystic, he will transcend life and myth to enter an inexpressible realm beyond form (354–55).

Campbell argues that "the standard path of the mythological adventure is a magnification of the formula represented in rites of passage: *separation—initiation—return* ... the nuclear unit of the monomyth" (30). As this is "some sort of dying to the world" followed by "the interval of the hero's nonentity, so that he comes back as one reborn," the primitive rites of passage, and by extension the adventure of the hero, all symbolize death and rebirth—the death of one's old pattern of life and a rebirth into one's new situation—and thus is the innate theme of the monomyth transcendence, moving beyond the self that one is in order to become the self that one is becoming (35–36). Campbell's primary example of such rites of passage, which he returns to repeatedly (10–11, 137–42, 154, 175), is the ancient initiation ritual practiced among Australian Aborigines. This rite is a perfect example of the separation—initiation—return pattern: The children to be initiated are first in the company of the tribal mothers, are then abducted by the masked adult male members of the tribe and taken to a ritual location (usually a cave or clearing) where the initiation ceremony is performed, and then are returned to the tribe as adult members, transfigured. The initiation ceremony itself is often a test that the initiates must survive; it may involve circumcision or scarification, to impress upon the initiates and the tribe that the children are being transformed; and it may even entail the death of one or more of the initiates, to impress upon the others the importance of the ceremony.[3] Moreover, much as the rites of passage entail a dying to the world so that the initiate comes back as one reborn, so too do "tribal ceremonies of birth, initiation, marriage, burial, installation, and so forth" (383). Thus is everyone the initiate and, by extension, the hero of the adventure. The message of myth is that, in this sense, everything happens to everybody.

The adventure's Separation or Departure Stage entails up to five incidents: receiving a call to adventure, which is sometimes a call to live or to die, in the guise of a blunder that reveals an unknown world or the appearance of a herald character from that world; refusing the call; receiving supernatural aid; crossing a magical threshold that leads to a sphere of rebirth; and being swallowed in the belly of the whale, a sojourn into the unknown symbolizing death and resurrection that may involve an underground journey that represents a descent into hell (36, 51). The herald character from the unknown world may be veiled, hooded, dark, in shadows, reviled by the world, evil, or a beast (52–53). Supernatural aid may be offered by an old man or crone, who provides a talisman in a setting suggesting a womb-like sense of peace, or by some guide, teacher, wizard, ferryman, hermit, or smith (one who works with his hands), who offers aid in a context that suggests danger or temptation (69–73). The threshold to the unknown world may be defended by a protective guardian or a destructive watchman (77–82). And in being swallowed in the belly of the whale, the single episode that is most elaborately replicated in science fiction films employing the monomyth, the hero may enter a temple guarded by gargoyles and may be mutilated, dismembered, or literally or symbolically killed (92).

The Initiation Stage includes up to six incidents: numerous tests endured in the road of trials, including the hero's assimilation of his opposite, shadow, or unsuspected self; meeting a mother-goddess, who may take the form of the Lady of the House of Sleep, the bad mother, or the Universal Mother; encountering a temptress; atonement with the father; apotheosis; and acquiring a boon (36, 110–11). To cope with the tests endured in the road of trials, the hero may be aided by the advice, talismans, amulets, or agents of his supernatural helper(s), or a "benign power" might protect him everywhere (97). A voyage to the underworld, which symbolizes death and rebirth and might also represent being swallowed in the belly of the whale, may be one of the tests in the road of trials (98). Another echo of being swallowed in the belly of the whale, the hero might also assimilate his opposite or shadow or unsuspected self "by swallowing it or by being swallowed" by it (108). That is, in literary terms, the adversary that the hero first mistook for his foil is ultimately found to be, if not his double, then most likely his shadow; the hero and his adversary have crucial superficial differences, but underlying these is a wealth of unsuspected similarity.

Following the road of trials is the meeting with the goddess, who is every woman, and with whom the hero may have a "mystical marriage" in a special location (118, 109). As the Lady of the House of Sleep, the goddess is a beautiful incarnation of the hero's "bliss," the object of his desire, and is reminiscent of the nourishing good mother (110–11). But the goddess might also be the bad mother, who is "absent, unattainable ... hampering, forbidding, punishing ... forbidden," or castrating (111). Or she might be the all-encompassing Universal Mother, who combines all opposites and represents all that is good and all that is evil (114–15). The inversion of the meeting with the goddess is an encounter with woman as the temptress; and woman is the temptress, not the goddess, to the hero who has not yet mastered life—to the hero who has not yet completed the tests and trials and/or who has yet to experience that subsequent apotheosis through which his consciousness is "amplified" to such an extent that he can comprehend and accept the Universal Mother (120–21). Such an unenlightened or untested hero perceives women and sexuality as being sinful (122–23).

Following his encounter(s) with the goddess and the temptress, the hero experiences atonement with the father. The father is an "initiating priest through whom the young being passes on into the larger world" because, after the initiate in the rite has been taken from the mothers, the fathers collectively preside over the rite of initiation (136). And, just as the goddess is both the nurturing and the castrating mother, so, too, is the father both the protective and the ogre father. Thus, the encounter with the father can be either negative or positive, can result in the death of the initiate—who may be eaten by the father—or his transfiguration, and may involve symbolic castration (in rites of circumcision) as well as rites of initiation (139). Once the hero is able to reconcile good and evil (and, by extension, the other pairs of opposites united in apotheosis), "He beholds the face of the father, understands—and the two are atoned" (147). The hero "transcends life" in attaining apotheosis, through the unification of these opposites, and this both reconciles him to the father and enables him to accept the Universal Mother, yet attaining apotheosis necessitates "abandonment of the attachment to ego itself" (147, 130).

This is required because apotheosis symbolizes attaining enlightenment, and the enlightenment experience—put most concisely—entails perceiving the universe without filtering it through the lens of the self or ego; that is, it is (at the least) a selfless/egoless perception of being one with everything. Campbell expresses this most succinctly in stating that "The essence of oneself and the essence of the world: these two are one" (386). "Apotheosis" is a Greek word that means exaltation to divine rank or stature, becoming god-like; the hero's entire adventure is encapsulated in his apotheosis, for "the adventure of the hero represents the moment in his life when he achieved illumination" (259). And the specific illumination achieved in apotheosis is the apprehension of "'The Cosmogonic Cycle' … the great vision of the creation and destruction of the world" (38). To Achieve enlightenment or illumination is to attain Nirvana, and Campbell defines Nirvana as "the extinguishing of the Threefold Fire of Desire, Hostility, and Delusion" (163). Being one with the universe in the enlightenment state, "we are what was desired and feared" (162). Hence, one is free from desire and hostility because there is nothing external to want or to attack. And the very nature of the enlightenment experience frees one from the delusion that one is distinct and separate from the cosmic all, a delusion fostered by the ego. Yet, in attaining freedom from this delusion, one is "shattered" as by "a thunderbolt"—that is, consciousness is annihilated—and this state of enlightenment is traditionally achieved by contemplating the unification of such opposites as eternity and time, truth and illusoriness, the god and the goddess, death and birth, and yang, the male principle, and yin, the female principle (171).

It is perhaps worth mentioning at this point that, while this all sounds very mystical, the enlightenment experience itself is not intrinsically or necessarily mystical. As discussed by Campbell, it is no more (or less) mystical than consciousness; viewing it in mystical terms impedes understanding it as an experience entirely grounded in human physiology. Echoing Campbell some fifty years later, psychologist David Wulff argues that "spiritual experiences are so consistent across cultures, across time and across faiths ... that it suggests a common core that is likely a reflection of structures and processes in the human brain" (Begley 53). Neurologist James Austin reasons that

> In order to feel that time, fear, and self-consciousness have dissolved ... certain brain circuits must be interrupted.... Activities in the amygdala, which ... registers fear, must be damped. Parietal-lobe circuits, which ... mark the sharp distinctions between self and world, must go quiet. Frontal-lobe and temporal-lobe circuits, which mark time and generate self-awareness, must disengage [52].

Mark Persinger "suspects that religious experiences are evoked by mini electrical storms in the temporal lobes" (55). And using "brain-imaging data they collected from Tibetan Buddhists lost in meditation ... to identify what seems to be the brain's spirituality circuit," Andrew Newberg and Eugene d'Aquili observe that "neurons in the superior parietal lobe ... had gone dark"; as "this region processes information about space and time ... determines where the body ends and the rest of the world begins," they hypothesize that intense meditation blocks "sensory inputs to this region" to "prevent the brain from forming the distinction between self and not-self.... [T]he left orientation area cannot find any boundary between the self and the world.... The right orientation area ... defaults to a feeling of infinite space. The meditators feel that they have touched infinity" (53). And, in fact, the mental process of unifying each of the pairs of opposites united in apotheosis—that mode of meditation that leads to the enlightenment experience—involves the contemplation of the infinite.

This movement from Meeting with the Goddess to Atonement with the Father to Apotheosis mirrors both the initiation ritual itself and "image of the bisexual god," the Bodhisattva, who is the "mystery of the theme of initiation" (Campbell 162). Beyond all human images of god, the Uncreated Uncreating as perceived in apotheosis (here represented by the Bodhisattva) is likewise androgynous; thus does apotheosis unite the opposites of male and female. And the opposites of good and evil are already united in both the concept of the Universal Mother and also in the concept of the protective/ogre father. As the oneness-of-being perceived in enlightenment is also that unity with the universe attained through death, for "the beatitude of the state of perfect being ... resembles death" (207; see also 12, 365–66, and 371), thus does apotheosis unite the opposites of death and life and also of eternity and time. (Here "eternity" is the Eastern notion of temporality, in which all moments always exist, while "time" is the Western notion of temporality, in which only the evanescent present moment exists.) And in apotheosis the unification of the male and female duality symbolizes the oneness of time and eternity (169). Strangely enough, while this is the monomyth's most crucial single episode, Apotheosis is also among those episodes most muted or entirely neglected in science-fiction films; yet "if one or another of the basic elements of the archetypal pattern is omitted ... the omission itself can speak volumes for the history and pathology of the example" (38). And the hero returns from his adventure with "the means for the regeneration of his society as a whole," the boon (38). The highest boon is enlightenment or revelation; immortality is a common but less desirable boon, for to the hero who attains enlightenment "Immortality is ... experienced as a present fact" and any quest for physical immortality is therefore superfluous; much less valuable still are the symbolic boons of wealth and power (189).

The Return Stage also contains up to six incidents: refusing to return; magic flight from the unknown world; rescue from outside the unknown world; re-crossing the threshold; attaining the power to cross the threshold freely; and the hero's realization that he is the vehicle of the cosmic cycle of change (37). While the Departure Stage (which contains the belly of the whale episode) is that stage of the monomyth most elaborately developed in science-fiction films, the Return Stage is that which is most often neglected. The Return Stage contains mutually exclusive episodes; thus, while elements throughout the monomyth may be omitted and the pattern of the whole left intact in any case, it is impossible for all the episodes of the Return Stage to occur in a single coherent narrative. The first possibility is that the hero may refuse to return or to bestow the boon upon/share the boon with his fellows (193). Or the hero's return could be a Magic Flight that may be furthered by supernatural means, if he has pleased the gods or is helped by a benign threshold guardian, or it may be "complicated by marvels of magical obstruction or evasion," if the hero has angered the gods or is opposed by the threshold guardian (196–97). Conversely, the hero might toss delaying objects behind him to hamper his pursuers (201). Or the hero might be rescued from outside the unknown world; that is, agents from the known world may have to enter the unknown world to retrieve him (207).

Several things may happen in re-crossing the threshold from the unknown back to the known world. First, the hero must overcome the temptation to refuse to accept everyday reality; then, amid much difficulty, the hero may convey the wisdom of the gods acquired in the unknown world (symbolically, the way to enlightenment) to the known world (218). Also, a dilation of time may occur in transiting from the unknown to the known world—the Brigadoon effect, in which (for example) a day in the unknown world is equivalent to a century in the known world (223). Or there may be specific dangers in returning to the known world, and the hero must be "insulated" to withstand them (225). Finally, the hero may return to the known world with a "talisman" acquired in the unknown world, a proof that he has experienced an adventure there (226). He becomes master of the two worlds if he gains the "freedom to pass back and forth" between them or if he accepts his transcendence and so "becomes ripe, at last, for the great at-one-ment" with the divine (229, 237). And he gains the freedom to live in the known world, to work in this mundane realm without anxiety, by retaining an awareness that he is the "conscious vehicle" of cosmic change (239).

Clearly, *The Hero with a Thousand Faces* is deeply and ubiquitously concerned (if not obsessed) with the concept of enlightenment; and, although Campbell never quite explicitly asserts this himself, he nonetheless suggests repeatedly that the volume as a whole, and the explication of the monomyth it contains, is in itself a way or path to enlightenment. Thus does he conclude *The Hero with a Thousand Faces'* initial chapter, on "Tragedy and Comedy," with the promise that

> we have only to follow the thread of the hero-path. And where we had thought to find an abomination [the Minotaur], we shall find god [experience enlightenment]; where we had sought to slay another, we shall slay ourselves; where we had thought to travel outward, we shall come to the center of our own existence; where we had thought to be alone, we shall be with all the world [25; see also 267, 269–70, and 319–20].

And Campbell's analysis of the monomyth and the cosmogonic cycle—which, like the monomyth, "is presented with astonishing consistency in the sacred writings of all the continents" (39)—entails a description of at least a part of the fractal matrix of thought upon which the aspirant must meditate to achieve enlightenment. (See Figure 1.) One half of this matrix is a meditation on the three wonders of the Bodhisattva, the traditional path. The aspirant must unify the oppositions of the castrating mother and the nurturing mother to apprehend The Goddess. Then she must unify the oppositions of the ogre father and the protective father to apprehend The Father. Then he must unify the oppositions of The Goddess (the female principle, yin) and The Father (the male principle, yang) to apprehend The Bodhisattva, the bisexual god. Simultaneously, she must unify the oppositions of time and eternity and then realize how the unity of the male and female principles in The Bodhisattva is like the unity of time and eternity. A similar process of unifying opposites occurs in the other half of this matrix of thought, which is derived from Campbell's discussion throughout *The Hero with a Thousand Faces* (see particularly 149–171): the aspirant must unify the oppositions of the void (within) and the world (beyond) and the oppositions of the self (within) and the Self (beyond), then apprehend how the unification of these first two pairs of opposites is like the unification of the second two pairs of opposites; simultaneously, the aspirant must unify

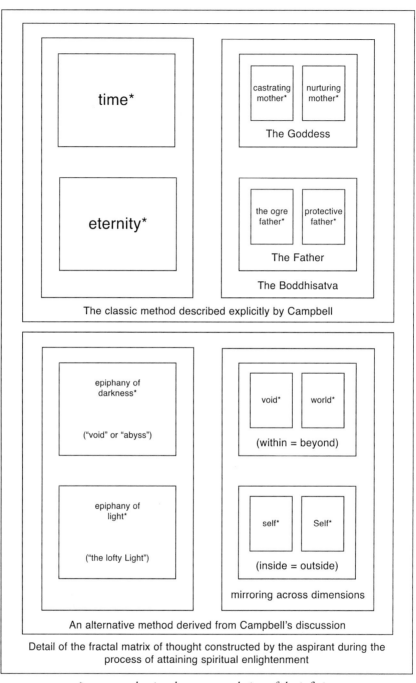

Figure 1. Detail of the Fractal Matrix of Thought Constructed by the Aspirant Engaged in the Process of Attaining Enlightenment.

the oppositions of the epiphany of darkness (the void or abyss) and the epiphany of light (the lofty Light) and then realize how the unity of "void is world" and of "self is Self" is like the unity of the epiphany of darkness and the epiphany of light. The aspirant may achieve enlightenment through either one of these meditations, but if she does not, then he must apprehend how the process represented by the first half of the matrix, the meditation on the three wonders of the Bodhisattva, is like the process represented by the other half of the matrix. It is tautological to note that successfully performing this mental exercise of comprehending the unity of opposites that touch on the infinite will ultimately result in the aspirant experiencing a state of enlightenment.

This matrix of thought engaged in by the aspirant to achieve enlightenment is fractal both because it involves the contemplation of infinities and also because it exhibits the repetition of similar elements on the same and on descending scales. "A visual representation of chaotic behavior," a fractal is an image "with an infinite amount of self-similarity" generated in "the realm of dynamical systems" by the "repeated application of an algorithm" or the reiteration of recursive geometric procedures (Laplante, 20, 3–4, 14–15). "Above all, fractal [means] self-similar" (Gleick, 103), and "'self-similarity' ... means a repetition of detail at descending scales" (Briggs and Peat, 90)—"pattern inside of pattern" (Gleick, 103)—as well as duplication across the same scale. Thus, in a fractal image "the structure of the whole is often reflected in every part," and any part might appear to be both "a small reproduction of the larger image" and a near-clone of innumerable like structures on the same scale (Laplante, 3). As the incorporation of the separate epiphanies of the Mother Goddess and the Father into the encompassing revelation of the bisexual god, the Bodhisattva, suggests (particularly as this is but one instance of the transcendence of dualities through the unification of opposites, yet represents all such instances), the very process of transcendence through which one is to achieve enlightenment has the fractal structure of self-similarity on the same and descending scales. This process is the attainment of revelation-within-revelation or of revelation-beyond-revelation, depending on how one looks at it; and both ways of looking at it are ultimately the same, just as both describe the same structure, the pattern of self-similarity on descending scales also exhibited in the temporal structure of the cosmogonic cycle (revealed to the hero in Apotheosis), with its progressively lesser cycles nested within each great round, and the analogous shells-within-shells physical structure of the cosmic egg, both of which Campbell discusses extensively (Campbell, 255–378; see particularly 274–78 for Campbell's description of the cosmic egg).

Not only does the thought process through which one attains enlightenment exhibit a fractal structure, but so does the monomyth itself, which represents and embodies this process, also exhibit a fractal structure. One can discern this structure by keeping in mind, first, that the Bodhisattva myth is a way to enlightenment that also reveals the monomyth's symbolic meaning, attaining enlightenment and conveying it to others, and, second, that the monomyth is a magnification of the formula represented in the rites of passage: separation—initiation—return, the monomyth's nuclear unit[4]; yet, as separation here is a symbolic death to the world, from which the hero returns as one reborn, the reenactment of this formula in these rites symbolizes death-and-rebirth as a metaphor for the initiate's transcendence of one stage of life to the next, so that each repetition of the death-and-rebirth motif within the monomyth is a symbolic reiteration of its overall separation—initiation—return structure on a smaller scale. Then, by relying solely on Campbell's explications of the monomyth's seventeen episodes, one can deduce that nearly every episode "mirrors the monomyth as a whole in at least one of three ways: by echoing its 'separation—initiation—return' structure symbolically in one or more death-and-rebirth incidents, symbols, or metaphors; by representing this structure literally in containing one or more initiation rituals *per se*; or by reflecting the symbolic action of the whole, which is attaining enlightenment and conveying it to others, through recapitulating in a relevant context one or more aspects of the Bodhisattva myth" (Palumbo, *Chaos*, 218; see 216–23 for a thorough analysis of each episode).

Of course, the monomyth is thoroughly fractal in numerous ways. Not only does it exhibit a thoroughly fractal internal structure, but it is also intrinsically fractal in both its derivation and its subsequent manifestations in that it appears in numerous works of fantasy (myths, fairy tales, folklore, etc.)—exhibits similarity across the same scale—prior to its articulation by Campbell in 1949 and has appeared in numerous other works since then, not only in the science fiction novels mentioned above (in addition to many other works of world literature), but also, most specifically, in the twenty-six science fiction films and two miniseries that are the subject of this volume. This strongly reinforces Campbell's contention that the monomyth is a naturally occurring phenomenon (the dream of humankind, and not something invented by Campbell) because fractal structures are characteristic of dynamical or nonlinear systems—that is, "the structures that provide the key to nonlinear dynamics prove to be fractal" (Gleick, 114)—and the real world is nonlinear because everything in it is part of the whole, interrelated and mutually interdependent; thus, the structures of real world phenomena are fractal. Reality's fractal self-similarity on the same scale is obvious in nature's ubiquitous reiteration-with-variations of everything, from sub-atomic particles, to microbes, to people, to galaxies, while self-similarity on descending scales is evident in turbulence, in the shapes of coastlines, clouds, and earth faults, and in branching in circulatory and bronchial systems as well as in plants. "Wherever chaos, turbulence, and disorder are found, fractal geometry is at play" (Briggs and Peat, 95), and the importance of dynamical systems analysis, also known as chaos theory, "comes from its re-visioning the world as dynamic and nonlinear, yet predictable in its very unpredictability" (Hayles, 143).

Although decades before the articulation of chaos theory by scientists in the 1970s, Campbell suggests the monomyth's fractal self-similarity on descending levels of scale in *The Hero with a Thousand Faces* in noting that mythology's ability "to touch and inspire deep creative centers dwells in the smallest nursery fairy tale—as the flavor of the ocean is contained in a droplet or the whole mystery of life within the egg of a flea"; thus is the monomyth, the sum of these "spontaneous productions of the psyche," the lucid dream of humanity (4). Moreover, in the cosmogonic cycle "universal consciousness" passes "from the deep sleep zone of the unmanifest, through dream, to the full day of waking; then back again through dream to the timeless dark" (266). Thus, the patterns of myth (i.e., the monomyth) are rationalized versions of the patterns of dream, and to say that passage between the manifest and the unmanifest proceeds through dream is also to say that it is mediated by myth. In astonishing congruence with this insight, "pioneering work of psychiatrist Montague Ullman and others ... indicates that even the structure of our dreams may be fractal. Researchers believe that the dream 'story' contains repetitions of the dreamer's central concerns. Reflections of these concerns can be found in both the overall 'story' and in its finer and finer details" (Briggs and Peat, 110). This is precisely the case with the pattern for the consciously controlled dream that is the monomyth. Its "story" (overall structure) and major concern, negotiating life's transitions through rites of passage, is reflected in component elements (the seventeen episodes) that embody themes of death and rebirth, transformation, and transcendence (its finer and finer details); yet nearly all of these elements are either reenactments of, symbolic of, or metaphors for the structure of the rites of passage itself: separation—initiation—return, the nuclear unit of the monomyth.

1

George Lucas' Original
Star Wars Trilogy

Andrew Gordon notes that "Viewers recognize that *Star Wars* [*A New Hope*] has no direct relation to external reality, but it does relate to our dreams of how we would *like* that reality to be" (325), and Steven Galipeau contends that, "Indeed, the entire *Star Wars* saga can be approached as a *cultural dream*" (1). One of the most successful motion pictures of all time, *Star Wars Episode IV: A New Hope* undeniably had a deep impact on the world psyche when it was released in 1977. One could easily argue that it has since had the most profound influence on American popular culture, of which it is profoundly derivative, of any film ever made. It was followed, and the initial trilogy completed, by the highly successful releases *of The Empire Strikes Back* in 1980 and *Return of the Jedi* in 1983. *Lord of the Rings* director Peter Jackson attests that "*Star Wars* smashed open the possibilities of what film could actually do. It was a seismic shift in how people perceived the cinema-going experience.... It was executed in a way that was so much more believable and so much more exhilarating than anything we had seen before" ("The Force Is with Them"). Today (2014) a Bing search of "Star Wars" pulls up 145,000,000 results, perhaps more than any other single two-word entry. (The current box office champion, 2009's *Avatar*, has 95,500,000 results; *Gone with the Wind* has 35,500,000 results; "The Beatles" yields 86,900,000 results; "Madonna" yields 67,600,000 results; and "Jesus Christ" yields 62,300,000 results.) Something akin to a revelation to its enormous audience, and unlike anything that had gone before it, *A New Hope* is to motion pictures what *Sergeant Pepper's Lonely Hearts Club Band* was a decade earlier to the music industry, only more so. And, by the measure of Bing results, while the Beatles actually may have been (and may still be) more popular than Jesus Christ, *Star Wars* is to this day more popular than either.

Consequently, while such a comprehensive and systematic analysis as this has not been attempted before, this is not the first essay to address the issue of the *Star Wars* trilogy's debt to Campbell's *The Hero with a Thousand Faces*. Robert G. Collins' "*Star Wars*: The Pastiche of Myth and the Yearning for a Past Future," which was published while *A New Hope* was still playing in theatres during the summer of 1977, attributes the phenomenal success of the film to three factors: its ground-breaking special effects, its many popular culture references, and its recycling of the Arthurian legend, one of the monomyth's sources. More accurately, Gordon's seminal article "*Star Wars*: A Myth for Our Time," published in 1978, while acknowledging the new film techniques employed, argues that *A New Hope* succeeds due to its combination of popular culture references and its use of Campbell's monomyth as its underlying plot structure. (Gordon, having seen only the first movie, does claim that all three stages of the monomyth are enacted in *A New Hope*, but, as is demonstrated below, it is actually the case that the full pattern of the monomyth is only developed throughout all three films of the initial trilogy.) Mary Henderson's 1997 Smithsonian Institution National Air and Space Museum Exhibition titled *Star Wars: The Magic of Myth* echoes Gordon's thesis in demonstrating in greater detail that prominent elements of the entire trilogy are its mythological allusions and its allusions to popular culture. Daniel Mackay takes issue with Henderson's assertion that the *Star Wars* trilogy is a myth in itself by arguing in "*Star Wars*: The Magic of the Anti-myth" that it is not a myth according to Campbell's own definition. Yet Jessica Tiffin almost simultaneously asserts, in "Digitally Remythicised: *Star Wars*, Modern Popular Mythology, and Madam and Eve," that the trilogy is "a myth in its own right" (67). (One might mention, here, that if the *Star Wars* trilogy is not, technically, a myth in itself, it is at the very least a science-fiction fairy tale; and fairy tales are, with myth and legend, a prominent source of Campbell's monomyth.) Finally, Galipeau's Jungian analysis of the trilogy in *The Journey of Luke Skywalker: An Analysis of Modern Myth and Symbol*, while it is only tangentially related to an analysis of the trilogy's use of Campbell's monomyth, argues that "*Star Wars* can be seen as adding to humanity's mythology" (5) and that all the characters in the trilogy are component parts of a whole personality working its way towards integration, self-awareness, and enlightenment.

The clue to solving the mystery of *A New Hope*'s (and, by extension, the entire trilogy's) incredible popularity may be Eric Rabkin's general dictum that "The delight of the fantastic is the discovery of old wine in new bottles" (11). Rabkin argues that fantastic literature is most successful when it repackages old and familiar tropes and formulas as something new and unfamiliar, and through this slight-of-hand subtly assures the audience that the new and unfamiliar is not to be feared because it is really something already known that is merely inhabiting a flimsy disguise. *A New Hope* in particular, and the *Star Wars* trilogy as a whole, provides two varieties of old wine in two types of new bottles, and thus exponentially increases its audience's delight in the fantastic. First, *Star Wars* successfully blends its use of the monomyth as its underlying plot structure, the really old wine, with its numerous allusions to much-more-recent elements of popular culture, old wines of a different vintage, and rebottles the result—not as fairy tale or fantasy or myth—but as science fiction. While Mary Henderson points out that "It is as if medieval legend had been sent into deep space" (12), Kelly and Parisi note that "Lucas' mythmaking is a novel convergence of Hans Christian Andersen and Isaac Asimov" (160). This creates a story that is already a blend of old wines in a new bottle. And Galipeau posits that "the story is at the core of the success of *Star Wars*" (2) while *Jedi* director Richard Marquand observes that "If there is one thing that I have learned from working on *Return of the Jedi* it is simply that the story is what really counts.... Special effects have their place—a very special place—in the *Star Wars* saga. But first and foremost comes the story" (*Return of the Jedi: Official Collectors' Edition*).

Yet the trilogy's ground-breaking special effects technology constitutes another kind of new bottle in which this story—already old wines in a new bottle—is repackaged as well. Collins argues that "one reason for the popular acclaim now accorded" *A New Hope* is that "writer-director George Lucas" is one of the few creators of "narrative film" to "have realized the unique capability of the medium," that "technical effects are genuinely creative as artistic technique" in this film in which "the visual magic [is] achieved by old materials given new movement" (1, 9–10 n). Mackay attributes "the phenomenal popularity" of *A New Hope* to its special effects more so than to its use of Campbell's monomyth: "*Star Wars* is an exciting spectacle movie, thoughtfully conceived, well-crafted, and featuring astonishing special effects thanks to innovations like the Dykstraflex Camera and the Electronic Motion Control System which, when used in concert with the creations of the film's crack model-building team, achieved the convincing illusion of immersing the audience in another world" (66). The end result, actress Carrie Fisher (Princess Leia) recalls, "was this sort of weird electric kind of reaction. One had never seen anything like it" ("Empire of Dreams"). Indeed, to see *New Hope*'s first extended shot of Darth Vader's enormous starship emerging out of the top of the screen in pursuit of Leia's smaller vessel in 1977 was a jaw-dropping movie experience. Still, Peter Jackson contends that "twenty-five years later, you don't remember the special effects. It's the characters who remain" ("The Characters of *Star Wars*"). And the characters are Jungian archetypes inhabiting a plot based on Campbell's monomyth. That these films are *still* so popular—Episode VII is due to be released in 2015—is a result of the "old wine in new bottles" appeal of both mythology and recent popular culture being repackaged as science fiction. But the added dimension of the unprecedented special effects technology it exhibits, which makes this material doubly new in a completely different way (than the intrinsic appeal of old wines in a new bottle already engendered by the story in itself), accounts for the unprecedented popularity of *New Hope* at the time of its release. It is not any of these elements—allusions to popular culture, the monomyth as underlying plot structure, or innovative film technology—in isolation, but their highly successful integration, that propelled *New Hope* to unparalleled popularity.

As the impact of the film's many allusions to the popular culture of the early twentieth century has faded with the passage of time, one also had to have seen *A New Hope* in 1977 to have fully experienced, not only the novelty of the special effects, but also the delight that the depth and breadth of these popular culture allusions engendered. Yet Tiffin argues that even in its 1997 re-release the trilogies' "appeal can be traced to the films' employment of popular cultural collage as much as to their investment in the initiatory scenarios of older forms such as myth, epic, and folklore" (66). Gordon generalizes that *A New Hope* is "a compendium of American pop and pulp culture ... *Star Wars* is literally constructed from bits and pieces of the usable past ... old movies, science fiction, television, and comic books—but held together at its most basic level by the ... the underlying structure of the 'monomyth'" (319, 315). And Lucas himself attests that "It's the flotsam and jetsam from the period when I was twelve years old.... All the books and films and comics that I liked when I was a child" ("*Star Wars*: The Year's Best Movie" 56). Happy "to unabashedly do all the things that have been done before" (Sherman 8), *A New Hope* in particular and the trilogy in general is especially indebted to space opera and science fiction, the western, old *Flash Gordon* and *Buck Rodgers* movie serials and comic strips, comic books generally, and a wide variety of old films.

Both Mary Henderson (149) and Gordon (317) note that *Star Wars'* genre is space opera, and both cite Brian Aldiss to argue that space operas "are, in their way, abstracts of the same impulses that lie behind traditional fairy tales" (Aldiss, 10). Gordon also attributes elements of *A New Hope* to the science fiction of Frank Herbert, Robert Heinlein, and Samuel R. Delany, to "the covers of science-fiction magazines and paperbacks," and to television's *Star Trek*, from which Lucas "lifts the conventions of 'deflector shields' and 'tractor beams'" (319). Gordon points out as well that "the scene in which Luke discovers his dead aunt and uncle is a reconstruction of a scene in John Ford's *The Searchers*," that Han Solo is "a gun for hire ... straight out of the old west," and that Chewbacca is Tonto to Han Solo's Lone Ranger (318). To these observations, Mary Henderson adds that "Mos Eisley's cantina is the frontier-town saloon, and Greedo is indeed the bounty hunter" (129).

Lucas acknowledges that in pitching the film in 1973 he explained that it was "based on the kind of Flash Gordon/Buck Rodgers comic book future" ("Empire of Dreams"). The crawl that begins each film, the convention of identifying each film as an "episode," the many wipes and fast dissolves, and the exhilarating pacing are all throwbacks to the *Flash Gordon* and *Buck Rodgers* movie serials of the late 1930s. Princess Leia's distinctive hairstyle in *A New Hope* is inspired by Queen Fria's coiffure in the Flash Gordon comic strip (see Mary Henderson 143). And Gordon sees Dr. Zarkov in Obi-Wan Kenobi, Dale Arden in Princess Leia, and a touch of Ming the Merciless ("the same black cape and … sarcastic courtesy") in Darth Vader (317). He also notes Vader's "uncanny resemblance" to Marvel Comics' Dr. Doom (319). Moreover, Mary Henderson points out that the Art Deco sets for Cloud City in *The Empire Strikes Back* were inspired by the Flash Gordon comic strips of the 1930s (182).

Although it may be a stretch to argue that *A New Hope* is especially influenced by *Forbidden Planet* (Gordon 317) or *The Wizard of Oz* (Gordon 317–18; Collins 2), to which there are some parallels, the first film and the trilogy as a whole draw significant inspiration from many types of movies in addition to the western. For example, Lucas acknowledges that "C-3PO was inspired by the robot in *Metropolis*" ("The Characters of *Star Wars*"), Fritz Lang's 1926 silent science-fiction film. Lucas also explains that "The pirate films and the romantic films of the '40s was definitely an influence on *Star Wars* … the Errol Flynn types of movies…. The whole premise of *Star Wars* is that it's a romantic fantasy in the great romantic traditions of mythology and King Arthur" ("The Birth of the Light Sabre"). Gordon notes that "In the tradition of Douglass Fairbanks and Errol Flynn, Solo is the bold and reckless captain of a pirate ship" and that "Luke and the Princess swing on a rope across a chasm in the Death Star, conjuring up Fairbanks and Flynn" (318). (Luke and Leia reprise this rope swing in escaping from Jabba the Hutt's sail barge in *Return of the Jedi*.) Collins (7), Gordon (319), and Mary Henderson (174) all recognize that the aerial combat scenes in *A New Hope* are based on old war film footage; and visual effects expert Ken Ralston remembers that "to help inspire the effects team at I. L. M. [Industrial Light and Magic] Lucas had spliced together aerial dog fights from old war movies…. We matched frame to frame onto the action of that as well as we could" ("Empire of Dreams"). Finally, Gordon surmises that "Japanese samurai films must have contributed to the conception of the half-religious, half-military order of the Jedi Knights [in *A New Hope*], and the laser sword battle between Ben and Vader is surely indebted to the stylized combat of such movies" (318–19); Mary Henderson points out that Obi-Wan Kenobi's, Yoda's, and the Emperor's costumes are inspired by Japanese robes, that "Darth Vader's mask and helmet resemble the mempo mask and *Kabuto* helmet from the Japanese feudal period," that "the Imperial TIE fighters pilots were given helmets that suggest Japanese

[World War II] flyers," and that Lucas was a fan of Akira Kurosawa's films (186, 189, 176, 133); indeed, Lucas acknowledges that R2-D2 and C-3PO are inspired by the two peasants who observe the action from "the lowest level" in Kurosawa's 1958 *The Hidden Fortress* ("The Characters of *Star Wars*").

While the dual impacts of the *Star Wars* trilogy's groundbreaking special effects *and* (although maybe less so) of its references to early-twentieth-century popular culture have both faded with time, the underlying effect of the elements of the monomyth that reside in our collective unconscious being repackaged as science fiction has not. Tiffin theorizes in 1999 that the trilogy's "appeal relies on our recognition of basic narrative patterns as much as modern cultural clichés, which is perhaps why the [1997] re-release has been successful despite the inevitable datedness of the films" (67). Collins asserts that *A New Hope* "confronts us as the first omnibus work of generalized myth in the film medium" (2). Sherman suggests that "the mass audience is eagerly reapplying the structure of ancient myths and fairy tales to achieve some degree of psychic order" (6). Gordon attributes *A New Hope*'s "fundamental appeal" at its deepest level to "the epic structure of what Joseph Campbell in *The Hero with a Thousand Faces* calls 'the monomyth'" (314). And Mackay insists that "The authority behind the *Star Wars* story is ... Joseph Campbell" (66). Lucas acknowledges his debt to Campbell repeatedly. In Campbell's *The Hero's Journey* Lucas states, "I had an idea of doing a modern fairy tale.... I wrote many drafts of this work and then I stumbled across *The Hero with a Thousand Faces*.... And I said, 'This is it.' After reading more of Joe's books I began to understand how I could do this.... It's possible that if I had not run across him I would still be writing *Star Wars* today" (180). In the 2004 re-release of the *Star Wars Trilogy* DVDs Lucas explains, "There is no particular character in mythology or in stories that connects directly with Luke Skywalker. Luke Skywalker is a hero, and it's more generic; it's more of a motif that comes out of the various books that are written about mythology and fairy tales, such as Joseph Campbell's *The Hero with a Thousand Faces*" ("The Characters of *Star Wars*"). And Bill Moyers, whose televised conversations with Campbell were filmed at Lucas' Skywalker Ranch, recalls that "Joseph Campbell said to me, 'The best student I ever had was George Lucas'" ("Empire of Dreams").

Everyone agrees that the *Star Wars* trilogy is a modern "fairy tale" (Gordon 314; Mary Henderson 12; Tiffin 69; Galipeau 1); and Collins is the first to observe that the opening words of each film, "long ago, in a galaxy far, far away," is a variation of the "classic fairy tale 'once upon a time'" (2). Yet *Star Wars* is also, as Lucas points out, "the traditional, ritualistic coming-of-age story" ("Empire of Dreams"). As such it resonates even more thoroughly with the separation-initiation-return structure of the monomyth, which is also the structure of the primitive initiation ritual. And the end result of the ritual is the culmination of an adolescent wish-fulfillment fantasy, magically to transform from a child to an adult member of the tribe. Appropriately, Luke's adventure is an adolescent wish-fulfillment fantasy as well. By the end of *Return of the Jedi* Luke has received everything he had wished for at the beginning of *A New Hope*. Initially he wants desperately to get off the moisture farm and go to the Academy to become a pilot. He wants to be where the action is; as he complains to the droids, "If there is a bright, shining center of the universe, this is the place farthest from it." C-3PO excites Luke's interest in the rebellion, and, when he meets Obi-Wan Kenobi, the audience sees both that Luke has an interest in joining the rebellion and that he has an even deeper interest in learning something about his father and, beyond this, a desire to connect with his father by becoming a Jedi Knight himself. By the end of *A New Hope* Luke has joined the rebellion and become the hero who has successfully piloted his X-wing fighter through the Death Star's trenches to launch his proton torpedo down the appropriate thermal exhaust port. At the climax of *The Empire Strikes Back* he learns more about his father than he had ever wanted to know. And by the conclusion of *Return of the Jedi* he has become a leader of the rebellion and a Jedi Knight, has certainly been where the action is, and has reconciled with his father in having precipitated in and witnessed Darth Vader's death-throes conversion back to the light side of the force and to his original Anakin Skywalker persona.

Qualities of the Hero

In fulfilling his adolescent fantasies, Luke exhibits most of the qualities of the monomythic hero and experiences most of the episodes of the adventure, yet in some instances qualities of the hero or episodes of the adventure are present in the films (or their prequels) but transferred to another, closely related character. For instance, Galipeau notes that "Lucas has boldly introduced a slightly altered version of the myth of the virgin birth" into 1999's *The Phantom Menace* ("Episode One," the first of the prequels), where "we learn that Anakin Skywalker has no father" but is apparently the result of impregnation by "midi-chlorians ... 'a microscopic life form that resides within all living cells and communicates with the force'" (263). We also learn in the prequels that Luke's mother, Queen Amidala, is indeed a crowned queen; thus, Luke's birth, too, is "special" in that he is the son of royalty and of a former Jedi Knight. In *A New Hope* Luke is introduced as an orphan, in that he is living with his "Uncle" Owen and "Aunt" Beru, and he is soon orphaned again when Imperial troopers searching for the droids slaughter his family. Beru had earlier observed to her husband that "Luke's just not a farmer," and Luke feels he is exiled from the more glamorous parts of the galaxy on the moisture farm, which he is anxious to abandon for the Academy that most of his friends have already left Tatooine to enter. Although he is not seeking his father, because he believes Anakin Skywalker had died long ago, Luke reveals in Obi-Wan's hut that he is anxious to learn any scrap of information he can about his father: "he has an insurmountable curiosity about his origins and a deep, inexplicable stirring to be about his father's business" (Sherman 7). And Luke becomes the "true son" who triumphs over pretenders by the conclusion of *Jedi*: He is instrumental in effecting Vader's death-throes conversion back to Anakin Skywalker (the persona who had been usurped by Darth Vader many years before) and in motivating Vader's assassination of the Emperor (who had almost simultaneously usurped the Republic's rightful, democratic rule of the galaxy).

The monomythic hero has no fear of death and possesses exceptional gifts. Luke demonstrates he does not fear death by volunteering for the attack run on the Death Star at the conclusion of *New Hope*, an act of courage that Han claims is "more like suicide" and that very few of Luke's fellow pilots survive; also, Vader observes to Luke during their duel at the climax of *Empire* that "Obi-Wan has taught you well. You have controlled your fear." As Vader pursues Luke through the Death Star's trenches in *New Hope* he notes to himself that "the force is strong in this one," and the Emperor concurs in *Empire* that "the force is strong with him." His unusually powerful connection with the force is Luke's exceptional gift, and it conveys a wide variety of talents: telekinesis, which Vader exercises in choking the occasional Imperial officer; the ability to levitate objects of any size, as Yoda demonstrates by lifting Luke's ship from the swamp on Dagoba in *Empire* and as Luke himself demonstrates repeatedly in retrieving his light sabre in the last two films and in elevating C-3PO for the Ewoks in *Jedi*; the ability to affect the decision-making processes of the "weak-minded," as Obi-Wan demonstrates as they enter Mos Eisley in *New Hope* and as Luke demonstrates when he enters Jabba's palace in *Jedi*; the ability, as Yoda tells Luke in *Empire*, to see "other places, the future, the past," which Luke exhibits in seeing his friends imperiled in the future in Cloud City while he is still on Dagoba, or to see "friends long gone," as when Luke has visions of Obi-Wan in the last two films; to predict the future, as both Yoda and the Emperor do in *Jedi*; to sense the presence of others strong in the force, as when Vader senses Obi-Wan's presence on the Death Star in *New Hope* and Luke's presence repeatedly in *Jedi*, or when Luke senses the proximity of Leia at the conclusion of *Empire*; and telepathy, as when Luke communicates with Leia immediately afterwards or when the Emperor reads Luke's mind at the climax of *Jedi* to discover that Leia is Luke's twin. Of course, the deficiency from which Luke's "world" suffers is the absence of freedom in a galaxy ruled by the ogre-tyrant Emperor and his henchman

Vader. This macrocosmic condition is echoed on the microcosmic scale by Luke's lack of freedom in being coerced into working one more "season" on the moisture farm, just as both this macrocosmic and microcosmic absence of freedom is reflected in Tatooine's lack of water, which in mythology often symbolizes some spiritual deficiency. And it is Luke's role, if not to make humankind comprehensible to itself, at least to make the world spiritually significant through reviving belief in the force and reinstating the order of the Jedi Knights, which he accomplishes symbolically in the ectoplasmic resurrections of Obi-Wan, Yoda, and Anakin at the conclusion of *Jedi*.

Luke fulfills the conditional qualities of the hero as warrior and of the hero as world-redeemer, but the conditional qualities of the hero as lover are fulfilled by Leia and Han, and the conditional qualities of the hero as saint or mystic are fulfilled by Obi-Wan in *New Hope* and by Yoda in *Jedi*. As an X-wing fighter pilot, Luke is a warrior for the rebellion who changes the status quo by destroying the Death Star at the climax of *New Hope* and by motivating Vader, through being victim of the Emperor's energy-bolt onslaught, finally to assassinate the Emperor at the climax of *Jedi*. Both Mary Henderson (53) and Galipeau (23) identify Leia as Luke's anima, the feminine aspect of the fully realized self, and Galipeau (38) also identifies Han as one of Luke's shadows, who represent unrealized aspects of the self. While it is unclear in *New Hope* whether Luke or Han will be Leia's love interest, Leia's and Han's romance proceeds slowly and somewhat subtly in *Empire*. Leia goes from being in denial about her feelings for Han at the beginning of the film—when she calls Han's romantic pretensions "delusional" and kisses Luke to demonstrate that Han "doesn't know everything about women yet"—to kissing Han passionately and confessing "I love you" (to which Han replies, "I know") towards the end, as he is about to enter carbon freeze. After defrosting Han in Jabba's palace in *Jedi*, Leia identifies herself to the temporarily blinded Solo as "someone who loves you"; and, while Han is willing to "get out of the way" of what he thinks is Luke's and Leia's love for one another at the end of the film, after the Death Star is again destroyed, the revelation that Leia is Luke's twin sister frees Han finally to reciprocate fully Leia's declared love for him. Having transformed from a selfish mercenary with a noble heart into a self-sacrificing hero and leader of the rebellion through the course of the three films, Han's accomplishments are rewarded by his anticipated union with Leia. As experienced Jedi Knights, both Obi-Wan and Yoda are mystics, and both enter an inexpressible realm on their "deaths": Rather than die during their duel in *New Hope*, Obi-Wan disappears, leaving his robes behind, when Vader takes a final swipe at him with his light sabre; and Yoda similarly disappears, leaving his clothes behind, when he "dies" in *Jedi*.

While he is clearly the hero as warrior, Luke is most prominently the hero as world-redeemer. He literally saves the fourth moon of Yavin from being destroyed by the Death Star (as Alderaan had been earlier) at the climax of *New Hope*, and he is instrumental in restoring freedom to the entire galaxy, through the death of the Emperor, at the climax of *Jedi*. The likeness between Luke and Vader (the most prominent of Luke's shadows)—the evidence that the hero and his father are one, the conditional quality of a world-redeemer—is emphasized throughout the three films. Lucas asserts, in fact, that "Luke is Darth Vader. He becomes the very thing he is trying to protect himself against" ("Empire of Dreams"). Early in *New Hope* Aunt Beru laments that Luke "has too much of his father in him"; Obi-Wan subsequently tells Luke that his father Anakin was "an excellent pilot," as is Luke; and Luke vows in this same conversation to become a Jedi Knight like his father. On Dagoba in *Empire*, Yoda realizes that there is "much anger" in Luke, as there had been in Anakin, and reiterates the observation that "there is too much of his father in him." And on Dagoba Luke has the dream-vision in a shallow cave of a light-sabre duel with Vader in which, when Luke decapitates Vader, Luke's face appears beneath Vader's mask. Later, as Mary Henderson points out, "When [Luke] steps out of the mist at the beginning of *Return of the Jedi*, he has become a mysterious cloaked figure like his father" (190). And, while Luke uses Anakin's light sabre in the first two films, when he appears in *Jedi* with a light sabre he had constructed himself the Emperor notes that it is "a Jedi's weapon, much like your father's." Soon thereafter, as he goads Luke and Vader into their final duel, the Emperor gloats, "You, like your father, are now mine." And when Luke draws his weapon first, "Luke becomes like the Darth Vader on the Death Star who waited, with weapon drawn, to challenge and kill Obi-Wan Kenobi" (Galipeau 126). But Luke is finally stayed from giving in to his anger and killing his father, the act through which the dark side of the force would consume him, by noting the similarity between himself and Vader on his own. Luke severs Vader's robotic hand, but then pauses in his assault, scrutinizes Vader's mechanical stump and looks at his own robotic hand—which replaces the hand Vader had severed at the climax of *Empire*—and "realizes that he is on his way to becoming the next Vader" (Mary Henderson 107). He then extinguishes and casts aside his light sabre, faces the Emperor, and declares, "Never! I'll never turn to the dark side. You've failed, Your Highness. I am a Jedi, like my father before me."

The Departure Stage

Luke is not quite as thorough in enacting all the episodes of the Stages of Adventure as he is at embodying the qualities of the hero, yet he still experiences nearly all of them. The call to adventure comes in the form of a blunder that reveals an unknown world or a herald character, and *New Hope* reveals two blunders that propel Luke towards his adventure and provides at least a half dozen heralds of the unknown world. The unknown world to Luke is the galaxy that exists beyond Tatooine, and the blunders both involve R2-D2. First, gunners on Vader's cruiser decide that the escape pod from Leia's ship containing R2-D2 and C-3PO must have "short circuited" because there are "no life forms aboard"; thus, they almost inexplicably fail to shoot it down. This is important because R2-D2 has technical data on the Death Star that reveals a fatal design flaw, the second, underlying blunder: the Death Star can be destroyed by a well-placed shot from a one-man fighter, and its defenses are not tight enough to protect it against such an assault. R2-D2, of course, is one of the many heralds; as he is a non-human character, he is the species of herald as fairy-tale beast, as is C-3PO, whom Mary Henderson sees as being an "unwitting herald" (29) in that he prophetically calls Luke "Sir Luke" (anticipating his Jedi Knighthood) during their first conversation. Chewbacca, another beast and the mate on the Millennium Falcon whom Luke encounters in the cantina before he meets Han, may be another herald of the worlds beyond Tatooine. But the herald is often a cloaked or hooded or masked figure, and *New Hope* has plenty of them. Leia is hooded in the message meant for Obi-Wan that R2-D2 plays for Luke—"Help me, Obi-Wan Kenobi. You're my only hope"—and it is the appearance of Leia's image that first intrigues Luke. Obi-Wan himself, who asks Luke to accompany him to Alderaan, is hooded when he first rescues Luke from the Sand People. The Jawas, who transport R2-D2 and C-3PO to Owen Lars' moisture farm, are also hooded. The Sand People who attack Luke in the Jundland wastes are masked, and so is Vader, who personifies the Empire that lies beyond Tatooine.

Next, the hero may refuse the call, and Luke does refuse. When Obi-wan invites him to participate in the adventure in telling him "You must learn the ways of the force if you're to come with me to Alderaan" to deliver R2-D2 to Leia's foster father, Luke responds, "I'm not going to Alderaan.... I can't get involved. I've got work to do.... There's nothing I can do about it right now." Only when he discovers later that storm troopers pursuing the droids have killed Uncle Owen and Aunt Beru does Luke recognize that "There's nothing here for me now. I want to know the ways of the force and become a Jedi like my father." After accepting the call the hero receives aid from an old man or crone, who provides a talisman in a setting suggesting a womb-like sense of peace, or from a guide, teacher, wizard, ferryman, hermit, or smith, who provides aid in a context suggesting danger or temptation. Obi-Wan is the old man who provides a talisman as well as Luke's guide and teacher. Before meeting him, Luke describes Obi-Wan to C-3PO as being a "kind of strange old hermit," and Owen refers to him as a "crazy old wizard." The talisman Obi-Wan provides is Anakin Skywalker's light sabre, which he gives to Luke in the peaceful surroundings of his Tatooine hut even before Luke accepts the call to adventure. Obi-Wan then guides Luke through the dangers of Mos Eisley to Han and Chewbacca, and he later instructs Luke in the ways of the force aboard the Millennium Falcon en route to Alderaan. (In *Empire* Luke meets another hermit and wizard in Yoda, who provides even more instruction in the ways of the force and whose hut on Dagoba, due to its cramped size, is more pronouncedly womb-like than is Obi-Wan's habitation on Tatooine.) Luke's ferryman is, of course, Han, who agrees to transport Luke, Obi-Wan, and the droids to Alderaan for an exorbitant fee and "no questions asked." Ironically, the smith is Anakin Skywalker, the Jedi who had constructed the light sabre Obi-Wan gives to Luke. (And Luke finally becomes his own smith in having constructed his own light sabre before *Jedi* begins.)

The Millennium Falcon's visually spectacular first jump to hyperspace from Tatooine is Luke's threshold crossing. It is a crossing that will ultimately lead to a rebirth of freedom in the galaxy, but Luke's adventure entails several symbolic rebirths of the hero as well. For example, Mary Henderson posits that Luke, Leia, Han, and Chewbacca emerge from the Death Star's "garbage masher as though reborn" (56) in *New Hope*, and Galipeau argues that Luke's escape from Vader by falling through Cloud City's tunnels at the conclusion of *Empire* is "rebirth imagery: a passage down a 'birth canal'" (165). Luke's leaving Tatooine also involves its share of benign and destructive threshold guardians. Mary Henderson sees Uncle Owen and Aunt Beru as "protective" yet "restrictive" guardians who attempt to keep Luke on Tatooine (30; see also Gordon 320). Gordon enumerates a series of destructive threshold guardians: "first the marauding Sandpeople, next a Stormtrooper guarding the entrance to the spaceport, and finally a foul-looking alien in the spaceport bar. In each case, Luke is saved by Ben," his protective guardian (322). The threshold guardian who comes closest to being a destructive watchman is the elephant-trunk-snouted alien spy who follows Luke and Obi-wan through the streets of Mos Eisley and informs on them to the storm troopers. Of course, the Imperial ships that try to block the Millennium Falcon's escape from Tatooine are also destructive guardians, and Han is the protective guardian who finally executes a successful jump to hyperspace.

Being Swallowed in the Belly of the Whale is the single episode that is most often replicated in science fiction films employing the monomyth; and, as in the *Star Wars* trilogy, it is also the episode most elaborately redeployed again and again with variations. The hero may have an underground journey that may also be a symbolic descent into hell and is often a symbolic death and rebirth; he may enter a temple guarded by gargoyles; and he may be literally or symbolically mutilated, dismembered, or killed. Mary Henderson sees Luke's and Obi-Wan's visit to the Mos Eisley cantina as a first "descent into the underworld" (39). Both Gordon (322) and Mary Henderson (47) view the Millennium Falcon being drawn into the Death Star by tractor beam as a journey into the belly of the whale, and Henderson points out that the interior of the Death Star is also a labyrinth the heroes must negotiate. She sees the garbage masher into which the heroes dive while within the Death Star as being both a "belly" and a symbolic "womb" from which they emerge as if "reborn" (53–4). And Galipeau points out that this experience shared by Luke, Han, Chewbacca, and Leia is foreshadowed by R2-D2 and C-3PO having had their own "Jonah-in-the-whale" adventure when they are captured by Jawas and held captive in the sand trawler (20).

"The wampa's lair is the first of a number of caves" in *Empire* (Galipeau 93). After Luke escapes from the wampa's cave, Han saves him from freezing to death in the Hoth night by stuffing him into the still-warm guts of a dead and frozen tauntaun, literally the belly of a beast. When the pair return to Hoth's Echo Base, Luke is healed inside a bacta tank; and Galipeau argues that his being inside both the tauntaun and the bacta tank "symbolically represent being returned to the womb" (96). As the Millennium Falcon's hyperdrive is disabled, Han, Chewbacca, Leia, and C-3PO escape Hoth by diving into an asteroid field and eventually hiding in a deep cave on a large asteroid, only to discover that they have flown down the gullet of a giant space worm whose closing jaws they narrowly evade as they exit the cave. Simultaneously, Luke and R2-D2 go to Dagoba in search of Yoda. There Luke descends into the shallow cave where he confronts and decapitates a vision of Vader only to discover his own face under Vader's mask. Mary Henderson sees Cloud City, where the heroes reunite, as a "mazelike enclosure" (82), another labyrinth, and she views Cloud City's carbon freezing chamber as "yet another symbol for hell, with its sulfurous fumes and red-yellow glow" (78). She also views both Jabba's palace on Tatooine, which Luke enters to rescue his friends in *Jedi*, and the second Death Star, which Luke enters later in pursuit of Vader, as additional underworlds (78, 106). Almost immediately after arriving at Jabba's palace, Luke is plunged into the Rancor pit, literally an underground lair, where the threat of literally being eaten is underscored by the remains of past victims that litter the pit and by the fact that the Rancor does eat one of Jabba's guards. After killing the Rancor, Luke (with Han and Chewbacca) is condemned to die by being thrown into the Sarlac pit in the Tatooine desert, prospectively another underground journey, where all will be "slowly digested over a thousand years."

Being swallowed in the belly of the whale suggests being eaten; Yoda warns Luke in *Empire* to "Beware the dark side: consume you it will"; and Mary Henderson points out that "throughout the trilogy, the imagery of the heroes being consumed is repeated over and over" (97). In addition to the threat of literally being eaten by the Rancor and the Sarlac in *Jedi*, Luke is almost eaten by a creature in the garbage masher in *New Hope*, is then almost masticated to death by the garbage masher itself, is hung by his heals to be lunch for the wampa in *Empire*, and is shortly thereafter symbolically consumed when shoved into the belly of the tauntaun. Moreover, in *Empire* R2-D2 is swallowed and spit out by a swamp creature on Dagoba while Han, Chewbacca, Leia, and C-3PO enter the gullet of the giant space worm in the asteroid field; and in *Jedi* the Ewoks first intend to cook and eat Luke, Han, and Chewbacca as "the main course at a banquet" in C-3PO's honor, but are saved by Leia's pleading and by Luke demonstrating C-3PO's "magic" in levitating his "throne." Jabba's palace on Tatooine is the closest thing to a temple that Luke enters; while it sports no gargoyles, it is inhabited by monstrous, brutish, tusked and horned inhuman guards. And Luke is mutilated by the Wampa in the beginning of *Empire* and dismembered by Vader cutting off his hand at the film's climax; moreover, he is symbolically dismembered in the middle of the film when he severs the shadow–Vader's head only to see his own face under Vader's mask. (Dismemberment is almost a motif in the trilogy, as the foul-looking alien in the cantina loses an arm to Obi-Wan's light sabre in *New Hope*, Luke severs the wampa's arm in *Empire*, and C-3PO is dismembered repeatedly: he loses an arm in the scuffle with the Sand People in *New Hope*, is thoroughly disassembled in Cloud City in *Empire*, and has one of his eyes plucked out by Jabba's pet Salacious Crumb in Jabba's palace in *Jedi*.)

The Initiation Stage

In the Road of Trials, the first episode in the Initiation Stage, the hero endures tests, is aided by the advice, talismans, or agents of his supernatural helper, discovers that a divine power protects him everywhere, and assimilates his opposite, shadow, or unsuspected self. In *New Hope* Luke must help get R2-D2 and the Death Star data to the rebel forces, must rescue Leia from the Death Star's detention level, and must destroy the Death Star. Obi-Wan's advice aids him in all three endeavors, but most memorably when Obi-Wan's disembodied voice urges Luke to "Use the Force" and turn off his targeting computer for his final run at the Death Star. In *Empire* Luke must disable Imperial Walkers during the rebellion's evacuation of Hoth, must "unlearn" what he has learned—abandon his notions of what is possible and impossible—to become a Jedi Knight, and must rescue Han, Chewbacca, C-3PO, and Leia from Vader in Bespin's

Cloud City without falling prey to the dark side of the force. Luke uses the Force and Anakin's light sabre to free himself from the wampa's cave and to disable an Imperial walker on Hoth, and he repeatedly uses both while on Bespin, particularly in his duel with Vader. A vision of Obi-Wan revives Luke as he lies on the frozen surface of Hoth and directs him to go to the planet Dagoba to continue his training with Yoda, who effectively becomes Obi-Wan's agent. And on Dagoba both Yoda and the voice of Obi-Wan advise Luke not to go to Bespin to rescue his friends before completing his Jedi training, but Luke does not heed them. In *Jedi* Luke must rescue Han—and also Lando Calrissian, C-3PO, R2-D2, Chewbacca, and Leia—from Jabba's palace, must assist the rebels in destroying the second Death Star, and must inspire Vader to turn back to the light side of the Force and assassinate the Emperor. While he does not use them in killing the Rancor, Luke uses both the Force and his own light sabre to rescue himself, Han, and Lando from the Sarlac pit (while Leia throttles Jabba with her own chain). A dying Yoda tells Luke, after he returns to Dagoba, "You must confront Vader. Then and only then [will you be a Jedi]." And Obi-Wan again appears to him to tell him, "Yoda will always be with you," to assure him that he must, indeed, face Vader, and to reveal to him that Leia is his twin sister. Luke uses his light sabre to disable a speeder bike on Endor, uses the Force to levitate C-3PO before the Ewoks, and uses both in his final battle with Vader.

The Force, of course, is the benign power that protects Luke everywhere. Both the corporeal and the disembodied Obi-Wan assure Luke repeatedly that "The Force will be with you ... always!" In *New Hope* Obi-Wan tells Luke that the Force "is an energy field created by all living things. It surrounds us and penetrates us. It binds the galaxy together." And Vader tells the Imperial officers on the Death Star that "The ability to destroy a planet is insignificant next to the power of the Force." *Star Wars* producer Gary Kurtz acknowledges that "The concept of the Force was an important one to the story. And the difficulty is trying to create a religious/spiritual concept that works in a very simple way, without heavy exposition and without it seeming to pull down the story" ("Empire of Dreams"). The *Star Wars* films solve this difficulty by turning again to ancient myth and to Campbell, who argues in *The Hero with a Thousand Faces* that mythology posits a "ubiquitous power" out of which all things arise (257). Gordon recognizes that this "ubiquitous power" is, in the *Star Wars* trilogy, the Force (323); and Galipeau sees the Force "in terms of the collective unconscious" as being "our psychic energy" (36, 49).

There are a lot of pairs of shadow characters in the *Star Wars* trilogy. Collins, Galipeau, Mary Henderson, and Lucas himself all see C-3PO and R2-D2 as shadows. While both are droids, Collins argues that C-3PO being "fretful" and "over-civilized" effectively complements R2-D2 being "determinedly ...

brave" (5). Contrasting C-3PO's anxiety to R2-D2's "adventuresome" spirit, Gali-peau notes that "They are opposites on a variety of levels" (15). Mary Henderson sees C-3PO and R2-D2 as shadows representing the ego and the subconscious mind, respectively (26, 29). And Lucas notes that in order to make the droids work as comic relief, "You have to create two characters who are very, very dif-ferent from each other" ("The Characters in *Star Wars*"). Lucas also points out that Luke and Obi-Wan are "opposites" and that in Luke and Han, "I have one character who is very selfless and one who is very selfish" ("The Characters in *Star Wars*"). Moreover, while both are brave, noble-hearted, heroic, and attracted to Leia, Luke is also willing from the beginning to believe in the Force while Han remains skeptical throughout *A New Hope* at least. Thus, Galipeau argues that "Han represents a shadow figure for Luke" (38). Han and Lando are shadows as well, as are Obi-Wan and Vader. But the most crucial shadows in the trilogy are Vader and Luke. Mary Henderson points out that "Vader is the shadow of Luke's bright side," as Luke's experience in the shallow cave on Dagoba in *Empire* indi-cates, and that "One personifies evil but carries within him the potential for redemption, while the other personifies good but carries within the potential for evil" (117, 120; see also 73). While Vader's (and the Emperor's) goal is to assimilate Luke by seducing him to the dark side of the force, Luke manages to subvert this objective by recognizing there is still some good and some humanity remaining in Vader and finally, through allowing himself (in refusing to take his father's life in anger) to be the suffering recipient of the Emperor's energy bolts, to re-convert Vader back to the light side at the climax of *Jedi*.

The goddess, of course, is Leia, the only notable female character in the trilogy. She is initially the Lady of the House of Sleep to Luke in *New Hope*, in which he falls in love with her at first sight on viewing the image of her generated by R2-D2, and he literally dreams of her in *Empire*. She becomes the bad mother who is forbidden and unattainable once Luke learns that she is his twin in *Jedi*. But she is most basically the Universal Mother who combines all opposites. She is Luke's love interest but also his sister. She is a princess and a damsel in distress, but also a member of the peremptorily dissolved Senate and a general in the rebellion who insists on taking charge of her own rescue from the Death Star. In *Jedi* she is slave girl, warrior, and lover; and she initially disguises herself as the ruthless and desperate bounty hunter Boushh, whom an impressed Jabba declares is "my kind of scum." She has her mystical marriage with Han on Endor at the trilogy's conclusion, when she learns from Luke and then tells Han that she is Luke's sister. And she is also a "temptress" to Luke in that he falls in love with her only to discover later that she is his twin.

While there is nothing to suggest that Vader is an initiating priest to Luke, such as some moment of baptism, Vader does offer confirmation to Luke when he acknowledges in *Jedi*, "Your training is complete. You are a Jedi." Vader's and the Emperor's plan for Luke is to effect a negative encounter with the father through their conspiracy to "turn" Luke to the dark side of the force, which Yoda had warned might "consume" him, a metaphor for being eaten by the father. In *Empire* Vader vows to the Emperor, "He will join us or die, Master." And Vader severing Luke's right hand at the conclusion of their first duel, just before revealing that he is Luke's father, is the symbolic castration or circumcision that signals this is an attempted rite of initiation, as Vader then intones, "Join me, and together we can rule the galaxy as father and son." But Luke declines, and he is only finally reconciled with his father after their second duel, in *Jedi*, ends with the Emperor dead at Vader's hands and Vader fatally wounded in the conflict. The son must see beyond the ogre-tyrant, Vader, manifestation of the father to apprehend the human face of the father, Anakin. This is precisely what happens after the Emperor's death: Vader asks Luke to help him remove his mask, reveals the face of Anakin Skywalker to Luke, acknowledges that Luke has "saved" him, and dies. The two are reconciled; Luke burns Vader's mask, environment suit, and cape in a warrior's funeral pyre to symbolize that the Vader manifestation of his father has been purged; and a redeemed Anakin Skywalker takes his place among the other deceased Jedi, Obi-Wan and Yoda, at the trilogy's conclusion.

This is Anakin's "apotheosis" (Mary Henderson 113), his transcending his humanity, which entails a conjunction of the opposites "good" and "evil." Comically, C-3PO has an "apotheosis" in *Jedi* as well, when "the Ewoks take [him] for some kind of deity" (Mary Henderson 105). But Luke's symbolic apotheosis, a more mundane elevation of the hero, is muted and occurs much earlier, when Leia awards medals of valor to Luke and Han at the conclusion of *New Hope*. However, Luke does receive the highest form of boon, revelation—although it is a thoroughly negative one—when he learns that he is Vader's son at the climax of *Empire*. And in restoring freedom to the galaxy in *Jedi* through being a party to the death of the Emperor, Luke returns to his society a symbolic boon of lesser value, the equivalent of wealth and power, signaled by the celebrations on Endor (and, in the 1997 director's cut, throughout the galaxy) that occur at the trilogy's conclusion.

The Return Stage

While the Departure Stage, on the whole, is the stage that is most fully developed in science fiction films that employ the monomyth, the Return Stage is the stage that is most neglected. This is true in the *Star Wars* trilogy as well, yet *Jedi*'s opening crawl informs the audience that "Luke Skywalker has returned to his home planet of Tatooine in an attempt to rescue his friend Han Solo from the clutches of the vile gangster Jabba the Hutt." His appearance on Tatooine at the beginning of *Jedi*, although he will not remain there, is Luke's return to the mundane world on which he had received the call to adventure. But there is no refusal to return, no magic flight, no rescue from outside the unknown world, and no re-crossing of the threshold; Luke just shows up. In a sense, though, he does return with a talisman of his quest in showing up with a light sabre he had made himself, which signifies that he has become a Jedi Knight in the several years between *Empire* and *Jedi*. Moreover, Luke has become master of the known and unknown worlds in having gained the freedom to cross the threshold to outer space freely by having returned freedom, generally, to the galaxy. And he seems to have accepted his transcendence. "Luke, as we meet him [in *New Hope*], is an unshaped figure, virtually without a personal psychology" (Collins 4). "Luke's character as the story begins is unformed and untested, innocent of a wider experience of the world and unaware of what lies ahead"; yet "Luke's journey through the three films transforms him from a rebellious and impatient teenager, itching for adventure, into a grown-up hero who has confronted his strengths and weaknesses and found the power to help save the world" (Mary Henderson 22, 20). The ectoplasmic resurrections of Anakin, Yoda, and Obi-Wan at *Jedi*'s conclusion signal that Luke is, and is conscious that he is, the vehicle of cosmic change; and the general celebration that follows signals that he can now work in the mundane world without anxiety.

The one remaining quality of the *Star Wars* trilogy that is relevant to Campbell's interpretation of the monomyth is its comic tone, which is most pronounced in *A New Hope*. Collins calls attention to *New Hope*'s "humor," a quality he feels "underlies the best of all science fiction" (8). Of course, as Lucas acknowledges, R2-D2 and C-3PO are "designed as ... comic relief" ("The Characters of *Star Wars*"), but there is much comedy in *New Hope* that is independent of the droids: Leia's comic cynicism and aggressiveness during her rescue from the Death Star, quite a lot of comically ironic dialogue, and a happy ending despite the destruction of Alderaan and the deaths of almost every pilot who joins Luke in attacking the Death Star, for example. Moreover, the trilogy concludes with arch-villain Vader's redemption and the return of freedom to the galaxy. Campbell contends in *The Hero With a Thousand Faces* that "Humor is the touchstone of the truly mythological" and that "It is the business of mythology ... to reveal ... the dark interior way from tragedy to comedy" because, while life is a tragedy when viewed from the perspective of the Western notion of time, because we die, it is a comedy when viewed from the perspective of the Eastern notion of eternity, because we live (180, 29; see also 45, 269, 288).

2

Before (and a Little After)
A New Hope: *The Time Machine,*
Logan's Run and *Time After Time*

Consideration of all the American science fiction films released before *A New Hope* only confirms that the first *Star Wars* film was the first American science fiction film to intentionally and systematically use Campbell's monomyth as its underlying plot structure. Three additional 1960s and 1970s films that lend themselves to such a treatment—George Pal's *The Time Machine* (1960), Michael Anderson's *Logan's Run* (1976), and Nicholas Meyer's *Time After Time* (1979)—do exhibit significant components of Campbell's monomyth, but the many missing elements not in these films suggest that the filmmakers were not intentionally attempting to replicate the monomyth's qualities of the hero or its stages of adventure. While the initial *Star Wars* trilogy omits only a couple of the qualities of the hero and only the first four episodes in the Return Stage, these three films from the '60s and '70s each omit a great deal more. All of them are considerably sketchier in attributing to their protagonists the ten qualities of the hero, and two of the three are missing crucial episodes from all three of the stages of adventure (*The Time Machine* and *Time After Time*, but not *Logan's Run,* which completely replicates only the Departure Stage). Yet, as time-travel stories, both Pal's *Time Machine* and *Time After Time* do provide another world in which the adventure occurs, another time period from that one in which the protagonist begins; George in *Time Machine* begins in 1899 but travels to 802,701 (among a few other temporal locations), and H.G. in *Time After Time* begins in 1893 but travels to 1979. Logan in *Logan's Run* also travels to another "world," the world outside the dome, and he is the only one of the protagonists from these three films to return to his society with a significant boon that he shares with his fellows.

Pal's *The Time Machine*'s protagonist, the time traveler (Rod Taylor), is named H.G. Wells but is known to his friends as "George." He is considerably more heroic than the unnamed protagonist of H.G. Wells' novella and, while he has almost the same qualities of the hero as does Wells' character, he experiences far more of the episodes in the stages of adventure than does Wells' time traveler. George does undergo a form of exile, does have an exceptional gift, does inhabit a world that suffers deficiencies, is destined (perhaps) to make humankind comprehensible to itself, and is the hero as lover and possibly also the hero as saint or mystic, but he lacks the other qualities of the hero and experiences only ten of the seventeen episodes of the adventure: the call to adventure, receiving supernatural aid, the initial threshold crossing, being swallowed in the belly of the whale, the road of trials, the meeting with the goddess, magic flight, crossing the return threshold, becoming master of both worlds, and attaining freedom to live. Logan 5 (Michael York) does have a species of virgin birth and is effectively an orphan in *Logan's Run*; his world of 2274 does suffer deficiencies, he may make humanity comprehensible to itself, and he is the hero as warrior and the hero as lover; but he possesses none of the other qualities of the hero. He does experience eleven of the seventeen episodes of the adventure, but he does not encounter a woman as temptress, has no moment of apotheosis, and does not enact four of the six episodes in the return stage: he does not refuse to return, he has no magic flight, he is not rescued from outside the unknown world, and he does not become the master of both worlds. The protagonist in *Time After Time* (Malcolm McDowell) is also named H.G. Wells, but he is known to his friends as "H.G." He feels he is a misfit (is exiled) in his own time, has an exceptional gift, feels that his world suffers deficiencies, and is the hero as lover, but he lacks the other qualities of the hero and experiences only seven of the seventeen episodes of the adventure: the call to adventure, refusing the call, receiving supernatural aid, the initial threshold crossing, the road of trials, the meeting with the goddess, and crossing the return threshold. Of these three films, *Logan's Run* echoes the monomyth most thoroughly. (See Figure 2 and Figure 3.)

Qualities of the Hero

While nothing is known about George's or H.G.'s nativity and parents in *Time Machine* or *Time After Time*, enough is revealed about Logan's birth in *Logan's Run*. Logan is a citizen of the dome, a fully automated twenty-third-century habitat that is completely cut off from the outside world and in which everyone lives "for pleasure" until their thirtieth birthday, when, to maintain

	The Time Machine	Logan's Run	Time After Time
Protagonist	George	Logan 5	H. G.
Special Birth		virgin birth	
Mother a Queen			
Orphan or Exile	stranded in 802,701	parents are unknown; trapped under dome; exiled from the dome	feels he is a misfit in 1893
Seeking a Father			
Triumphs over Pretenders			
Possesses Special Gifts	inventive genius		inventive genius
Does not Fear Death			
World Suffers Deficiencies	war	trapped under dome; death at 30; no love, marriage, or family	no social utopia as yet
Provides Spiritual Significance			
Makes Humanity Comprehensible to Itself	will return to 802,701 to help the Eloi to build a new world	citizens feed from the dome and death at 30 into the outside world	
Hero as Warrior		a sandman who frees citizens from the dome	
Hero as Lover	Weena	Jessica	Amy Robins
Hero as Ruler			
Hero as World Redeemer			
Hero as Saint or Mystic	disappears into time at film's conclusion		

Figure 2. Qualities of the Hero in *The Time Machine*, *Logan's Run*, and *Time After Time*.

population balance, they are incinerated in a ritual called "carousel" unless they are "renewed" (but Logan learns from the dome's computer system early in the film that no one is ever renewed). *Logan's Run* begins in the dome's nursery, where Logan is looking at newborns and reveals that he does not know which child is his or who his child's "seed mother" is. Everyone is born in "breeders"— are, in essence, test-tube babies—and thus Logan's, like everyone else's under the dome, is a virgin birth. Also, as he, like his unknown offspring, does not know who his parents are, Logan (again like everyone else under the dome) is effectively an orphan. Jessica 6 (Jenny Agutter), who escapes the dome with Logan in the course of the film, laments at one point, "I wish I'd known my mother"; and when they encounter the "old man" (Peter Ustinov), the only

	The Time Machine	Logan's Run	Time After Time
The "Other World"	802,701	outside the dome	1979
Call to Adventure	herald: model time machine; blunder: moves forward from 1966	blunder: dome computer retrograms Logan and sends him to Sanctuary	herald: Jack the Ripper; blunder: explaining machine to guests
Call is Refused		Logan objects to retrogramming and to running	at first lacks the "nerve" to use his machine
Supernatural Aid	Weena is George's guide to 802,701	ankh; Jessica as guide, "old man," & "doc"	Amy Robbins is H. G.'s guide to 1979
Threshold Crossing	time-lapse photography; mannequin & Sphinx	symbolic rebirth; "doc," Francis, sandmen, "Box"	visual and audio effects; museum guard
Swallowed in the "Belly of the Whale"	interred in stone; down ventilation well; into Sphinx pedestal	way is further underground; "Box"'s cave; mutilated in "New You"	
Road of Trials	Morlocks as shadows	Francis as shadow	Jack the Ripper = shadow
Meeting with Goddess	Weena; 802,701	Jessica; outside the dome	Amy Robbins; 1979
Woman as Temptress			
Atonement with Father		(Logan meets "old man")	
Apotheosis	(theme of cyclical return)		
Receiving the Boon		life outside the dome	
Refusal to Return		(Jessica does not want to)	
Magic Flight	ambushed by Morlocks; reinstalls levers		
Rescue from Outside			
Re-crossing the Threshold	time dilation; flowers from future as talisman	the "old man" as talisman	time dilation; Amy as talisman
Master of Two Worlds	retains time machine		
Freedom to Live	frees Eloi from Morlocks and returns to 802,701	frees citizens from dome; now they don't die at 30	(rids the world of Jack the Ripper in 1979)

Figure 3. Stages of the Adventure in *The Time Machine*, *Logan's Run*, and *Time After Time*.

human being they meet outside the dome, Logan is surprised that the old man knew his own father and Jessica is amazed that he was "grown" inside his mother and not in a breeder.

All citizens of the dome are in exile from the outside world, and Logan is exiled from the dome when he undergoes a "retrogram" procedure that resets his "life-clock" from twenty-six, his age, to thirty, the age at which all dome citizens must endure carousel. Logan is a "sandman," a policeman who chases and executes "runners," citizens who have reached the age of thirty but refuse to experience carousel and instead try to escape the dome to "Sanctuary," a fabled place of refuge in the outside world. The dome's computer system retrograms Logan to establish the fiction that he is a runner (although sandmen allegedly never run), and Logan is given the mission to pass as a runner, to escape the dome, and to find and destroy Sanctuary. His choice, then, is either to be killed in carousel prematurely or to exile himself from the dome as a runner.

George is an exile for much of *Time Machine* as well. He inadvertently travels from 1899 to 802,701—a time he despises after he sees the human-looking, surface-dwelling Eloi's decayed books—and is stranded in that year once the monstrous, subterranean Morlocks drag his time machine into their Sphinx-surmounted pedestal. After destroying the Morlocks' underground realm, but before he recovers his machine, he observes, "I was imprisoned in a world in which I just did not belong"; he then tells Weena (Yvette Mimieux), the Eloi he had saved from drowning and to whom he rapidly falls in love, "I don't really fit here, any more than you would in my time." While he is not similarly exiled to 1979, H.G. in *Time After Time* does feel that he is out of his proper element, an exile, in the present, 1893, and that he belongs in what he believes will be a utopian future. All three protagonists experience some mode of exile, but no one's mother is assumed into heaven or crowned a queen, no one consciously seeks a father, and no one triumphs over any type of pretender to demonstrate that he is the true son.

As inventors who have accomplished the impossible in creating their time machines, both George and H.G. possess the same exceptional gift, inventive genius; Logan, however, does not possess any exceptional gift. While he may be unusual in 2274 in that he has any occupation at all, he displays no special talents as a sandman other than the ability to use a futuristic sidearm. Also, he demonstrates a healthy and somewhat ironic fear of death in first objecting strenuously to having had four years removed from his life-clock and then in attempting to run rather than die in carousel (despite the fact that he thinks, correctly, that no one will readily aid him because no one will readily believe he is a runner). While George exhibits notable bravery in saving Weena from drowning, in saving her from abduction by Morlocks during his first night in 802,701, and especially in afterwards going into the Morlocks' domain, "below," to save Weena again and to search for his machine, he never quite demonstrates that he does not fear death. And *Time After Time*'s H.G. is considerably less courageous than *The Time Machine*'s George: H.G. had not yet "worked up the nerve" to use his machine until his friend John Stevenson (David Warner), whom the police have just discovered is Jack the Ripper, steals it to escape into the future; only then does H.G. use the machine (which automatically returns to its point of origin unless a key is turned to prevent it from doing so) to pursue Jack to 1979 and "save" what he assumes will be a future utopia from a "madman."

All three protagonists inhabit worlds that suffer deficiencies, however. Both H.G. and George want to go to the future because they are dissatisfied with their present. H.G. ironically predicts that, in contrast to 1893, in three generations "the social utopia will have come to pass. There'll be no war, no poverty, and no disease either. Men will live as brothers, and on terms of total equality with women as well." George's dissatisfaction with 1899 is a bit more pointed. His friend Dr. Hillyear (Sabastian Cabot) notes that "There's a war on in South Africa," and George's December 31, 1899, newspaper bears the headline "Boer Army Has Won Another Victory. Our Armies Are in Retreat." George laments that human progress has been nothing but the finding of ever more efficient means of killing one another, and he hopes the future will be different. But, just as H.G. is proven to be mistaken about the future in *Time After Time*, so too is George mistaken about the future in *The Time Machine*. Unlike the time traveler in Wells' novella (who stops in the year 30,000,000 after traveling to 802,701), George makes three stops on the way to 802,701: 1917, when he learns that his friend Filby (Alan Young) had died a year earlier in the great war; 1940, when he observes the bombing of London in World War II; and 1966, when he observes "atomic satellites" devastate London in what is apparently the beginning of World War III. Even in 802,701 George has not escaped the specter of war, for the "talking rings" in an abandoned museum tell him and Weena that "the war between the East and West, which is now in its 326th year, has at last come to an end" and that some, the ancestors of the Morlocks, have gone underground due to the lack of oxygen in the atmosphere. While the deficiency in George's 1899 is the seemingly perpetual presence of war, and that in H.G.'s 1893 is the persistence of a host of social ills, the deficiency in Logan's world of 2274 is threefold: everyone is imprisoned under the dome and entirely unaware of the existence of the world outside; everyone dies when they reach the age of thirty; and romantic love, marriage, and family are unknown concepts.

While none of these protagonists do anything to make the world spiritually significant, Logan and George do perform acts that possibly have the end result of making humanity more comprehensible to itself. When Logan returns to the dome, after his journey to the world outside and his discovery that Sanctuary does not exist, he gives this information to the dome's computer, which then overloads and explodes because it is given data that conflicts with what it believes to be "fact." This guts and ruptures the dome itself, and at the conclusion of *Logan's Run* all the dome's citizens are freed into the outside world, whose very existence is a revelation to them, and are simultaneously freed of the obligation to die at thirty, a necessity that exists only under the dome. At the conclusion of *The Time Machine* Filby believes that George, who has disappeared back into time after telling his dinner guests the story of his adventure in 802,701, has returned to that year to be reunited with Weena and "to help the Eloi build a new world." While this is the last time period to which the time traveler would have gone in Wells' novella, it is plausible that George would return to 802,701 in Pal's film in that there is a Weena to return to and in that George had told Weena earlier that he wants to "reawaken" the Eloi's submerged "spirit of self-sacrifice." His ostensible return to 802,701 to rekindle civilization is precisely an attempt to make humankind comprehensible to itself once more.

All of these films' protagonists possess at least one of the monomyth's conditional qualities, and all three are at least the hero as lover. Although in Wells' novella Weena is not so human, dies before the conclusion, and is more of a pet than a love interest in any case, George does fall in love with her (and she does survive) in the few days he is in 802,701 in Pal's film. Weena flirts with George after he saves her from the Morlock underworld; they then nuzzle and almost kiss, but are interrupted when the other Eloi point out to George that the Sphinx's pedestal, which contains his machine, is open; and George does try to take Weena back in time with him but is prevented when the pedestal doors slam shut behind him. Thus it is believable that he might have returned to 802,701 to be with her, as Filby surmises, at the film's conclusion. George accomplishing the impossible task of traveling in time is symbolized, finally, by Weena (at least to Filby), and his apparent return to 802,701 may lead to their bridal bed. But since he does disappear into time at the film's conclusion, he may also be the hero as saint or mystic, who enters an inexpressible realm beyond form.

Logan is the hero as lover and the hero as warrior. In the course of escaping the dome he falls in love with Jessica, a woman he had tried to bed earlier in the film and a runner sympathizer who helps guide him out of the dome and shares his adventure. At the film's conclusion they look forward to "marriage" (being sexually committed only to one another) and to growing old and raising a family together, all impossibilities under the dome; thus, accomplishing the impossible task of escaping the dome has led to their bridal bed. But Logan is a sandman, a type of warrior, also, and he absolutely changes the status quo in destroying the dome and freeing its inhabitants to experience the world outside. H.G. in *Time After Time* is the hero as lover only. Although she is initially more smitten with him, during the course of their adventure in 1979 H.G. does fall in love with Amy Robbins (Mary Steenburgen), a bank officer who is his guide to 1979, and she returns to 1893 with him to be his wife. (The film notes that Amy Robbins was the historical H.G. Wells' wife.) Accomplishing the impossible task of traveling in time more unequivocally leads to the bridal bed in this film than it does in *The Time Machine.*

The Departure Stage

All three protagonists receive a call to adventure as well. In *Time Machine* George is provided with both a herald character, of sorts, and a blunder that reveals the unknown world of 802,701. He begins his tale to his dinner guests by reminding them of the demonstration he had given them the previous week, when he had sent a miniature model of his time machine irrevocably into the future as his first experiment in time travel. This model machine—or perhaps its symbolic inhabitant, Dr. Hillyear's bent cigar—is the herald, the first object to travel in time. The blunder is George's mistake in continuing to move forward in time after he is caught in the nuclear bombardment of London in 1966. Had he gone back towards 1899, he would have escaped any effects of the blast, which induces a volcanic eruption. But since he persists in moving forwards, he is covered with lava and "encased in stone" for over 800,000 years, until the stone erodes away and he finally stops his machine in 802,701. H.G., too, commits a blunder that reveals the unknown world of 1979, one that also provides him with a herald, when he shows the time machine to his November 5, 1893, dinner guests and explains how it operates. He does not know that his friend John Stevenson is Jack the Ripper; and when the police come to arrest Jack in H.G.'s home that same evening, Jack evades them by escaping into time in H.G.'s machine, thus becoming the first time traveler and H.G.'s herald to the future in *Time After Time*. Exclaiming, "What have I done? I've turned that bloody maniac loose on utopia!" H.G.—who had previously not had the "nerve" to use his machine, his form of refusing the call—then follows Jack into the future to save it when the empty machine returns to 1893. The blunder in *Logan's Run* is performed by the dome's computer system when it retrograms Logan to age thirty against his will and sends him outside the dome as a runner to locate and destroy Sanctuary, a place that does not exist. Logan's call to adventure features no herald—he and Jessica are the first runners to ever make it to the outside world—but Logan does attempt to refuse the call in objecting to being retrogrammed and in initially refusing to run, yet he has no choice.

And all three protagonists receive some form of "supernatural aid." Logan takes an "ankh"—a key to "the last gate" to the outside world—from a dead runner and uses this talisman in escaping the dome. His guide to the circuitous route out of the dome is Jessica. Once outside they meet a hermit in the "old man," who lives alone with hundreds of cats. And before he begins his journey to the outside world Logan meets a smith in "Doc," a plastic surgeon to whom he goes for facial reconstruction after the dome's computer retrograms him, but "Doc" receives orders from the computer to kill Logan instead. In having invented and fabricated time machines, both George and H.G. are their own wizard, ferryman, and smith. George also receives some small amount of aid from Weena, who becomes his guide to 802,701 and takes him to the museum of "talking rings." Similarly, except that she is considerably more helpful, Amy is H.G.'s guide to 1979 San Francisco.

All three protagonists cross a threshold to an unknown world as well. A variety of visual special effects signals H.G.'s threshold crossing to 1979 in pursuit of Jack the Ripper, and these are accompanied by a soundtrack composed of historical audio clips that represent the passing of the intervening century. H.G. arrives in 1979 in a San Francisco museum exhibit about H.G. Wells, "A Man Before His Time," that contains the time machine. Yet there is no suggestion in *Time After Time* that this threshold crossing leads to any sphere of rebirth, and the only threshold guardian is the museum guard who ousts H.G. from the machine. The threshold crossing in *Time Machine* is also visually spectacular; time-lapse photography illustrates the ever-increasing speed with which George—at first tentatively, then with greater velocity—hurls himself into the future. As George may have returned to 802,701 at the film's conclusion to spark a rebirth of civilization and intellectual curiosity in humankind (as represented by the Eloi), his initial threshold crossing may, indeed, have led to a sphere of rebirth for humanity. But his threshold guardians are symbolic at best. The mannequin in Filby's Department Store window, across the street from his lab, is at first the barometer of George's temporal progress; he observes the passing changes in fashion with amusement, and this equation of traveling through time with alterations in fashion—which are harmless and cyclical (like the alternating days and seasons that pass in the time-lapse photography sequence)—suggests that the mannequin is George's symbolic protective guardian. His symbolic destructive watchman is the Sphinx he sees on arriving in 802,701, which represents the Morlocks who will impound his machine and threaten Weena.

Logan's protracted threshold crossing, which extends from his attempt to receive plastic surgery in "New You" to his finally arriving in the outside world, does unequivocally lead to a sphere of rebirth and is defended by several protective guardians and destructive watchmen. The unfulfilled promise of "carousel" is that some of its participants will be "renewed," have their life-clocks reset. The time left on each citizen's life-clock is represented by a crystal imbedded in the citizen's palm. It is clear when the citizen is born, turns green during youth, turns red during adulthood, and turns blinking red when the citizen approaches the age of thirty. Logan's crystal starts to blink after he is retrogrammed, but it turns clear (as does Jessica's) when he reaches the outside world. Francis 7 (Richard Jordan), a sandman who pursues Logan and Jessica into the outside world, notices the change in Logan's crystal and exclaims, "Logan, you've renewed!" Symbolically, Logan has been reborn in escaping the dome; and all the dome's citizens are likewise symbolically reborn when all their crystals turn clear once they leave the shattered dome at the film's conclusion.

"Doc," who is ordered to attempt to kill Logan in "New You" to get him running, is one of the first of *Logan's Run*'s destructive watchmen. Another is Francis, Logan's friend and fellow sandman who tries to prevent him from leaving "New You" and who pursues him all the way to the outside. Logan next encounters a group of protective guardians in the runner sympathizers who inhabit the bottom-most levels of the dome; they attack him at first, not believing that a sandman would run, but then accept him and aid him in his attempt to find Sanctuary once Jessica and Holly (Farrah Fawcett-Majors), Doc's assistant and another protective guardian, testify that Logan really is a runner. However, the runner sympathizers are attacked by a squad of sandmen, more destructive watchmen, as Logan and Jessica begin their trek down the tunnel that leads to the "last gate" to Sanctuary. They use the recovered ankh to pass through the last gate, the most specific threshold they traverse, and (still pursued by Francis) go beyond the dome's hydro-electric system to reach an ice cavern inhabited by "Box," a robot whose "job" it is to freeze and encase in ice every runner who reaches him. This has been the fate of all of the 1,056 "unaccounted for" runners that Logan has been sent to follow; and Box, whom Logan manages to disable, is yet another destructive watchman. After defeating Box, Logan and Jessica exit the ice cavern, another specific threshold crossing, to discover the rising sun in the outside world. The last remaining destructive watchman is Francis, whom Logan finally kills in hand-to-hand combat outside the dome.

Logan and *Time Machine*'s George are swallowed in the belly of the whale during or during and after their threshold crossings, respectively, but H.G. does not experience any trace of this episode in *Time After Time*. Logan begins under the dome, which is already symbolically underground; and, until they reach the freight elevator that takes them to Box's ice cavern, Logan's and Jessica's journey towards the world outside the dome is always down into deeper and deeper subterranean levels. They descend further beneath the dome after Logan is almost killed in "New You," reach a level designated "Cathedral" (which is inhabited by violent juveniles called "cubs"), and then attain an even lower level where they encounter the runner sympathizers, who tell them that the continued way to Sanctuary is still "always down." This underground journey symbolizes death and rebirth for Logan in that his life-clock is blinking, indicating that it is time for him to die, when he begins his descent but turns clear, indicating that he has "renewed," when he exists the ice cavern. Box's ice cave, still an underground location even though it is virtually at ground level, is the symbolic hell; and the lost souls/*memento mori* there are the 1,056 "unaccounted for" runners, who are all encased in ice. Logan is symbolically mutilated in "New You" when his left cheekbone is "narrowed" by laser surgery; and he is mutilated further, with a laser slash across his chest, when "Doc" turns all the facility's lasers on him in the first attempt to kill him.

George endures three distinct underground journeys in *Time Machine*, and all are symbolic descents into hell. He is first interred in stone for 800,000 years after the atomic satellite's detonation provokes a volcanic eruption in 1966 London; the flaming lava coursing through the ruined London streets indicates that this is a symbolic descent into hell, and George notes, "Only my speed through time saved me from being roasted alive and encased in stone forever." He is knocked unconscious for several hours after he falls from his spinning machine once it stops too precipitously in 802,701; and this, with his 800,000-year interment itself, is the symbolic death from which George arises as if reborn when he recovers consciousness. After Weena and some other Eloi are taken by the Morlocks into the Sphinx's pedestal, George descends into the Morlocks' underground domain via one of their many ventilation wells to rescue Weena and try to finds his machine. He is told that those who enter the pedestal "never come back. No one can bring them back"; and this is one indication among many that this is another, more elaborate subterranean hell. The Eloi who have been herded underground are the lost souls, the whip-wielding Morlocks are the demons tormenting them, and the ubiquitous skeletons of those Eloi the Morlocks have already eaten are the *memento mori*. (Of course, that the Morlocks eat the Eloi, and undoubtedly would eat George as well, introduces the concept of being ingested into this belly of the whale episode.) George finally sets fire to this subterranean realm, relocating to a more symbolically appropriate location the forest fire that consumes Weena in Wells' novella; and these flames, too, reinforce the message that the Morlock's domain is hell. After he has freed the Eloi and destroyed the Morlock's realm, George discovers that the doors to the pedestal are open, and he enters to recover his machine. This is his third underground journey, as the doors to the pedestal close behind him; and the flaming, smoking ruin that is the interior of the pedestal is yet another symbolic hell. George is attacked by Morlocks and kills one of them before he manages to escape in the time machine, but he goes forward in time again, at first, and sees the remains of the dead Morlock, another *memento mori*, decompose to a skeleton and then decay into dust. And this film also features something like a temple guarded by gargoyles in the pedestal into which George must go to retrieve his machine, as this entrance to the Morlock's domain is surmounted by the gargoyle-like Sphinx.

The Initiation Stage

Of course, all three protagonists must endure tests in the road of trials, and all must face and assimilate a shadow. George must retrieve his machine from the Morlocks' realm to return to his own time, must save Weena from being taken and eaten, and must destroy the Morlock's underground domain by rallying the Eloi to throw wood down the ventilation wells into the raging fires below. The Morlocks eat meat, have an affinity for machinery, and exhibit some curiosity—characteristics they have in common with George but do not share with the Eloi—yet they are also monstrous parodies of human beings; thus, they are the Eloi's opposites but George's shadows. (The Morlocks are the time traveler's shadows even more so in Wells' novella, in which the time traveler is also more pointedly a shadow to the Eloi as well.) George assimilates the Morlocks by destroying their habitat and, ostensibly, their hold over the Eloi.

H.G. must stop Jack the Ripper from initiating a murder spree in 1979 and, specifically, must stop him from killing Amy. He is only partially successful, as Jack does take five victims—but not Amy—before H.G. finally puts an end to his rampage by sending him "into infinity" through removing the time machine's "vaporizing equalizer" and thus sending Jack hurling through time without the machine when Jack tries to escape into time once more at *Time After Time*'s conclusion. And Jack is H.G.'s shadow: both are professional men from the 1890s—H.G. is an inventor and social critic, and Jack is a medical doctor—but H.G. is a "gentleman," which he demonstrates in his behavior to Amy throughout the film, while Jack, a homicidal maniac, is, as he admits to H.G. at the film's conclusion, "no gentleman." Logan must escape from the dome and, once he discovers that Sanctuary is a myth, return to share this knowledge with his society; his shadow is Francis, Logan's friend and another sandman—but one whose life-clock has not been retrogrammed—whom Logan kills after they both escape from the dome.

As all three protagonists are the hero as lover, all three have a meeting with the goddess; and all have a mystical marriage in a special location with the goddess as the Lady of the House of Sleep. While they are under the dome Jessica, a runner sympathizer, does not want to have sex with Logan because he is a sandman—even though she had put herself "in the circuit" and he had "chosen" her. However, he eventually convinces her he is a runner, and she then falls in love with him and wants to accompany him to Sanctuary. She finally says "yes" to Logan—and vows, "All I want is to be alive and with you. That's all"—after they have reached the outside world, learned that Sanctuary does not exist, and discovered that their palm crystals have turned clear; so the special location in which they have their mystical marriage is the natural world outside the dome.

As Weena represents "the slumber of human consciousness" to George, she, too, is the Lady of the House of Sleep. The special location of their mystical marriage is the year 802,701, to which George may have returned at *Time Machine*'s conclusion. While she falls for him in *Time After Time* before H.G. fully reciprocates her feelings, Amy is the Lady of the House of Sleep to H.G. in that, as a 1979 feminist, she embodies some of the utopian ideals—specifically equality between the sexes and "free love"—that had prompted H.G. to invent his time machine in the first place. They have sex in 1979, the special location of their mystical marriage, after Amy assures the gentlemanly H.G. "I'm practically raping you."

Yet the Initiation Stage is the stage of adventure that is most neglected in these films. None of them features a woman as temptress. And the only hint of anything like an atonement with the father in any of them is Logan's friendly encounter outside the dome with the "old man," a father-figure in *Logan's Run* merely in that he is the only old man either Logan or Jessica has ever seen. Similarly, the only vestige of any moment of apotheosis in these films is the suggestion of a theme of cyclical return in *Time Machine*. The emphasis on the repeating cycles of nature in this film—evident in its insistence on the existence of repeating cycles of war and peace as well as in the time-lapse photography's graphic depiction of the cycles of nature—is a reversal of the theme of entropy in Wells' novella. Where the time traveler's sojourn to the terminal beach of the year 30,000,000 in the novella demonstrates that the cycles of nature will eventually break down, George's stops in 1917, 1940, and 1966 in the film only reaffirm that there are cycles of war and peace as well as cycles in nature. And the content of the monomythic hero's apotheosis is the cosmogonic cycle, the ever-repeating cycle of the universe's destruction and recreation. Finally, while George does save Weena and devastate the Morlocks' underground realm in *Time Machine*, and while H.G. does save Amy and rid the world of Jack the Ripper in *Time After Time*, the only really significant boon any of these protagonists receive that is of use to his original societies is Logan's revelation that Sanctuary does not exist but that there is a habitable world outside the dome, which ultimately frees the dome's citizens and gives them the additional boon, not of immortality, but at least of extended life beyond the age of thirty.

The Return Stage

The return stage is muted in these films, too, just as it is in the *Star Wars* trilogy. It is Jessica who does not, at first, want to return to the dome, not Logan, who is determined to share his discovery of the outside world with his fellow citizens. He and Jessica reenter the dome through its hydro-electric facility, but there is not much of a magic flight and no rescue from outside the unknown world in *Logan's Run*. Nor is there any refusal to return, magic flight, or rescue from outside the unknown world in *Time After Time*, as H.G. and Amy return to 1893 apparently without incident. While George in *Time Machine* is quite anxious to return his present (to January 5, 1900, five days after his departure), in Filby's opinion he then abandons his present for 802,701 and Weena after his story is met with incredulity by his dinner guests. His return to the present is both opposed and furthered by "magic" means. The Morlocks, who had taken his machine into the pedestal, entice him inside after he destroys their domain by opening the doors for him; but they then trap and ambush him, and would have killed him had he not been able to escape into time. This escape is furthered by extraordinary means in that George had removed the levers that control the machine before the Morlocks had taken it—which is why they never operate it—and he is finally able to reinstall the levers and use his machine before the Morlocks completely overpower him.

During the return threshold crossing there is a dilation of time for both George in *Time Machine* and H.G. in *Time After Time*, and each of the three protagonists returns with a talisman of his quest. George leaves his own time period on December 31, 1899, and returns to it on January 5, 1900; he is gone for five days, but appears to spend only two or three days in 802,701. Similarly, H.G. arrives in 1979 on November 5 and leaves 1979 on November 10, having spent five days in the future, but he is in the process of setting his machine to return him to the same date on which he had left 1893, November 5, at the film's conclusion. He returns to 1893 with Amy, the talisman of his quest. As in Wells' novella, George returns to 1900 with the flowers from 802,701 that Weena had given him and—as the species is unknown in his present—offers them to his dinner guests as proof that he had travelled into the future. The talisman of Logan's quest in *Logan's Run* is the old man whom Logan and Jessica bring back to the dome with them as proof that the outside world exists and that the life-clocks kill those who would be able to continue living in that other world.

Logan conveys wisdom from the unknown world outside the dome to the citizens of the dome when he tells them at *Logan's Run*'s conclusion that "No one has to die at thirty. Live. Live! Live and grow old." Jessica adds, "There is another world outside." And Logan concludes by saying, "The life-clocks are a lie. Carousel is a lie. There is no renewal, only death." In a reversal of what occurs in the monomyth, rather than accept the known world under the dome, he and Jessica have accepted the everyday reality of the world outside the dome, of the "other" world, having determined that life outside the dome is preferable to death at thirty. Also, now that he has Amy to bring back with him and after having seen that the future is not what he had anticipated, H.G. seems more reconciled to life in 1893 at the conclusion of *Time After Time* than he had been at the film's beginning. Only *Time Machine*'s George does not accept the everyday reality of either the known or the unknown worlds; while he is thoroughly demoralized by the human condition in 802,701, he also finally abandons his present, which he feels is flawed as well, to resume his travels in time.

None of these protagonists has any transcendent experience to accept, and George is the only one of them who becomes the master of both the known and unknown worlds by gaining the freedom to cross the threshold freely in having retained and reused his time machine. He agrees with Filby, before he begins to tell his tale, that he has "all the time in the world," and Filby reiterates that "He has all the time in the world," the film's last line of dialogue, at *Time Machine*'s conclusion. In contrast, *Time After Time*'s H.G. intends to "dismantle" his machine once he returns to 1983. And there is no returning to the gutted dome in *Logan's Run*.

Yet all three protagonists attain the freedom to live. Logan can live in the other world outside the dome—but not in the original, know world under the dome—without the anxiety of knowing he will die at age thirty, and he is conscious that he is the vehicle of the cosmic change of having freed his fellow citizens. Near the beginning of *Time Machine*, before he sends his model into the future, George asks Dr. Hillyear, "Can man control his destiny? Can he change the shape of things to come?" By the end of the film George has discovered—in having freed the Eloi from the Morlocks' predations—that, indeed, one can change the shape of things to come; he may have returned to the future, not only aware that he has been the vehicle of a cosmic change, but also determined to change the future even further. *Time After Time*'s H.G. returns to 1893 free of the anxiety of having loosed a madman on the future, but this is a far less cosmic change than those engendered by George or Logan.

3

Early '80s Cult Films:
Escape from New York, *Tron*, *Dreamscape* and *The Last Starfighter*

Following the stunning cultural impact and spectacular financial success of *Star Wars Episode IV: A New Hope* (1977), science fiction films reinterpret the monomyth most relentlessly during the final seven years of the second science fiction film boom of 1977–1985, which *A New Hope* established and which a film that reproduces the monomyth's plot structure even more meticulously, *Back to the Future* (1985), punctuated. In addition to *Time After Time* (1979), the two *Star Wars* sequels (1980, 1983), and *Back to the Future* (see Chapter 6), these films from the second science fiction film boom also include the first three *Star Trek* films (1979, 1982, 1984; see Chapter 8), *Dune* (1984; see Chapter 4), *The Terminator* (1984; see Chapter 5), and a cluster of somewhat less-celebrated films released between 1981 and 1984: *Escape from New York* (1981), *Tron* (1982), *The Last Starfighter* (1984), and *Dreamscape* (1984). Each of these four films reiterates the monomyth more completely than does *The Time Machine*, *Logan's Run*, and *Time After Time*; and each provides a different take on the monomyth in that each conceptualizes a different kind of "other world" in which the hero experiences the adventure—respectively, a penal colony, cyberspace, outer space, and the inner space of another's dreams, the subconscious. Joseph Henderson points out that "it is only the specific forms of these archaic patterns that change, not their psychic meaning" (157). Thus, while the other world is conceptualized differently in each film—making them seem distinctly unique, superficially—all are strikingly similar otherwise, not only in exhibiting the same underlying plot structure generally, but also in the specifics of each protagonist's character-ization and in the details of each adventure; all these protagonists embody or

48

omit many of the same qualities a monomythic hero might possibly possess, and their adventures likewise include or ignore many of the same episodes that hero might possibly experience.

The protagonists in *Escape from New York*, *Tron*, *The Last Starfighter*, and *Dreamscape* are, respectively, "Snake" Plissken (Kurt Russell), Kevin Flynn (Jeff Bridges), Alex Rogan (Lance Guest), and Alex Gardner (Dennis Quaid). All are orphaned or exiled, at least socially, and all possess exceptional gifts; but only Flynn and Gardner (in *Tron* and *Dreamscape*) triumph over pretenders, and only Gardner risks his life willingly. None has a special birth or virgin mother, none is seeking a father, and none make humanity more comprehensible or the world more spiritually significant; but each of their worlds suffers symbolic or real deficiencies, and each protagonist possesses at least one conditional quality: While all but Plissken (in *Escape from New York*) save the world, none identifies with a father-figure; while Plissken, Flynn, and Rogan (in *The Last Starfighter*) are warriors, none changes his world's status quo significantly; moreover, Rogan is also a lover, Flynn is also a mystic, and Gardner is also both a lover and a mystic.

Almost every science fiction film that utilizes this plot structure strongly emphasizes the departure stage, omits one or more key elements of the initiation stage, and radically downplays the return stage; these films are no exception. Each protagonist experiences both modes of the call to adventure; all but Flynn (in *Tron*), who has no choice, at first refuse; and each receives supernatural aid, crosses a threshold defended by a destructive watchman, and is literally or symbolically mutilated, dismembered, or killed while experiencing a literal or figurative underground journey that, for Plissken and Gardner (in *Escape from New York* and *Dreamscape*), is also a symbolic descent into hell. Each endures tests, and each except Plissken assimilates his shadow; all encounter a goddess and a father-figure, but not a temptress; none experience apotheosis; and while all receive some kind of "boon," only Plissken's is a tangible object, and he alone refuses to share it with his society. Only Plissken and Flynn (in *Escape* and *Tron*) experience a magical flight or any dramatic re-crossing of the threshold; only Gardner and Rogan (in *Starfighter* and *Dreamscape*) acquire the ability to cross the threshold freely; only Gardner and Flynn (in *Dreamscape* and *Tron*) return to the world free of anxiety; and only Rogan (in *Starfighter*) attains any semblance of transcendence—as he is the only protagonist to evolve significantly during the adventure—or any sense of being the vehicle of cosmic change. (See Figure 4 and Figure 5.)

	Escape from New York	Tron	The Last Starfighter	Dreamscape
Monomythic Hero	"Snake" Plissken	Kevin Flynn	Alex Rogan	Alex Gardner
Special Birth				
Mother a Queen				
The Hero is an Orphan or in Exile	totally disaffected criminal anti-hero exiled to "life" in Manhattan penal colony	disaffected, underachieving corporate drop-out exiled to cyberspace	fatherless; his social alienation is exaggerated by his Beta Unit's social ineptitude	fatherless; he is a disaffected social outcast and hustler who is wasting his talent
Seeking a Father				
The Hero Triumphs over Pretenders	(Plissken humiliates President and Hauk, finally, by switching tapes)	Flynn (1) replaces Dillinger as Encom exec after (2) helping Tron crash the MCP	(Rogan finally acknowledges that deceased Beta Unit had replaced him)	Gardner (1) defeats Tommy Ray in President's dream and then (2) kills Blair
The Hero Possesses Exceptional Gifts	former war hero and glider pilot with a dogged determination to survive anything	computer genius and incomparable videogame player has "user power" in cyberspace	incomparable videogame player with "the gift" to be "the best starfighter ever"	an "authentic genius" who has "the old God-given gift" of telepathy
The Hero Does not Fear Death	(inverted, as avoiding death is his motivation)	risks "de-resolution" to save "programs"	(inverted, as he is extremely reluctant)	voluntarily risks his life to save Buddy, President
The Hero's World Suffers Deficiencies	imperialist police state mired in war lacks meaning and leadership	corporate corruption; threat that MCP will control the world	nothing ever happens in Rogan's trailer park or his life	rogue spy chief Blair plots to assassinate the President
Provide Spiritual Significance				
Make Humanity Comprehensible				
Hero as Warrior	but inverted: war hero perversely preserves the hellish status quo	but inverted: as a warrior, he changes only the "other world"	but inverted: as a warrior, he changes only the "other world"	
Hero as Lover			Rogan returns to space w Maggie	Gardner "takes" Jane on a train
Hero as Ruler				
Hero as World Redeemer	(inverted: while able, he refuses)	(yes, but isn't one with the father)	(yes, but isn't one with the father)	
Hero as Mystic		a "user" who can affect cyberspace		telepath can enter and affect dreams

Figure 4: The Qualities of the Hero in Four Less-Celebrated '80s Cult SF Films.

Qualities of the Hero

Plissken, Flynn, Rogan, and Gardner are all in some way exiles. Fatherless and thus partially orphaned, *Starfighter*'s Rogan is also a social outcast who cannot go to Silver Lake with his girlfriend, Maggie (Barbara Bosson), and his buddies (who call him "Mr. Seri-o-so") but must remain at the Starlite Starbrite

	Escape from New York	Tron	The Last Starfighter	Dreamscape
The "Other World"	walled-in Manhattan as a penal colony	cyberspace within Encom's computers	outer space, most specifically Rylos	inside another person's dreams
The Call to Adventure	blunders: Plissken and Air Force One captured; heralds: two dead convicts, Hauk, and Romero	blunder: Dillinger denies Flynn access to Encom's computer; heralds: CLU & Sark in Flynn's lightcycle game	blunder: Starfighter game is not in Vegas; herald: Centauri's voice, as voice of the game, issues call	blunder: Gardner takes Blair's agents' help; heralds: running woman in dream, Tommy, and Sims
The Call is Refused	until Hauk blackmails Plissken with arterial time bombs	(Flynn literally has no choice, but refuses to believe it at first)	repeatedly, but Beta Unit & Grig finally talk Rogan into it	until Novotny blackmails Gardner with IRS audit
Supernatural Aid (& a Talisman) Provided by	Hauk (arterial bombs, etc.), Cabby, and Brain	Dumont, Alan (code, but to Tron), Laura, RAM, Yori, & MCP	Centauri (communo-crystal) and Grig	Novotny (dream-link device) and Jane, Novotny's colleague
Crossing the Threshold to a Sphere of Rebirth; Guardians, Watchmen	Plissken flies into Manhattan "dead already," condemned and aided by Hauk	MCP digitizes Flynn, a reborn CLU, after Alan and Laura get Flynn into Encom	to Rylos, threatened by Xur and the Zando-Zan, protected by Centauri & Beta Unit	Gardner enters six dreams, guarded by Novotny and Jane, attacked by Tommy
Swallowed in the "Belly of the Whale"	Manhattan is hell; Plissken is mutilated, symbolically dead	CLU reborn as Flynn sucked "down" into cyberspace	symbolic death and dismemberment, real underground journeys	President's nuclear nightmare: Snakeman in underground hell
Road of Trials/Shadow	retrieve president & tape/(establishment)	game grid to MCP, Tron, Alan/ Dillinger	beat game & destroy armada/ (Beta Unit)	save worker, Buddy, President/ Tommy
Meeting with Goddess		(Yori, but she's with Tron, not Flynn)	Rogan returns to space with Maggie	Jane is "Lady of the House of Sleep"
Woman as Temptress				
Atonement with Father	Negative: Hauk and President are ogres to the end	(no atonement with father-figure Walter or his avatar Dumont)	Centauri turns up alive after Rogan defeats armada	Gardner saves President & avenges Novotny's death
Apotheosis	(Plissken determines humanity's fate)	(Flynn manipulates cyber simulations)	(Rogan validated on Rylos and Earth)	(Gardner manipulates dream realities)
Receiving the Boon	president & tape: Plissken gets to live	data file: Flynn becomes senior exec	Rogan returns to space with Maggie	Gardner goes to Lexington with Jane
Hero Refuses to Return	Plissken destroys tape & hope of peace		(returns for Maggie only to go back)	(Gardner and Jane depart in dream train)
Magic Flight	across mined bridge with Brain's map	Flynn evades pursuit with "user" powers		
Rescue from Outside	Hauk's winch pulls Plissken over wall	Tron receives "code" from Alan		(by Novotny , displaced to 1st dream)
Re-crossing Threshold: Time Dilation; Danger; Talisman of Quest	(arterial time bombs may explode); President and two tapes are talismans	cyber time reckoned in nanoseconds; data file incriminating Dillinger is talisman	Rogan returns, briefly and uneventfully, with gunstar and Grig as talismans	
Master of Two Worlds			immediately returns to Rylos in gunstar	Gardner can enter dreams unassisted
Freedom to Live		Flynn promoted to "senior exec"	as starfighter, returns to rebuild the fleet	Gardner assassinates Blair

Figure 5: The Stages of the Adventure in Four Less-Celebrated '80s Cult SF Films.

trailer park to fix "Elvira's electric" while his mother goes to work. Unlike his friends in his aspirations, too, Rogan wants to do "something with my life" other than "hang out here, watch you shine your pick-up, go to the drive-in, get drunk and throw up every Saturday night, go to City College like everybody else. Forget it." Further dejected when he does not receive the student loan that would have provided an alternative, Rogan's alienation is echoed (and absurdly exaggerated) by the "spaced out" social ineptitude of his Beta Unit, a physical duplicate that alien starfighter-recruiter Centauri (Robert Preston) leaves behind as a "courtesy replacement" on transporting Rogan to the planet Rylos: A "robot," the Beta Unit is comically incapable of interacting successfully with Rogan's friends and particularly with Maggie, who complains, "It's like you're a million miles away."

Another fatherless social outcast, *Dreamscape*'s Gardner is a disenchanted telepath who has abandoned any productive relationship with society to spend his life "always playing the horses and hustling the ladies." *Escape*'s Plissken is a far more thoroughly alienated anti-hero: A former war hero turned criminal and sentenced to "life" for armed robbery in a future–1997, he is exiled to the New York Maximum Security Penitentiary—a walled-in Manhattan (transformed in 1988 into an escape-proof prison) overseen by Police Commissioner Hauk (Lee Van Cleef), who accurately observes that "the survival of the human race [is] something you don't give a shit about," either, when Plissken tells him, "I don't give a fuck about your war, or your President." And *Tron*'s Flynn is not only another self-appointed social outcast—having abandoned his career for the semi-seclusion of his video arcade, "Flynn's," after former Encom co-worker Ed Dillinger (David Warner) steals his computer-game designs—but is also literally exiled to cyberspace when he is digitized by Encom's computer system's Master Control Program, the "MCP."

Rogan merely reveals, finally, that he had been replaced by the since-deceased Beta Unit; and one could argue that Plissken defeats or at least humiliates the President (Donald Pleasence) and Hauk, representatives of America's implicitly illegitimate power structure, by switching the critically important tape he had been sent to retrieve with Cabby's (Ernest Borgnine) tape of "Bandstand Boogie"; but both Gardner and Flynn triumph over pretenders much more emphatically. *Dreamscape*'s Gardner and psychotic telepath Tommy Ray Glatman (David Patrick Kelly), his shadow, are dream-link researcher Dr. Paul Novotny's (Max von Sydow) only remaining psychic protégés, and both are the far older man's symbolic sons; Gardner, Novotny's initial protégé, had "walked out" on the scientist and his experiments nine years earlier and has since been replaced by Tommy Ray, who is jealous of his status as Novotny's prize dream-linker when Gardner reenters the picture. Yet, as a covert telepathic assassin in training, Tommy Ray is secretly "head of [US] covert intelligence" Bob Blair's (Christopher Plummer) protégé, too; and his symbolic identification as the evil "son" (of Novotny) who has usurped "true son" Gardner's place is reinforced by the fact that Tommy Ray had not only murdered his biological father but is also complicit in father-surrogate Novotny's execution by Blair's agents. After Tommy Ray proves that the subject dies in reality if a dream-linker slays her in her dream, Blair plans to eliminate the President (Eddie Albert) by sending Tommy Ray into his dream to assassinate him; and, although he had failed to save his mentor, Novotny, Gardner triumphs over Tommy Ray by saving the President, another father-figure to both, when he follows Tommy Ray into the dream, defends the

President, and finally assumes the appearance of Tommy Ray's dead father in order to distract Tommy Ray long enough to allow the President to impale and kill him. Gardner finally avenges Novotny, ironically, by assassinating Blair—another usurper, in plotting to kill the President—in one of Blair's dreams.

The hero's triumph over pretenders is most explicit, if equally redundant, in *Tron*. Dillinger had stolen ace software-writer Flynn's computer game designs and passed them off as his own, taking both the credit and the promotion to "senior exec" that should have gone to Flynn (who had then resigned), and at some point had usurped Encom founder Walter Gibbs' position in the company as well. Subsequently, the MCP—which, in running Encom and giving orders to Dillinger, has already usurped the usurper—plots to take over the world by taking control of key military computer systems. Flynn aids titular "security program" Tron in crashing the MCP, thus triumphing over the cybernetic pretender, and the immediate result is release of the secure data file revealing that Dillinger had appropriated Flynn's work, which constitutes a triumph over the corporal pretender. Consequently, in the film's final sequence (titled "New Boss" on the DVD) Flynn replaces Dillinger in the company helicopter and, implicitly, as Encom's "senior exec," thus sealing his triumph over the human pretender to the position that should have been his years ago.

Flynn's exceptional gifts are his genius as a software writer and his incomparable skill as a videogame player. To locate the secure file that will incriminate Dillinger, Flynn hacks into Encom's system so expertly that Dillinger must shut it down until Flynn can be "neutralized"; and "the best program that's ever been written" is the program Flynn had created to infiltrate the system—"CLU," his original avatar in cyberspace (also portrayed by Jeff Bridges) before it is destroyed and the digitized Flynn takes its place. Not only a "hotshot" and "the best programmer Encom ever saw," Flynn can also "play video games better than anybody," a skill that enables him to survive and escape the "game grid" on which the MCP plans to wear the digitized Flynn down before finally "de-resing" him. Moreover, as he is a "user," not a "program," the digitized Flynn not only immediately intimidates Dillinger's cyberspace avatar Sark (a "program" who knows that "a user wrote us") but also exhibits "user power"—the ability to manipulate "simulations" in cyberspace (everything that seems to be there, anticipating *The Matrix*'s Neo) as well as to bring programs back from imminent de-resolution and to prevent his own de-resolution.

Incomparable videogame-playing ability is *Starfighter*'s Rogan's exceptional gift, too. After he breaks "the Starfighter record" on the trailer park's game—and, as the sole recruit from Earth, he must be the only human being who ever has—Centauri appears, praises his "virtuoso performance" as "the best, my boy, dazzling, light-years ahead of the competition," and shanghais him to Rylos, where Ambassador Enduran's acknowledgement that Rogan "has the gift" prompts Centauri to assert that "he could be the best starfighter ever.... Face it, Alex, you're a born starfighter." *Dreamscape*'s Gardner is "an authentic genius" with "tremendous gifts"—specifically his telepathic ability, "the old God-given gift" to "work your way into the conscious mind"; Novotny now wants to unleash Gardner's gift on the unconscious, dreaming mind, but Gardner prefers to fritter it away in "always callin' 'em right on the nose" at the race track. And, in addition to being a former war hero decorated by the president, *Escape*'s Plissken exhibits a truly dogged determination to survive, can fly a gullfire—a prerequisite for completing the mission Hauk forces him to accept—and is "their best man," in The Duke of New York's (Isaac Hayes) opinion, or at least "the best I have" available, in Hauk's.

Yet, while all exhibit bravery, the protagonist who comes closest to having no fear of death—the only one to risk his life voluntarily who always has a choice—is *Dreamscape*'s Gardner, who altruistically insists on entering the nightmares of a troubled boy, Buddy Driscoll, "to save the kid," despite knowing that Novotny has already "lost one psychic," Sims, to Buddy's dreams. Gardner also decides to go back to the lab to "stop Blair," who has threatened his life, after having already escaped from him once; and he finally decides to enter the President's dream to confront Tommy Ray, who is the more-experienced and more-vicious dream-linker. *Tron*'s Flynn is suddenly hi-"jacked" into cyberspace and has no choice, but once there he risks de-resolution in attempting to save two "programs," RAM and YORI. Similarly, Centauri "kidnaps" *Starfighter*'s Rogan and takes him to Rylos without first telling him why. Once there, Rogan balks at chanting "Victory or death" with the other starfighter "recruits"; initially refuses to enlist; only returns to Rylos, after Centauri first takes him back home, because the "interplanetary hit-beasts" dispatched to Earth to kill him, the Zando-Zan, will inevitably succeed if he remains there; fears that the battle his alien navigator Grig (Dan O'Herlihy) urges him to fight, as the last remaining starfighter after their base is destroyed, will be "my slaughter"; and only agrees to be a starfighter, finally, to see if the plan he devises to defeat the Ko-Dan Armada will actually work. Inversely, fear of death is *Escape*'s Plissken's only motivation; he wants no part of Hauk's mission, beyond his initial plan to abort it immediately and fly the gullfire to Canada, but is forced to undertake it after Hauk has explosive capsules injected into his circulatory system that will kill him in twenty-four hours if he doesn't succeed.

And Plissken, Flynn, Rogan, and Gardner all inhabit worlds that suffer deficiencies. Plissken's America is an "imperialist" police state at war with Russia, China, and its own home-grown terrorists that is governed by a self-absorbed president who appears to lack compassion, sincerity, and respect for anyone's life but his own; while the film's conclusion implies that the war will soon escalate into a nuclear catastrophe, in the abstract this world is devoid of leadership and meaning, the very qualities symbolized by the two things Plissken is sent into Manhattan to retrieve, the president himself and a tape recording vital to the success of a faltering, nearly concluded peace conference. Flynn's world is not only steeped in corporate corruption but is also in imminent danger of being taken over cybernetically by Encom's MCP. Nothing different ever happens in Rogan's trailer park or in his life. And Gardner's America is afflicted by a rogue intelligence chief, Blair, determined to assassinate a president he fears will be compelled by his dreams to "give away the farm" at an impending peace conference.

Flynn, Rogan, and Plissken are warriors. But, while Flynn and Rogan at least make a difference, especially in affecting their own lives, none change the larger status quo significantly; and Plissken ultimately decides, perversely, to preserve it. A former Special Forces war hero, Plissken is already a warrior; but, in finally switching the tapes, he dooms his world to the status quo of remaining on the brink of Armageddon and implicitly refuses to be a world-redeemer. The digitized Flynn is placed among the "programs" hijacked into cyberspace to fight to the death (de-resolution) as "warriors" on the MCP's "game grid." He assists Tron in preventing the MCP from taking over cyberspace, and thus saves the external world as well, but the only change effected in that world is that a validated Flynn replaces a disgraced Dillinger as Encom's "senior exec"; however, as cyberspace is spectacularly transformed when the MCP crashes, Flynn helps Tron change the status quo within Encom's computer system dramatically, an inversion in which the warrior-hero changes the status quo of the "other world" rather than that of his own world. Similarly, in finally becoming a starfighter and defeating the Ko-Dan Armada, Rogan becomes a warrior and changes the status quo—imminent defeat—of his "other world," Rylos and the other "civilized worlds" the Armada threatens; yet, while he saves "hundreds of worlds, including Earth," nothing on Earth changes—except that he and Maggie leave it behind to pursue what will surely be a more eventful life in outer space.

Thus, *Starfighter's* Rogan is also the hero as lover: Accomplishing the impossible task of defeating the Armada with only one ship leads to a reunion with Maggie that will take their love to the stars. And *Dreamscape's* Gardner is both a lover and a mystic: Novotny's beautiful but reluctant colleague Dr. Jane DeVries (Kate Capshaw) persistently resists ladies' man Gardner's sexual advances at the lab, even though he seduces her on a train in her dream when she once falls asleep, and in the film's final scene they begin a three-day train trip (on a train with the same conductor that had appeared in her dream) that she promises will be "as good as" her dream. As entering either the "dreamscape" of another's subconscious or cyberspace is "to enter an inexpressible realm beyond form," Gardner's telepathic ability to enter and affect another's dreams makes him a mystic as well as a lover, while Flynn's ability to wield "user power" in cyberspace makes him a mystic as well as a warrior.

The Departure Stage

Each of these films contains every episode, and nearly every nuance of every episode, in the monomyth's departure stage (although strict adherence to sequence, like reference to every heroic quality or to every episode, is unnecessary). Each film's call to adventure entails both a blunder that reveals another world and an appropriate herald; yet, unlike the monomyth itself, each film actually begins in the "other world," too, if only fleetingly. Anticipating the opening sentence of Gibson's *Neuromacer* (1984), *Tron* visually conflates cyberspace and the real world by morphing schematized microchip circuits into city streets viewed from above as its title sequence segues to the first scene, set in Flynn's arcade, which immediately re-enters cyberspace by going inside the game Flynn is playing, "Lightcycle," to introduce the other world's lightcycle-riding heralds—the "programs" CLU, Flynn's initial avatar, and Dillinger's evil avatar Sark, his opponent. (That the "programs" in cyberspace always call external reality "the other world," while the film's captions consistently refer to it as "the real world," only reinforces this conflation.) Ironically, the blunder that inserts Flynn into cyberspace is Dillinger's decision to shut down Flynn's level-seven access to Encom's computer, to prevent him from hacking it from outside the system; but Dillinger underestimates the ease with which Flynn can hack the system from within, the only alternative left him. Flynn persuades former co-workers Alan (Bruce Boxleitner) and Laura (Cindy Morgan) to sneak him into the facility, where he accesses the computer from Laura's station; and the MCP then prevents him from locating the data file incriminating Dillinger by severing his access to the system again in the only way it can, by digitizing him into cyberspace using Laura's experimental "matter transform sequence," a teleportation device at her station that employs a laser to disassemble matter and store its pattern as computerized data that can be transmitted to and reassembled elsewhere.

Similarly, *Starfighter*'s title sequence begins in outer space only to zoom quickly to Earth and, finally, to the Starlite Starbrite trailer park, where mysterious herald-character Centauri will eventually offer Rogan "a little proposition" after he breaks "the Starfighter record." But Centauri is herald to the "other world" of outer space long before he turns up in person, as his is the voice of the Starfighter game that "calls" Rogan "TO DEFEND THE FRONTIER

AGAINST XUR AND THE KO-DAN ARMADA" at the film's beginning. And the blunder in *Starfighter* is that the game is in Rogan's trailer park at all: Centauri explains, "It's all a big mistake.... That particular Starfighter game was supposed to go to Vegas, not some flea-speck trailer park.... So it must be fate, destiny, blind chance, luck, even, that brings us together."

Gardner's blunder in *Dreamscape* is to be in a situation that makes it seem like a good idea to get into a car with agents Blair has sent to recruit him for Novotny's dream-link project, who kidnap him; Gardner does so only to avoid being beaten again by some bookies who had already chased him all over the race track and cornered him in the ladies' room. *Dreamscape* begins in its "other world," too, in the President's terrifying dream of a running woman, the first of the film's heralds, being consumed by a nuclear blast. Two additional heralds are the two telepaths, already working with Novotny, who have entered another's dreams before Gardner does: the mysterious Sims, who is carried out "in a basket" after he is nearly killed by the "monster" in Buddy's dream, and the evil Tommy Ray.

In addition to Plissken's blunder in getting caught while attempting a heist, the fundamental blunder in *Escape* is the monumental security breach that has allowed terrorists to seize Air Force One and crash it into Manhattan, where the evil herald who introduces Plissken to this other world by forcing him to undertake the rescue mission, Hauk, receives the Duke of New York's ransom demands from a resident herald, the bizarre-looking inmate Romero. And this film, too, begins in its other world: Two shadowy convicts attempting to escape Manhattan by paddling a raft across the night-dark Hudson—*Escape*'s first two heralds—are blown to bits by a police helicopter in the first scene. Plissken initially refuses the call, ironically, in appearing at first to accept the mission in return for Hauk's offer of a full pardon, for he has no intention whatsoever of really rescuing the president but plans instead, as Hauk has guessed, to "turn the gullfire around and head for Canada"; only later does he reluctantly accept the mission, and thus the call, upon learning that explosive charges implanted in his arteries will kill him if he doesn't return with the president and the tape within twenty-four hours—and even then he tries to beg off the first chance he gets, on the grounds that the president is probably dead already, as soon as he finds the president's locator beacon on a drunken bum.

Dreamscape's Gardner, too, rejects the call at first only to be blackmailed (albeit with a less fatal threat) into accepting it later: After Blair's agents deliver him to Novotny, Gardner tells the scientist, "I'd have to be out of my mind to hook up with that machine of yours.... I don't think I want to get back on that merry-go-round with you"; he changes his mind only when Novotny threatens him with a five-year I.R.S. audit of his gambling winnings. And *Starfighter*'s

Rogan refuses the call repeatedly. He "declines the honor of becoming a starfighter" almost immediately after learning that that is why Centauri had taken him to Rylos, on hearing the other recruits chant "Victory or death." However, after Centauri reluctantly returns him to Earth, Rogan realizes even more reluctantly that he must go back to Rylos—once the Beta Unit convinces him that, if he doesn't, Xur's Zan-do-Zan will hunt him to extinction, that he's "got no choice, 'cause if you stay down here, you're dog food.... At least up there you have a fighting chance in a gunstar." But, back on Rylos, Rogan wants to give up again when he discovers that the base has been destroyed, that his is the only gunstar left, and that he is the last starfighter; and he is still determined to quit after destroying an Azurian ship that had ambushed his gunstar, but Grig finally changes Rogan's mind—while lamenting that Rogan's plan to ambush the Ko-Dan command ship single-handedly might work, if only there were a starfighter left to implement it—by pointing out that the Ko-Dan will eventually reach Earth, if not stopped by Rogan at "the frontier," and by appealing to Rogan's inner starfighter. Only *Tron*'s Flynn does not refuse the call, and that is only because the MCP digitizes him without warning and he literally has no choice. But—like *Starfighter*'s Rogan, who keeps saying "I don't believe this" and "I've got to be dreaming" en route to and once on Rylos—*Tron*'s Flynn, too, initially refuses to believe he is in "the other world" of cyberspace at all and tells himself, "Oh, man ... this isn't happening; I only think it's happening," that it must all be "a dream."

After accepting the call the hero receives supernatural aid from an old man or crone, who provides a talisman in a setting suggesting a womb-like sense of peace, or from a guide, teacher, wizard, ferryman, hermit, or smith who offers aid in a context of danger or temptation. Albeit an alien in disguise, Centauri is the old man in *Starfighter* who, after initially returning Rogan to Earth, provides a talisman in giving him the "communo-crystal" with which he can, and does, contact Centauri again to seize a "second chance" to be a starfighter. As he transports Rogan from Earth to Rylos, back to Earth, and then back to Rylos again, Centauri is also a "ferryman"; but Grig is a "ferryman," too, as Rogan's gunstar navigator who returns him to Earth at the film's conclusion, as well as the "teacher" and "guide" who instructs him in how to operate the gunstar's weaponry and in starfighter lore. Dr. Novotny is the old man in *Dreamscape* who provides Gardner with a talisman, the "dream-link" device itself; as its inventor and creator, he is a "wizard" and "smith" as well; and as its operators he and Jane are also the "ferrymen" and "guides" who transport Gardner into another's dreams.

Hauk is the old man in *Escape* who supplies Plissken with weapons, night-vision goggles, a walkie-talkie, the explosive capsules in his bloodstream that motivate him, a "master life clock" that constantly tells him how much time is left, the gullfire glider that will take him into and (theoretically) out of Manhattan, a "tracer" bracelet through which he can be tracked for fifteen minutes, and the "homing device" that will lead him to the president's "beacon." Although the gullfire is also necessary initially, Plissken's arterial time bomb is the most crucial item and the one most like a talisman. More so than Hauk in providing the gullfire, however, penal colony inmate Cabbie is Plissken's "ferryman"—a Charon-like figure in the film's comically insistent identification of Manhattan with hell—as well as the "guide" who warns Plissken of the penal colony's dangers and leads him through its bonfire-lit streets to Brain (Harry Dean Stanton). And Brain is another "guide"—who leads Plissken to the Duke of New York and finally to the president, and who also provides the map that gets Plissken most of the way back across the mined 69th Street Bridge—as well as the "wizard" and "smith" who, as the penal colony's resident scientific genius, invents and manufactures whatever the Duke demands.

The old man in *Tron* is "Tower Guardian" Dumont, Encom founder Walter's avatar in cyberspace, who sacrifices himself to Sark's "inquisition" in order to give Tron, Alan's avatar, an opportunity to interface with Alan, his "user"; but it is Alan who provides a talisman—the new "code" for Tron's "identity disk" that will disrupt the MCP—and he provides it, not to Flynn, but to Tron. Yet Flynn does encounter guides, ferrymen, and a smith: RAM, a "program" who orients Flynn to cyberspace and later joins Flynn and Tron in battling the MCP, and YORI, Laura's cyberspace avatar who accompanies Flynn from the "game grid" to the MCP control tower, are guides; Alan and Laura, who sneak Flynn into Encom's computer facility, as well as the MCP, who digitizes Flynn with Laura's "matter transform sequence" laser, are ferrymen; and Alan, who has written the "code" that enables Tron to crash the MCP, is the smith.

The hero next crosses the threshold to an unknown world that leads to a sphere of rebirth and may be defended by protective guardians or destructive watchmen. Of course, Flynn crosses the threshold when digitized by the MCP, the destructive watchman that monitors him hacking Encom's computers; and this is a symbolic rebirth *per se* in that the digitized Flynn replaces in cyberspace his "de-resed" avatar CLU (portrayed by the same actor, Jeff Bridges), who had been crushed earlier while attempting to escape the Lightcycle "game grid." But Flynn also crosses a literal threshold, moments before this, when Alan and Laura, his protective guardians, smuggle him into Encom's high-security area through an enormously thick, vault-like passageway.

Escape's Plissken crosses the threshold by flying his gullfire across the Hudson into Manhattan; this is his sphere of rebirth twice over because, as Hauk tells him, he is metaphorically "dead already" due to the explosive charges in his arteries that will be nullified only if he succeeds, and because if he does succeed he will also receive a "full pardon" from his "life" sentence. Hauk is both the destructive watchman, in implanting the arterial explosives to control Plissken, and the protective guardian, in also providing the gear that enables Plissken to survive and complete the mission. *Starfighter*'s Rogan crosses the departure threshold twice, when Centauri twice flies him to Rylos; his destructive watchmen are Xur, whose sneak attack kills the other starfighters on Rylos, and the Zan-do-Zan, whose attempts to assassinate Rogan back on Earth are foiled by protective guardians Centauri and the Beta Unit; space is Rogan's sphere of symbolic rebirth in that the Beta Unit, his double on Earth, dies ramming a Zan-do-Zan with a stolen truck, yet Rogan later returns from space, again, alive after all. (Echoing Rogan's symbolic rebirth with what appears to be a literal resurrection, Centauri is wounded by a Zan-do-Zan on Earth and seems to die after returning Rogan to Rylos; but he eventually reappears and explains, "I was merely dormant while my body repaired itself.")

While Rogan crosses the departure threshold twice, *Dreamscape*'s Gardner crosses it six times, each time he enters another's dream, and the symbolic rebirth occurs during the first link, after the initial threshold crossing: Inside a steel-worker's dream ostensibly only as an observer, Gardner tries to prevent the dreamer from falling off of a skyscraper under construction only to fall to his apparent death himself, yet he merely awakens before he can hit the ground when Novotny disconnects him from the dream-link device. Gardner subsequently enters the dreams of Mr. Weber (George Wendt as a comically jealous husband), Buddy, Jane, the president, and Blair. Novotny, who promises beforehand to "bring [Gardner] back out" of the first dream, and does, is a protective guardian, as is Jane, who watches over Gardner's body later, when he enters the president's dream. In addition to Blair's agents in the real world—who spy on, abduct, and try to kill Gardner—the dream world's destructive watchmen are the monstrous Snakeman in Buddy's nightmare and Tommy-Ray-as-the-Snakeman in the president's nightmare.

Sometimes literally or symbolically consumed, the hero has a death-and-rebirth experience in being swallowed in the belly of the whale that is frequently a literal or symbolic underground journey representing descent into a literal or figurative hell that may contain serpents, devils, lost souls, flames, and *memento mori*. The hero might also enter a temple guarded by gargoyles, and he may be literally or symbolically mutilated, dismembered, or killed. *Dreamscape*'s imagery conflates the trope of being eaten with that of the underground journey as a symbolic descent into hell through its visualization of Gardner's threshold crossings into the subconscious, which are simultaneously like being swallowed down a huge gullet and like plunging down a nastily organic computer-graphics tunnel.

The last dream-link, in which Gardner kills Blair, is brief and anti-climactic; but Gardner enters each of the five earlier dreams via this gullet-like tunnel except Buddy's, in which this initial symbolic descent is replaced by two less-stylized and even more nightmarish underground journeys that occur within the dream itself: After Buddy and Gardner follow the Snakeman down an enormous length of surreal stairs, Buddy decapitates the Snakeman and its head tumbles into a bottomless abyss. The very presence of the Snakeman in Buddy's nightmare suggests a symbolic descent into hell; and the climactic fifth dream, in which Tommy Ray threatens the president, is redundantly hellish. Not only does Tommy Ray become the Snakeman within this dream, but, like all the President's recurring nightmares, this one, too, is set in a flaming, devastated Washington that has suffered a nuclear blast like the one that awakens the president in the film's opening dream-sequence. This climactic dream also contains lost souls as *memento mori* in the form of the hideously burned, cadaverous passengers on the train carrying the President through this hellish landscape; already having been killed symbolically in the steelworker's dream, earlier, Gardner is mutilated in the president's nightmare when Tommy Ray-as-the-Snakeman bites him; and Tommy Ray subsequently pursues Gardner and the president down into a bombed-out subway station and finally into a flaming underground cavern.

Not only is *Tron*'s Flynn, too, symbolically killed when the MCP squashes CLU, Flynn's initial avatar in cyberspace, but the imagery of Flynn being sucked into cyberspace, which the MCP refers to as "down here," is strikingly similar to that of Gardner entering a dream—an almost identical descent down a computer-generated tunnel, minus the icky organic element—suggesting that this is another symbolic underground journey; also, all the hijacked "programs" forced to compete on the "game grid" are this other underworld's lost souls. And *Starfighter*'s Rogan is not only symbolically killed when the Beta Unit sacrifices itself to stop a Zan-do-Zan, he is also symbolically mutilated when the Zan-do-Zan wounds his robotic double, earlier, and is symbolically dismembered earlier still when the Beta Unit removes its head to fix an "ear malfunction." Yet *Starfighter*'s underground journeys are literal: The starfighter base to which Centauri takes Rogan is inside a mountain-like asteroid, and Rogan later pursues an Azurian ship into and all through the "caves"—an incredibly intricate tunnel system—of another asteroid, where he hides until the Ko-Dan Armada passes by.

While its underground journey is primarily figurative, *Escape* features the most insistently evoked, and the most comic, symbolic hell to be found in these films. Not only does the female terrorist who pilots Air Force One "down" into its streets call Manhattan "the human dungeon of [the president's] own imperialist prison"—much as its guards always refer to entering it as "going down" or "moving down"—but the aptly nicknamed "Snake" Plissken "free falls" in via glider and finally climbs out over a wall; even its serpent must figuratively descend into this man-made hell and ascend from it. And Manhattan-as-penal-colony is relentlessly depicted as hell. During his briefing Plissken is told "Once you go in, you don't come out," that potential inmates are first given the option "to terminate or be cremated," and that "the crazies"—lost souls he later sees emerging from manholes and boiling up through the floor of a decayed Chock Full o' Nuts—"live in the subways ... the underworld." Decorated with such *memento mori* as heads on stakes, the night-dark streets of Manhattan are initially illuminated by flaming debris from Air Force One and, thereafter, by trash can fires and bonfires. The first inhabitant to appear, Romero, resembles a demon; the first legible graffito is the word "devils" on the walls of the World Trade Center's fiftieth floor; and the first words Plissken hears are lyrics to The Velvetes' parody of "Everyone's Going to New York" that inform him, "This is hell." Moreover, Plissken has to die, albeit symbolically, to enter; not only does Hauk gloat that Plissken is "dead already," due to the tiny time bombs in his arteries, but every major character Plissken meets in Manhattan echoes this idea by referring to an apparently widespread rumor of his demise. Cabby, Brain, and Brain's "squeeze" Maggie (Adrienne Barbeau) all tell him, "I thought you were dead"; the Duke ruminates, "I've heard of you," knocks him unconscious with a crowbar, then concludes, "I heard you were dead"; and when a woman in Chock Full o' Nuts marvels, "I heard you were dead," Plissken responds, "I am." Even Hauk thinks Plissken is dead, on finding his night goggles in the briefcase that contains the Duke's ransom demands, until Plissken activates his "tracer." Symbolically killed to start with, Plissken is also mutilated when shot with a flaming arrow while negotiating Broadway in Cabby's cab and again when mauled by a gigantic, club-wielding brute in the Duke's boxing ring.

The Initiation Stage

The monomyth's initiation stage begins with the road of trials, a series of tests in which the hero is assisted by the talismans, advice, or agents of those who had provided aid, and during which he may also assimilate or be assimilated by his shadow or unsuspected self. Plissken's trial in *Escape* is to survive the mission and return with the president and tape, and everything Hauk provides except the homing device is useful. Rogan's initial trial is to break the record in *Starfighter*, which Centauri notes he "may have thought ... was a game, but it's a test ... a test." In *Starfighter* Rogan must subsequently evade the Zan-do-Zan, fight an Azurian ship and wipe out its base, devise a plan to disable the Ko-Dan command ship, and destroy the Armada, all of which he can accomplish only after using the "communo crystal" to recall Centauri, who returns to Earth in time to save Rogan from the first Zan-do-Zan. And the Beta Unit is not only Centauri's agent, left on Earth to assist Rogan by acting as Zan-do-Zan bait in his absence, but is also Rogan's shadow in being a physical double that lacks his social skills. However, Rogan only assimilates the Beta Unit in that the Unit is destroyed in Rogan's stead while preventing a Zan-do-Zan from alerting Xur that the last starfighter is still alive. Flynn's initial test in *Tron* is also a game; he must first play and survive cyberspace jai alai and Lightcycle on the "game grid" before undertaking his other trials, escaping the grid and surviving the journey to the "control tower" in order to assist Tron, a security program written by Alan that is also "going after the MCP." Thus, Tron is Alan's agent who, in an inversion, does not assist but is assisted by Flynn (as well as by Dumont) in using the new "code" Alan provides. In exposing his dishonesty and replacing him as "senior exec" Flynn assimilates Dillinger, who is Flynn's shadow in being "another software engineer ... not so young, not so bright, but very, very sneaky," who has taken credit for Flynn's game designs and occupies the position that should have been Flynn's.

While *Escape's* Plissken humbles the establishment generally but has no such specific shadow self to assimilate, *Dreamscape's* Gardner and Tommy Ray are developed as shadows more meticulously than any other pair of characters in these films. Another psychic and telepath recruited by Novotny, Tommy Ray first appears in Gardner's apartment, where he plays Gardner's sax and dons Gardner's jacket while attempting to dissuade him from becoming another dream-linker; and both develop the ability to dream-link without Novotny's machine. Yet—as he uses it to discover the cause of his comic foil Mr. Webber's "terrible anxiety" (fear that literally everyone is "schtupping his wife," in an epic parade of infidelities) as well as to aid the falling steelworker, enable Buddy to confront his "monster," and save the President—Gardner's dream-linking is essentially altruistic while Tommy Ray is training to be Blair's psychic assassin and has killed Mrs. Matusik in her dream as a trial run for slaying the president in his. Blair "had no doubts about Tommy" but "wonders" if Gardner, too, "will cooperate" in murder, and orders Gardner's execution after quickly realizing that he won't. Yet Gardner finally does become a psychic assassin, ironically but still altruistically, in becoming the Snakeman and killing Blair in his dream— much as Tommy Ray had become the Snakeman and attempted to kill the president in the president's dream. And Gardner, too, is aided by the talisman, advice, and agents of his supernatural helper, Novotny, in negotiating a road of trials: He must wake before the fall kills him in the first dream-link, save Buddy in the third, and save the President in the fifth; and while Gardner uses Novotny's machine to enter the first two of these dreams, survives them through Novotny's intervention and by heeding his advice, and succeeds in the third by using information from Novotny's files—the fact that Tommy Ray had murdered his father and a photo of the corpse—it is Novotny's colleague Jane who assists Gardner in entering the President's nightmare, without the machine, after Novotny's death.

The hero might also encounter a goddess, a temptress, or both. None of these films contain a plausible temptress, and only *Dreamscape* and *Starfighter* feature a prominent goddess, a woman with whom the hero may have a mystical marriage in a special location and who might assume the guise of the Universal Mother, the bad mother, or the Lady of the House of Sleep. As a dream researcher in a sleep lab, Jane is Gardner's goddess as the Lady of the house of Sleep. While she initially resists his advances, their mystical marriage begins in the dream in which he seduces her on a train; and its consummation will occur on the same train, now inexplicably a part of waking reality, for she promises at the film's conclusion that their three-day trip to Lexington "will be ... as good as the dream," that she soon will be the bliss-bestowing reply to his desire. As a "program" who has forgotten her identity, Laura's cyberspace avatar YORI is also a Lady of the House of Sleep, but not Flynn's; although he restores her memory and brings her back from the brink of de-resolution, the closest they come to a mystical marriage is to share a passionate kiss at a moment when both believe that Tron—her lover in cyberspace, just as Alan is Lori's lover in reality—is de-resed. *Escape*'s only prominent female character, Maggie, has no romantic involvement with Plissken. Yet, somewhat as in *Dreamscape*'s conclusion, *Starfighter*'s Maggie finally returns with Rogan to space, the locus of their mystical marriage, even though she does not exhibit qualities that associate her with any particular version of the goddess.

The hero might also experience atonement with the father or a father figure. None of these protagonists has a father, and only Gardner in *Dreamscape* and Rogan in *Starfighter* experience anything like atonement with a father-figure, just as only they have a mystical marriage with a goddess. Centauri is Rogan's initiating priest in recruiting him to be a starfighter, yet Rogan at first turns him down; after Rogan changes his mind and defeats the Armada, however, a muted atonement occurs when Centauri, whom Rogan had believed dead, unexpectedly turns up alive after all. But some fathers and father-figures die for good in *Dreamscape*: Not only has Tommy Ray murdered his own father, but the Snakeman kills Buddy's dream-father in Buddy's nightmare; and not only do Blair's agents murder Novotny, but in the President's nightmare Tommy Ray kills another father-figure, in ripping out a policeman's heart, before becoming the Snakeman to attack yet another, the President. Gardner saves the President but fails to save his and Tommy Ray's principal father-figure, Novotny, the initiating priest who had enabled both to enter another's dreams. Yet Gardner, who had "walked out on" Novotny and his experiments nine years earlier, achieves a measure of atonement in avenging Novotny's death by killing Blair.

However, this episode can be a negative encounter that might involve an initiatory rite of circumcision and may also demonstrate each generation's violent impulse towards the other generation. Thus, the father can be or can appear to be a tyrant or ogre, and the son and father figures are atoned only after the hero sees beyond this negative manifestation. Plissken also encounters two father-figures, Hauk and *Escape's* President; but both are ogres, both encounters are negative, and there is no atonement because Plissken sees nothing but their negative manifestations. Never depicted favorably, *Escape's* President is most obnoxious after Plissken saves his life—when he immediately aborts, albeit temporarily, Plissken's critically timed escape over Manhattan's walled perimeter to gun down the Duke, who had humiliated him earlier, and then, in his subsequent audience with Plissken, when he seems more interested in getting a close shave, literally, than in the lives lost to secure his release. But Hauk is the principal father-figure in *Escape*, the initiating priest who forces Plissken to enter Manhattan by threatening his life, an initial violent impulse, for which Plissken promises to kill him later, a reciprocated violent impulse. Yet Hauk attempts a reconciliation with Plissken, after Plissken succeeds in the mission, by offering him a job and noting, "We'd make one hell of a team, Snake," but is rebuffed when Plissken, who throughout the entire film has told everyone to "Call me Snake," responds, "The name is Plissken."

The initiation stage's penultimate episode is apotheosis, transcending one's humanity to become god-like, which symbolizes attaining enlightenment—but this is commonly ignored or severely muted in science fiction films that reiterate the monomyth, especially if they have little to do with enlightenment or transcendence thematically, and these films are no exception. *Escape* ignores this episode completely, but Plissken nonetheless determines humanity's fate in destroying the tape. However, as in *A New Hope*, a worldly elevation of the hero at the film's conclusion often substitutes for apotheosis, and in *Starfighter* Rogan is hailed by the multitudes on Rylos after he defeats the Armada and again by his trailer park's residents during his brief return to Earth. Still-more-subtle vestiges of apotheosis occur in *Dreamscape* and *Tron*. Tommy Ray claims to be the "god" of the dream world because he can enter it without assistance and manipulate anything in it; but Gardner finally exhibits the same abilities and thus assumes the mantle of dream-world "god" after defeating Tommy Ray. As a "user," Flynn exhibits a similar ability to manipulate "simulations" in cyberspace, and, as those "programs" who believe in "users" also believe that they are god-like, this, too, is an implicit, much watered-down intimation of apotheosis.

Receiving the boon is the final episode in the initiation stage; the highest boon is enlightenment, but the hero usually seeks such lesser gifts as immortality, power, or wealth. Flynn's boon in *Tron* is release of the data file incriminating Dillinger that he had been after all along, and as a consequence he attains wealth and power as Encom's new "senior exec." Basically, Gardner in *Dreamscape* and Rogan in *Starfighter* get the girl, merely a symbol of wealth and power at best. Plissken receives the gift of his own life, a prosaic variation on immortality, when his arterial time bombs are neutralized in *Escape*; but those more tangible boons he retrieves from Manhattan, the President (whom he detests) and the tape (which he destroys), have the greatest (but unrealized) potential to regenerate his dystopic society.

The Return Stage

Yet this potential is literally thrown away in *Escape*'s final frames when Plissken tosses the tape on which Hauk claims "the survival of the human race" depends into the Hudson and leaves the president with Cabbie's tape of "Bandstand Boogie"; thus, he also refuses to share with humanity his other boon, extended life, in refusing to share the tape. Such a refusal to return or to give the boon to humanity is the first potential episode of the return stage, and *Escape* is one of the few science fiction films utilizing the monomyth to include it so pointedly and conclusively. *Starfighter* is more subtle, as Rogan does briefly return to Earth at the film's conclusion, but only to go back to space immediately afterwards. Several other incidents that may happen during the return stage, like this one, also exclude the possibility that others can occur; and only some episodes—rather than most or all, as in earlier stages—are likely to appear in any given narrative. The hero's return could also be opposed or furthered by "magic" means, he might toss delaying objects behind him to impede pursuers, his attempt to return could end in failure, or he could be rescued from outside the other world; in crossing the return threshold, the hero might convey new wisdom to the known world, accept the known world, experience a dilation of time, encounter dangers in returning to the known world that require him to insulate himself, or return with a talisman of his quest; and, on returning, the hero may become the master of the two worlds by acquiring the ability to pass freely between them, or he might attain the freedom to live, to work in the known world without anxiety or as a conscious vehicle of the cosmic cycle of change.

While Rogan's merely temporary return from space *per se* is entirely uneventful—his gunstar simply lands on Earth—Plissken's return from Manhattan is a magic flight fraught with danger; his final refusal to share the boon is chronologically displaced to the film's conclusion, then, as *Escape* is the most attentive of these four films to this often-neglected stage's subsequent incidents. Opposed by mines planted along his only escape route, the 69th Street Bridge, Plissken's return is furthered by Brain's map, which shows where they are placed. Yet Brain, Cabbie, and Maggie perish in crossing the bridge, and their corpses and collateral debris may be seen as delaying objects impeding the mob of inmates still pursuing Plissken and the President, who murders their last companion, the Duke, while Plissken attempts to scramble over the wall. Hauk's winch pulls them over this return threshold, the wall around Manhattan, and negotiating this final obstacle constitutes a rescue from outside the other world. The President and both tapes are the talismans of Plissken's quest, of course; however, in a final inversion, the greatest danger Plissken faces in returning is not a consequence of re-crossing the threshold but, conversely, that his arterial time bombs will explode if he doesn't re-cross it in time.

Opposed by cyber-ships pursuing him en route to the MCP control tower, Flynn's return from cyberspace in *Tron* is furthered by the "super powers" he wields as a "user," which enable him to create an alternate route, as well as by the "code" Tron receives from Alan, which constitutes a rescue from outside the other world. After Alan's "code" disrupts the MCP, however, Flynn merely and quite inexplicably ascends back "up" the same computer-graphics tunnel to be reassembled again in "the real world," still in the same frozen posture, at Laura's computer station. Thus, his return also involves a dilation of time, which is reckoned in "nanoseconds" in cyberspace, so that his adventure there took virtually no time at all in the real world. And the data incriminating Dillinger that immediately appears on Laura's monitor is the talisman of his quest.

Starfighter's Rogan also returns with talismans, the gunstar and Grig, and in immediately going back to Rylos to begin rebuilding the starfighter fleet he demonstrates that he is both master of the two worlds, in being able to move between them so easily, and that he has attained the freedom to live, in accepting himself as a starfighter and a vehicle of cosmic change, an implicit transcendence. But there is no transcendence for anyone in *Escape*, which exhibits only the most cursory and negative hint of apotheosis; and Flynn merely receives a promotion in *Tron*, although as Encom's new "senior exec" he does acquire freedom to live in the world without anxiety. The return stage is most thoroughly ignored in *Dreamscape*, wherein rescue from outside the other world is severely displaced to the initial dream-link only, from which Novotny retrieves Gardner, while Gardner merely awakens from the climactic fifth dream, in which he saves the

President, as well as from the final dream, in which he assassinates Blair. Yet, by eliminating Blair, who is still determined to kill him, Gardner nevertheless attains freedom to live in the world without anxiety, too. And, in another chronological displacement, his ability to enter Jane's dream (and then the President's and Blair's) without using Novotny's machine demonstrates that he is another master of the two worlds as well.

It is not that surprising that these four films most often pay scant attention to the monomyth's return stage—as some of its incidents are mutually exclusive, so that no narrative is likely to include them all, and as the economy of science-fiction/action-adventure cinema often mandates that a film's conclusion should follow shortly after its climax, which most often in these films is an element of the first episode of the initiation stage, the hero succeeding in one of the tests in the road of trials or in assimilating his shadow. For instance, Gardner defeating his shadow, Tommy Ray, in the act of saving the President—thus conflating assimilating the shadow self with succeeding in the road of trials—is the climax of *Dreamscape*. Similarly, at *Tron*'s climax Flynn finally exposes Dillinger as a fraud, thus assimilating his shadow, as a consequence of escaping the game grid and assisting Tron in destroying the MCP, the last of the tests in Flynn's road of trials. Rogan defeating the Ko-Dan Armada, the last test in his road of trials, is the climax of *Starfighter*. And Plissken retrieving the President in time to have the explosive capsules in his circulatory system neutralized, the last test in his road of trials, is the climax of *Escape*. In dealing out of sequence with whatever attention is paid to the remainder of the initiation stage—or in relegating aspects of the initiation stage to being elements of the film's conclusion—these films conveniently skip from the road of trials to the return stage, which is then in its turn severely deemphasized. For example, YORI shares a kiss with Flynn prior to *Tron*'s climax and thus out of sequence, when they believe Tron has been de-resed. And Gardner consummates his romance with Jane and avenges Novotny's death by killing Blair at *Dreamscape*'s conclusion, yet these incidents are the culminations of his encounter with the goddess and atonement with the father, respectively. Similarly, Rogan returns to Earth to be reunited with Maggie at the conclusion of *Starfighter*, and Plissken's ultimate failure to reconcile with either the President or Hauk leads immediately to his failure to share the boon (the contents of the tape) with humanity at the conclusion of *Escape*.

There is no encounter with a goddess in *Escape*, the encounter is brief and underplayed as well as out of sequence in *Tron*, which also contains no reconciliation with the father or a father figure, and there is no temptress in any of these four films. While the absence of any temptress figure may merely be an aspect of the dramatic economy of each of these individual movies, this lack of any woman as temptress is in any case related to the far more crucial absence of any moment of apotheosis in these films. The woman as temptress is the goddess as perceived by the unenlightened hero, and thus an inversion of the goddess. There is no transition in these films from the protagonist perceiving woman as the temptress to his perceiving woman as the goddess because the hero's enlightenment or transcendence, which such a transition would signal, is not an issue in any of these films. This is because none of these films contain a moment of apotheosis, which is the momomyth's most specific representation of the hero's transcendence and attainment of spiritual enlightenment as well as the symbolic meaning of the hero's adventure as a whole.

The hero's apotheosis represents attaining enlightenment, is symbolized by an annihilation of consciousness that entails the merging of time and eternity, and is characterized by a symbolic transcendence of duality—representing a return to that lost unity that had preceded creation and epitomized by the lotus flower, which has many petals yet is one organism—that is signaled by the unification of such opposites as time and eternity, good and evil, male and female, birth and death, truth and illusion, or friend and enemy. The moment of apotheosis symbolizes transcendence—the transformation of the self as a result of the hero's entire adventure, including his success in passing the tests of the road of trials and assimilating his shadow or opposite—and transcendence is the implicit theme of the monomyth. It is in this way that the monomyth is everyone's story, and each of us the hero: We all must continuously negotiate the path from the being we are to the being we are becoming, the path of transcendence, of the continuous rediscovery of the self. Yet in experiencing no moment of annihilation of consciousness the protagonist of each of these films experiences no apotheosis, either: They each go through the outward form of the monomythic adventure without experiencing its core event, the transformation of the self through the particulars of the adventure; without experiencing its implicit theme, transcendence; and thus without experiencing its deepest resonance with the human condition, the continuous rediscovery of the self.

This may point to an absence of interest in, or engagement with, deeper spiritual issues in the mass media's reflection of American life in the 1980s. This is entirely consistent with what occurs in *Star Wars Episode IV: A New Hope*, the seminal film that is the immediate antecedent of these four films' uses of the monomyth as their underlying plot structure: Luke Skywalker similarly experiences the adventure of the hero but has no moment of apotheosis. But in *A New Hope* the absence of apotheosis makes even less sense than it does in *Escape*, *Tron*, *Starfighter*, or *Dreamscape*. The protagonists of these four films are fundamentally static characters who do not evolve significantly during the course of the adventure, who do not transcend themselves (even though Rogan finally does accept that he is a starfighter); thus, as each film avoids the spiritual element of the monomyth through this absence, it may be appropriate in the context of each individual film that the protagonist has no apotheosis. But Luke does transcend his initial state as a whining, callow youth at the beginning of *A New Hope*. He is a confidant hero of the rebellion at this film's conclusion and a relatively somber Jedi Knight by the end of the initial *Star Wars* trilogy. Yet the closest these films come to any hint of apotheosis is the mundane elevation of the hero—the bestowing of medals—at the conclusion of *A New Hope* and the even-more-abstracted celebrations of the fall of the Empire at the conclusion on *Return of the Jedi*.

Other SF films from the 1980s that utilize the monomyth as their underlying plot structure likewise characteristically exhibit heroes who do not experience apotheosis. Like Luke Skywalker, Sarah Connor (with the help of Kyle Reese) is a monomythic hero who transcends her initial characterization as an inept L.A. waitress to become "the mother of the future" but still experiences no moment of apotheosis in *The Terminator*. Like the protagonists of these four films, Marty McFly is the monomythic hero as a fundamentally static character who experiences no moment of apotheosis in *Back to the Future*. And while Deckard transcends his humanity to merge with the Ilia-probe in *Star Trek: The Motion Picture* (1980) and Spock recovers his "katra" in *Star Trek III: The Search for Spock* (1984), none of the first eleven *Star Trek* films—each one of which also utilizes the monomyth as its underlying plot structure—contains a moment of apotheosis that specifically entails an annihilation of consciousness. However, unlike what is seen in SF films from the 1980s, the protagonists of those SF novels from the second half of the twentieth century that most successfully utilize the monomyth as their underlying plot structure do transcend themselves, do change significantly from the beginning of the novel to the end, and do experience apotheosis.

Gully Foyle "evolves" from an amoral "cipher" to become humanity's savior and a prophet who has grown a conscience, and is about to bestow the gift of space-jaunting on humankind, in Bester's *The Stars My Destination*; his apotheosis occurs when he experiences the crossed-senses of synesthesia (an annihilation of consciousness) and manages to jaunte through time (a conflation of time and eternity) while trapped and on fire in the sub-basement of St. Pat's Cathedral at the novel's climax (Bester 17, 14). Charlie Gordon goes from being a retarded adult to being a genius and then back to having an I.Q. of 68 again—and in the process develops a new persona and comes to learn about himself and his life—in Keyes' *Flowers for Algernon*; his apotheosis occurs during the out-of-body experience he has during his last visit with Dr. Strauss, a psychiatrist and neurosurgeon, in which Charlie feels that he is "on the verge of blending with the universe," loses "all feeling of body or sensation ... as the atoms of my-

self merge into microcosm," and envisions "a multipetaled … flower, *un*multiplying, *un*dividing itself back from the many toward the one," the "swirling lotus," a symbol of enlightenment (Keyes 197–98). Paul Atreides is forced to grow from being the pampered scion of a noble house to being a fugitive nomadic warrior and hardened rebel leader, finally becoming the Bene Gesserit's "kwisatz haderach" and the Emperor of the known universe, in Herbert's *Dune*; his apotheosis occurs when he finally transmutes the Water of Life and enters the plane of apotheosis for the three weeks in which he lies in a deathlike trance, his consciousness annihilated, while exploring his prescient visions. His prescience is itself essentially a conflation of time and eternity, but in transmuting the Water of Life he also unites within himself the male-and-female polarity through becoming a male Bene Gesserit Reverend Mother. And Severian goes from being an apprentice in the Torturer's Guild to becoming Earth's Autarch (the ruler of South America) in Wolfe's *The Book of the New Sun*; his apotheosis is the "actuality" of becoming Autarch in that the "ritual" of "Assimiliation" in which he has just officiated, and which symbolizes this rite of investiture, "belongs to the seventh and highest … level" of "transcendence" (*Citadel* 229, 228). In becoming "the Autarch, who in one body is a thousand," Severian becomes "Legion" by absorbing the personae of his predecessors (226, 211)—becomes many in one, like the lotus flower—and in this sense experiences that loss of the distinction between himself and others that is characteristic of the enlightenment state.

Thus, one cannot merely argue that the absence of transcendence and apotheosis in these four (and other) films reflects a universal lack of interest in, or engagement with, deeper spiritual issues in late twentieth-century American life, as American science fiction novels from the same period that similarly utilize the monomyth do contain protagonists who both transcend themselves and experience moments of apotheosis. Rather, the absence of apotheosis and transcendence in these films suggests that it is more specifically the mass media of film that—following the example of the *Star Wars* films—finds emotional traction in utilizing the monomyth as a plot structure but sees little added value in retaining the "Apotheosis" episode and the spiritual element of transcendence it encapsulates, which lie at the core of the monomyth. Indeed, the four films under consideration in this chapter depict protagonists who evince little transcendence, in addition to having no moment of apotheosis signifying transcendence. This absence strips the monomyth of its spiritual dimensions and leaves the form of the monomyth, which is still dramatically compelling, while abandoning its substance. That these protagonists all receive lesser gifts than the ultimate boon of revelation or enlightenment is related to the downplaying of apotheosis in these films, as apotheosis symbolizes the attainment of enlightenment, and the conjunction of opposites associated with apotheosis is a part of the thought process adepts use to attain a state of enlightenment.

This absence of transcendence and apotheosis mirrors a constricted concept of the "hero" in these four early 1980s films that is also seen in the relative absence of altruistic motivation and a relative inability to change the status quo. While all are brave, the only protagonist to risk his life voluntarily who always has a choice is *Dreamscape*'s Gardner. His altruism in entering first Buddy Driscoll's and finally the President's dreams is not shared by Snake Plissken (who only wants to escape to Canada), by Alex Rogain (who is finally motivated to be a starfighter primarily to see if his plan to defeat the Ko-Dan Armada will work), or by Kevin Flynn (who is essentially trying to survive in and escape cyberspace, and who has a personal score to settle with Dillinger and the MCP). While all these protagonists exhibit the ability to behave heroically when the situation forces their hands, only Gardner exhibits the archetypal hero's inclination to sacrifice himself solely for the benefit of others that is also seen in non-contemporary heroes Luke Skywalker in the *Star Wars* films and the *Enterprise* crew generally in the *Star Trek* films. And, even so, Gardner is an especially cynical individual who has heretofore chosen to live his life quite selfishly in devoting himself entirely to the racetrack and "the ladies." Gardner is the only one of these protagonists who is not the hero as warrior; yet in saving the president and killing Blair he affects the status quo—but by preserving it—more immediately than does Flynn or Rogan, who also preserve it in defeating the MCP and the Ko-Dan Armada, or especially Plissken, who anti-heroically chooses to preserve the precariousness of the world's status quo by destroying the tape that is the only chance of averting war. It seems that, in American society in the 1980s, it is expecting too much to expect that heroism can change the world. Moreover, such unfettered heroism as Luke Skywalker's or Captain Kirk's is believable only if it occurs "long ago, in a galaxy far, far away" or in a strikingly utopian twenty-third century. Such a noble strain of unselfish and effective heroism is too much to expect from characters who inhabit a world much like our own—the protagonists of *Escape from New York*, *The Last Starfighter*, *Tron*, or even *Dreamscape*.

4

Dune: Herbert's Novels, Lynch's Film and the Scifi Channel's Two Miniseries

Each of Frank Herbert's six *Dune* novels—*Dune* (1965), *Dune Messiah* (1975), *Children of Dune* (1981), *God Emperor of Dune* (1981), *Heretics of Dune* (1984), and *Chapterhouse: Dune* (1985)—contains the monomyth, but in most of these works the monomyth's "Stages of Adventure" are enacted by a secondary character and not by the novel's protagonist. While protagonists Paul Atreides and his son Leto II, the series' two most prescient characters, are the monomythic heroes in *Dune* and *Children*, respectively, the monomythic heroes in the remaining four novels are the series' three most prominent Duncan Idaho gholas— Idaho-2 in *Messiah*, Idaho-4 in *God Emperor*, and Idaho-5 in *Heretics*—and the Miles Teg clone in *Chapterhouse*.[1] A seriously flawed production that was well-received by neither the public nor the critics, and almost surely the worst film to be considered in this study, David Lynch's 1984 version of *Dune* unsuccessfully attempts to compress Herbert's epic novel into a 145-minute movie. While exhibiting good casting and good production design, and while it is fairly faithful to the first third of Herbert's story, Lynch's film thereafter degenerates into near-incoherency. More popular but only marginally more successful aesthetically, the 2000 SciFi Channel remake, *Frank Herbert's Dune* (which runs for 265 minutes), takes the time to be more faithful throughout to Herbert's novel but lacks the efficacious casting, cinematic production values, and excellent art design elements of Lynch's film. In being more faithful to the original novel, however, the SciFi version of *Dune* is also more faithful to the original novel's extremely thorough treatment of Paul as a monomythic hero, although Paul is a monomythic hero in Lynch's film as well.

Yet neither version, while both may elaborate such qualities as the hero's special gifts, puts any particular emphasis on the elements of the monomyth evident in Herbert's story overall; ironically, while based on a work that employs the monomyth extensively, neither Lynch's film nor the SciFi Channel's miniseries makes any clear attempt to exploit this. It is as though the creators are unaware of the fact that in replicating Herbert's story they are replicating Campbell's monomyth as well. This is true of the SciFi Channel's less-successful 2003 sequel, *Frank Herbert's Children of Dune*, also. Encompassing both Herbert's *Dune Messiah* and Herbert's *Children of Dune*, this second SciFi miniseries set in the Dune universe is, even at its 266-minute running time, too short to contain adequately the complexities of Herbert's two most-immediate sequels to *Dune*. While duplicating the action of Herbert's sequels, *Frank Herbert's Children of Dune* fails to communicate adequately the motivations and thought processes behind much of that action—particularly in Part I, which recapitulates the plot of *Dune Messiah*. Thus, while Leto II, the miniseries' protagonist, is still a monomythic hero in the SciFi Channel's *Frank Herbert's Children of Dune*, the Duncan Idaho ghola, a secondary character, does not come across in this miniseries as a monomythic hero as well, even though he performs the same acts as does the Idaho ghola of *Dune Messiah* and *Children of Dune*.

Qualities of the Hero

Each of the monomythic heroes in Herbert's *Dune* series is the product of a special or virgin birth and possesses exceptional gifts. Royal-born Paul—the son and heir of Duke Leto and his concubine Jessica, a Bene Gesserit—is *"a freak"* in *Dune*; the unanticipated culmination of the Bene Gesserit breeding program who appears a generation too soon, he is a genetic mutation who possesses the unique abilities of a Kwisatz Haderach, "a male Bene Gesserit whose organic mental powers would bridge space and time" (*Dune*, 195, 522). These powers include having prophetic dreams, being able to sense when someone is speaking the truth, the computer-like computational abilities of a mentat, and prescience, the somewhat problematic and limited ability to perceive the past, the present, and the future. Paul's birth is also special in that it is in defiance of the Bene Gesserit orders to Jessica to bear a daughter to Duke Leto. Paul's son Leto II's birth and abilities are even more exceptional. "An aware, thinking entity before birth" (*Messiah*, 244), Leto II gestates in a monstrously accelerated pregnancy that kills his mother, Chani, in childbirth and is "born with a totality of genetic memory" (*Children*, 4)—with full access to the memories of all his ancestors—as well as with the potential to develop all of Paul's abilities and to merge with Dune's sandtrout, a symbiotic union that also grants Leto II the powers of extended life, super-speed, super-strength, and invulnerability. Reproduced in an axlotl tank from cell scrapings, *Messiah's* and *Children's* Duncan Idaho ghola (like the subsequent Idaho gholas and the Miles Teg clone of the later Herbert sequels) is literally a virgin birth. Every Idaho ghola shares with the original Idaho, an Atreides lieutenant, the distinction of being the greatest swordsman in history; and Idaho-2 is a Zensunni philosopher and a mentat as well. Moreover, he is also the first ghola ever to regain the memories and persona of the original from whose dead cells he was cloned.

Lynch's and the SciFi Channel's Paul are also born to royalty in defiance of Bene Gesserit orders that Jessica produce a daughter, who was to have been wed to a Harkonnen heir, and he is also the Bene Gesserit's Kwisatz Haderach born a generation too soon. In addition to the abilities Paul possesses in Herbert's *Dune*, Lynch's Paul (Kyle MacLachlan) also exhibits "precise control" in using against mechanical "fighters" the Atreides' "weirding modules" (sound-based weapons that are entirely absent in Herbert's and the SciFi Channel's *Dune*). Later, Lynch's Paul trains the Fremen in the use of these weirding modules and eventually discovers that his Fremen name, Muad'Dib, is a "killing word." Moreover, Lynch's Paul is more adept in using the Voice—the Bene Gesserit ability to control others through vocal tone—than is Herbert's Paul, and he has more elaborate prescient visions: he uses the Voice to prompt their Harkonnen guards to remove Jessica's gag in the ornithopter in which they are being taken into the desert to be killed, and he is subsequently able to produce the destructive effects of the weirding module without the module; after Duke Leto dies, Paul has a vision of a Guild navigator demanding his own death, of Duke Leto's death, and of Feyd-Rautha, the Harkonnen heir. Finally, after he transmutes the Water of Life, Lynch's Paul acquires the power to command Arrakis' worms. The SciFi Channel's Paul also acquires the power at least to summon the worms; this Paul magically makes water flow in Stilgar's Seitch Tabr as well, after the Fremen recognize him as "Duke Muad'Dib" and their "mahdi" or messiah; and that Paul has prescient dreams is emphasized more in the SciFi Channel's *Dune* than in either Herbert's or Lynch's *Dune*. While Herbert's Paul dreams only of Chani, and while Lynch's Paul dreams of both Chani and Feyd-Rautha (Sting), the SciFi channel's Paul dreams repeatedly of Leto's death, of the Fremen shouting his name, of Chani, of the "jihad" his actions will provoke, of the eventual terraforming of Arrakis, that Jessica is pregnant with his sister Alia, and that the Fremen will demand that he "call out" Stilgar for a duel to the death to determine the leadership of all the Fremen.

Although he has no mechanical Tleilaxu eyes, as does Herbert's Idaho-2, Duncan Idaho is resurrected as a ghola in the SciFi Channel's *Children of Dune*, just as he is in Herbert's *Dune Messiah*; and the SciFi Channel's Idaho-2 is also a mentat, if not a Zensunni philosopher. Yet, even though the miniseries' Idaho-2 serves precisely the same plot functions and performs precisely the same acts as does Herbert's Idaho-2, because the miniseries' audience is given little insight into his thought processes and emotional states, the SciFi Channel's Idaho-2 falls short of seeming to be a monomythic hero. The climax of Herbert's *Dune Messiah* occurs when Idaho-2 recovers his original's persona and memories after Paul utters the key phrase "She is gone" in reference to Chani's death in childbirth. This phrase triggers Idaho-2's genetically programmed response to kill Paul, but the deep conflict between this compulsion and the original Idaho's lifelong loyalty to the Atreides prompts Idaho's original persona to emerge. (This is what the Tleilaxu had been after all along. Their convoluted plot is, not to kill Paul, but to co-opt him by offering to make him a perfect duplicate of his deceased wife upon proving, immediately after Chani's death, that a ghola can recover its original's persona.) Herbert's climax to *Dune Messiah* has terrific narrative impact, not only because it is believed to be impossible for a ghola to recover its original's persona, so that Idaho-2 doing so is a tremendous surprise, but also because it is at this moment in the novel that the climax of the monomythic subplot involving Idaho-2—in which the ghola's symbolic death and rebirth, crucial trial, atonement with the father (Paul, the Emperor, as father-figure), and apotheosis all occur simultaneously—intersects the climax of the main plot involving Paul, in which Chani dies and the Tleilaxu's true plan to co-opt Paul with the promise of a perfect ghola duplicate is revealed. What is missing in the miniseries is any sufficient development of the novel's monomythic subplot achieved through providing insight into Idaho-2's psychology. Why it is that the original Idaho's persona re-emerges is left to the viewer's imagination, and it is not sufficiently clear that this is a symbolic death and rebirth, a trial overcome, atonement with a surrogate father, and a moment of apotheosis for the ghola.

Leto II's birth and the drama that surrounds it is the climax to Part I of the *Children of Dune* miniseries, just as it is the climax to Herbert's *Dune Messiah*. In both versions, the newborn Leto II communicates presciently with a now-blind Paul and prompts Paul to see through his eyes in order to kill Scytale, the Tleilaxu face dancer who offers to create a ghola duplicate of Chani while simultaneously threatening to murder Leto II and his twin sister Ghanima in their crib. But Leto II then exhibits a greater number of exceptional gifts in the miniseries than he does in Herbert's novel. Not only does the miniseries' Leto II communicate with Paul's consciousness within him, as does Herbert's Leto II, but he also has prescient visions (he tells his sister Ghanima) of running across the desert at super-human speed, his skin covered with sandtrout. Not only does

Leto II know all about Paul without being told, but he also is able to fly an ornithopter without any training, and he and Ghanima are the first to realize they have "already lost" Alia to possession by the Baron Harkonnen who resides in her ancestral memories. Moreover, Leto II exhibits the Voice in talking with Jessica and, while he is being force-fed spice in Jacurutu, has visions of the greening of Arrakis killing off the sandworms. However, while it is clear that he does acquire super-speed and super-strength from merging with the sandtrout, it is not as apparent in the miniseries that Leto II also acquires extended life and invulnerability from this symbiosis.

Each of Herbert's monomythic heroes is an exile or orphan, most are seeking a father in some way, and several triumph over pretenders as the true son. Already exiled from Caladan to Arrakis, Paul is partially orphaned by Duke Leto's death and must flee Arrakeen, the Imperial city, to live in a desert exile among the Fremen while seeking vengeance against those who had killed his father; he defeats Feyd-Rautha—the deceased Baron Harkonnen's designated heir, and thus a pretender to Paul's ducal fief—in a duel at *Dune*'s conclusion. Leto II is orphaned at *Messiah*'s conclusion by Chani's death in childbirth and by the blind Paul's disappearance into, and apparent death in, the desert. In *Children*, Leto II echoes his father's flight from Arrakeen when he exiles himself from Seitch Tabr to the deep desert in pretending to fall victim to House Corrino's attempt to assassinate him, and he eventually abandons his humanity (another mode of exile) in merging with the sandtrout. Suspecting that the wandering desert "Preacher" may be his "father" in disguise (34), Leto II seeks and finally confronts The Preacher, recognizes him as his "father," Paul (340), and then triumphs over three pretenders: Assan Tariq (the Preacher's guide and surrogate son), Alia (Leto II's aunt, who rules as Regent), and Farad'n (the former Emperor's grandson and scion of House Corrino). Idaho-2 (like the subsequent Idaho gholas and the Teg clone) suffers two uniquely different forms of exile: being separated from his persona, until it is restored by some psychic conflict that forces it to reassert itself, and being separated from one's own time, as he is reborn more than fifteen years after his death into a world radically different from the one he had known. Thus, Idaho-2 (again like the subsequent Idaho gholas and the Teg clone) sublimates the monomythic hero's search for the father into a desperate quest for knowledge of a more immediate predecessor, an obsession with recovering his original persona, the driving desire to "*know myself as I once was*" (*Messiah*, 131).

Like Herbert's Paul, Lynch's and the SciFi Channel's Pauls are also exiled from Caladan to Arrakis and subsequently flee, with Jessica, into a still more desperate exile in the desert after Duke Leto is killed. Paul's initial exile from Caladan is emphasized most in the *Dune* miniseries: unlike the Pauls of the novel and of Lynch's film, who are enthusiastic about the adventure of relocating to Arrakis, the SciFi Channel's Paul is angry over having to leave Caladan "for a dry speck of dust in the middle of nowhere"; and the SciFi Channel's Princess Irulan (who appears and interacts with Paul much earlier in the miniseries than she does in either the novel or the film) observes in conversation with Paul at the Arrakeen banquet that he has been "exiled to Arrakis." That Paul seeks vengeance for his father's death is also emphasized in the *Dune* miniseries, in which Paul vows in the desert to "avenge" his father's death and not to stop until he has destroyed the Baron and the Emperor. As in the novel, in both the film and the miniseries Paul kills Feyd-Rautha in a climactic duel after Paul's Fremen forces have retaken Arrakeen. That this is a triumph over a pretender is also most clearly established in the miniseries, in which Feyd-Rautha, in challenging Paul to the duel, acknowledges that he is the Baron Harkonnen, now that his uncle is dead.

Idaho-2's modes of exile and his quest for knowledge of his original personality are both relatively understated in the *Children of Dune* miniseries. Like Herbert's Leto II, Leto II in the miniseries is orphaned shortly after his birth—when Chani dies in childbirth and the blind Paul subsequently "wanders alone into the desert to die" and appears to be crushed by a sandworm at the conclusion of Part I. Yet the miniseries' Leto II tells Stilgar in Part II that he believes Paul may not be dead and that he may be called upon to "demystify" his father, "to destroy his legacy." Subsequently he leaves Seitch Tabr for Jacurutu in search of Paul. While the miniseries' Leto II does not triumph over Assan Tariq, who is the Preacher's guide but is not so evidently his surrogate son in the miniseries, he does triumph over the Regent Alia, who takes her own life with a crysknife during their climactic confrontation. Leto II's triumph over Prince Farad'n—whom his mother, Princess Wensicia (Susan Sarandon), had plotted to place on the throne by attempting to assassinate Leto II and Ghamina—is muted by the fact that Farad'n denounces his own mother, reveals her plot against Leto II and Ghanima, and banishes her at the miniseries' conclusion. Also, the form of Leto II's triumph over Farad'n, Farad'n's bethrothal to Ghanima, seems less dangerous and intimidating to Farad'n in the miniseries than it does in Herbert's novel. And in the novel Leto II further emphasizes his triumph over Farad'n by renaming him Harq al–Ada and making him his scribe, events which do not happen in the miniseries.

Each of Herbert's monomythic heroes demonstrates that he has no fear of death. For example, one expressed purpose of Paul's initiation as a sandrider is to show "Shai-hulud" that he has "no fear" (*Dune* 384), and Paul freely offers his life to a dying Thufir Hawat at *Dune*'s conclusion, while Leto II clearly orchestrates his own death throughout *God Emperor of Dune*. As in Herbert's

Dune, Lynch's Paul transmutes the water of life even after remembering that Reverend Mother Mohiam had told him that "all the men who have tried have died." As in Herbert's novel, Paul in the SciFi Channel's *Dune* recites the litany against fear as he flies his and Jessica's ornithopter into the desert storm to escape Harkonnen pursuers after Duke Leto is killed; he had also recited the litany earlier, when being tested with the box and the gom jabbar by Reverend Mother Mohiam on Caladan. Leto II is completely without fear in the *Children of Dune* miniseries. While Irulan is terrified as a worm almost swallows their ornithopter, Leto II and Ghanima find Arrakis' sandworms "beautiful." Nor does Leto II fear the part Palimbasha and the Laza Tigers have to play in Wensicia's plot to kill him and Ghanima. Finally, Leto II also does not fear the quest for Jacurutu or the dangers of pursuing Paul's "golden path," of merging with the sandtrout and losing his humanity; as the sandtrout bond to his skin at the miniseries' conclusion, Leto II faces down a coriolis storm while reciting the litany against fear.

Each of Herbert's monomythic heroes also inhabits a world that suffers symbolic deficiencies and acts either to make the world spiritually significant or, in some way, to make humankind more comprehensible to itself. Water, of course, is what is lacking on Arrakis, and this absence is symbolic of the Fremen's lack of freedom at the hands of their Harkonnen oppressors. Paul—whom the Fremen accept as their "Lisan al–Gaib" or "Mahdi," the "messiah" of "prophecy" who will "lead them to true freedom"—teaches the Fremen that "they're a people" as well as "how to escape their bondage" (*Dune* 101, 451); only reluctantly does he found the new religion of Muad'Dib that sweeps across the universe with his Jihad and that diminishes the Fremen by making many of them religious bureaucrats preoccupied with political infighting. Twenty years after Paul becomes Emperor, Stilgar laments that the Arrakis of *Children* lacks the "cleaner values" of his old Fremen days, yet by the novel's conclusion Leto II claims that he is "here to give purpose to evolution and, therefore, to give purpose to our lives," that he will "create a new consciousness in all men" (*Children* 3, 346, 406). The monomythic hero's role in making the world spiritually significant and humankind comprehensible to itself is also played out on a microcosmic scale in that struggle for self-knowledge with which Idaho-2 (as well as the subsequent Idaho gholas and the Teg clone) is obsessed.

In Lynch's *Dune* Paul learns that "water is life" on Arrakis, a planet on which "not one drop of water falls"; and after Paul retakes the capital city of Arrakeen and establishes himself as Emperor, it inexplicably rains on Arrakis, signifying symbolically that the Harkonnen yoke has been lifted and the people freed from their oppression. Early in the SciFi Channel's *Dune* Atreides mentat Thufir Hawat tells Duke Leto that the Fremen have a legend of a "messiah, who will guide them to true freedom." In both adaptations, of course, Paul's leadership liberates the Fremen from the Harkonnens and his establishment of the cult of Muad'Dib imposes a monolithic spiritual significance throughout the known universe. It is very clear in the *Children of Dune* miniseries that Paul's empire is corrupted by the ritual symbolism of Muad'Dib's religion. Arriving on Arrakis after twenty years' absence, Jessica notes that "the hypocrisy of ritual still thrives"; and Paul disguised as The Preacher then appears to tell Jessica and the multitude that "the blessings of Muad'Dib have been corrupted." Many Fremen are concerned that the "greening of the desert has proceeded too rapidly" and have withdrawn support from Alia and the Atreides, while Jessica warns that, despite Alia's assurances, the Fremen "must not abandon the desert." Moreover, Leto II talks to Stilgar of the "corruption infecting Arrakis" and tells Stilgar that the old Fremen inhabiting his ancestral memories are "repulsed by this alien life," by the changes the religion of Muad'Dib and the wealth of Empire have wrought on Arrakis, and that a crucial part of Leto II's mission is to "demystify" his father and "destroy his legend." He does this symbolically in denouncing Alia, the spiritual leader of the cult of Muad'Dib, and precipitating her suicide at the miniseries' conclusion.

While each of Herbert's *Dune* series' monomythic heroes exhibits at least two of the five conditional qualities of the hero, Herbert's Paul embodies all five. He is warrior, lover, ruler, world-redeemer, and mystic. Herbert's Leto II encompasses all of these qualities except lover. And Herbert's Idaho-2 is a warrior, a lover, and a mystic. Within an acceptable degree of latitude, each of Herbert's heroes also fulfills that specific destiny associated with each aspect of the hero that he embodies. For example, consider Paul's correspondence to each quality of the hero and the ways in which Leto II and Idaho-2 are also heroes as mystics. Irulan writes that Paul "*was warrior and mystic, ogre and saint*" (*Dune* 466). As warrior, he changes the status quo by driving the Harkonnens from Arrakis and toppling the Corrino dynasty. He is a lover in his relationship with Chani; yet his triumph is ironically symbolized by another woman, Irulan, whom he claims as "bride" at the novel's conclusion because she is his "key to the throne, and that's all she'll ever be" (471). Born and bred "to rule" (31), Paul initially becomes a ruler as military and spiritual leader of the Fremen, then as Emperor of the known universe; while he does not literally seek his father, who is dead, he does flee Arrakeen into the unknown regions of the desert "to avenge my father" (226), and he returns as the lawgiver who establishes a new political and spiritual order, decreeing that "we live by Atreides law now" (*Messiah* 205). Claiming Dune as his "ducal fief" because "it comes to me through my father," Paul takes his father's place when he finally puts his "father's ducal signet" ring on his finger immediately before launching the assault on Arrakeen (*Dune* 428);

in becoming a world-redeemer by then freeing Arrakis from Harkonnen oppression, to avenge his father, he learns that he and the father are one.

A mystic by virtue of his prescient abilities, Herbert's Paul transcends life and myth to enter an inexpressible realm beyond form on at least two occasions. He falls into the deathlike trance in which he experiences "the vision of pure time" after he transmutes the Water of Life, an act that fully awakens his prescience (360), and he disappears again "into the desert—like a Fremen" after he is blinded at the conclusion of *Messiah* (272). This act of fealty to their customs makes Paul a "saint" (253, 279) to the Fremen, some of whom believe "that he had entered the ruh-world where all possible futures existed, that he would be present henceforth in the *alam al-mythal*" (273), "the mystical world of similitudes" (*Dune* 513). Indeed, Leto II believes that "Paul Atreides had passed from the universe of reality into the *alam al-mythal* while still alive" (*Children* 339). Paul had previously explained that, due to his prescience, "I am in the world beyond this world here. For me, they are the same.... I live in the cycle of being where the war of good and evil has its arena"; his priesthood teaches that "*he has gone on a journey into the land where we walk without footprints*" (*Messiah* 205, 271). Although it is a quality already inherent in his prescient abilities, Hwi Noree in *Emperor* notes that Herbert's Leto II is also a "mystic" (392). His ancestral "other memories" constitute the inexpressible realm beyond forms that he enters, in his frequent memory "*safaris,*" during his 3000-year lifetime; and after his death this realm beyond forms is the "endless dream" in which he lives on as "pearls of awareness" within the sandworms (and their progeny) to which his death in *Emperor* gives birth—and in which he attains the "formless" realm of "immortality" by becoming an undying myth (36, 423, 420). As a Zensunni philosopher and a Mentat, Herbert's Idaho-2 is a mystic as well. While Idaho-2 does not enter an inexpressible realm beyond form in *Messiah* or *Children*, both Idaho-5 and the Teg clone use their no-ship prison to escape the universe of the *Dune* series for an unknown destination in an unknown universe—another inexpressible realm—at the conclusion of *Chapterhouse*.

Paul in Lynch's film and in the SciFi Channel's miniseries fulfills the conditional qualities of the hero in much the same way as he does in Herbert's novels. Lynch's film notes, in fact, that in his two-year struggle against the Harkonnens prior to his retaking Arrakeen, after teaching the Fremen his "weirding way" of battle, Paul as warrior had brought "spice production to a standstill." And Paul falls in love with Chani in the desert in all three versions of *Dune*. Yet Paul is not betrothed to Irulan at the conclusion of Lynch's film—as he is in the miniseries as well as in the novel—but is left implicitly to live happily ever after with Chani. Appearing much earlier in the miniseries than she does in either the novel or the film versions of *Dune*—if one discounts her roles as commentator and prologue, respectively—Irulan in the miniseries tries to "interest" Paul in her during the banquet in Arrakeen in Episode I, accuses her father angrily of being complicit in the overthrow of the Atreides in Episode II, and (replacing Lady Margot Fenring) goes to Giedi Prime (the Harkonnen homeworld) to observe Feyd's 100th gladiatorial combat and to seduce Feyd in Episode III. As he does in Herbert's *Dune*, in the miniseries (but not in the film) Paul as ruler changes the ways of the Fremen, which he terms "mindless ritual," by refusing to call out Stilgar in a duel to the death to assume leadership of all the Fremen. Leto II's "Golden Path" will save humanity from future stagnation, and he is thus another world-redeemer, in both Herbert's *Children of Dune* and in the miniseries; and in both versions he and his father, Paul, are one in that Paul's consciousness lives on in Leto II as an element of his ancestral memories. As in *Messiah*, Idaho-2 and Alia become lovers in Part I of the *Children of Dune* miniseries and are married when Part II begins. Idaho-2 is a mentat, and thus a mystic, in the miniseries as well; but as he is not presented as a monomythic hero in the miniseries, this element of his characterization is relatively understated there.

The Departure Stage

The other world to which the hero travels to have his adventure is conceptualized somewhat differently in the film version of *Dune* than it is in the novel or the miniseries. In mythology typical "regions of the unknown" include the "desert" or "alien land" (Campbell 79). As Arrakeen, Arrakis' Imperial city, is an outpost of the Empire—in the miniseries, as in the novel, the "unknown world" of *Dune* is not so much the entire planet Arrakis as it is specifically its mysterious and literally unknown deep desert, home of the Fremen, to which Paul and Jessica flee in escaping the Harkonnens. While "Arrakis is an unknown," it is only in the desert that Paul "passed ... into the deep unknown" (*Dune* 152, 227). Thus, the Atreides travel to Arrakis between chapters in Herbert's *Dune*, just as they do so between scenes in the SciFi Channel's miniseries, whereas the escape from Arrakeen into the deep desert and ultimately to Stilgar's Seitch Tabr occupies some 100 pages in the novel and is, likewise, much more elaborate in the miniseries than it is in Lynch's film. In the novel and the miniseries it is this protracted journey from Arrakeen to Seitch Tabr that is the threshold crossing. However, in Lynch's film the threshold crossing is the trip from Caladan to Arrakis on a Guild highliner, which is depicted, and this passage is effected through a Guild Navigator "folding space" by using the spice.[2] Thus, while the return to the known world in the novel and the miniseries is Paul's return to Arrakeen after his victory, in Lynch's film the return is merely symbolic: the torrential rains that miraculously fall on Arrakis at the conclusion of the film associate Arrakis with Caladan, the Atreides' ocean homeworld, and only represent Paul's return to his planet of origin through symbolically transforming Arrakis into another waterworld.

The hero receives a call to adventure in the form of a blunder that reveals the unknown world or the appearance of a herald from that world—usually a beast, some shadowy, veiled or hooded, mysterious figure, or someone dark, loathly, and evil who may literally call the hero to live or to die. As Dr. Yueh's treachery precipitates Paul's and Jessica's flight, one blunder that reveals this unknown world of Arrakis' deep desert in Herbert's *Dune* is the Atreides'—and particularly Jessica's—failure to recognize that Yueh is the traitor about whom they have twice been warned (by the Shadout Mapes and by Lady Margot Fenring). Another blunder is Atreides mentat Thufir Hawat's miscalculation in underestimating by a factor of ten how many troops the Harkonnens will pay the Guild to have transported to Arrakis. And a third blunder is Reverend Mother Gaius Helen Mohiam's failure to recognize that Paul may be the Bene Gesserit Kwisatz Haderach arrived one generation before his time, as she knows that Paul has prophetic dreams and has witnessed herself that he can withstand more pain than any female child who had also been tested with the box and gom jabbar. The six heralds in Herbert's *Dune* are Reverend Mother Mohiam, "an old crone ... a witch shadow—hair like matted spiderwebs, hooded 'round darkness of features," who appears at Castle Caladan to administer this test that will determine immediately if Paul will live or die (3); the evil Baron Harkonnen, a "*beast*" with loathly habits who first appears "half-hidden in shadows" and "a shadow among shadows" as he reveals the plot that is meant to encompass Paul's death as well as Duke Leto's (181, 14, 17); the Shadout Mapes, a Fremen servant who is almost killed by a hunter-seeker meant for Paul; Stilgar, the Fremen Naib from the desert who appears "in hood and black veil" at the Atreides war council (92); the mysterious and hooded imperial planetologist Dr. Kynes, who first takes Paul into the desert; and the terrifying "monster" worm that Paul sees there devouring a spice harvester (124).

In Lynch's *Dune* and the SciFi Channel's miniseries the blunder that reveals the unknown world is only the Atreides' failure to recognize that Dr. Yueh may be the traitor about whom they have been warned (by only the Shadout Mapes). In their conversation early in the film, Jessica realizes that Yueh is "holding something back" but does not press him due to his "Imperial conditioning," which should make it impossible for him to take another's life. In the miniseries Jessica tells Paul to look upon their impending relocation to Arrakis as "the adventure of a lifetime," and it is Paul who opines on Arrakis that Yueh cannot be the traitor due to his "Suk conditioning." Hawat's miscalculation is not mentioned in the film or the miniseries, and Reverend Mother Mohiam's failure to realize that Paul may be the Quisatz Hadderach receives less emphasis in both than it does in the novel. Moreover, there are only three heralds—but not precisely the same three—in both the film and the miniseries. In the film Reverend Mother Mohiam is appropriately hooded when she arrives on Caladan to give Paul the test with the box and gom jabbar, yet Paul and Jessica do not meet Stilgar until after their escape into the desert. However, in the miniseries it is a hooded Stilgar who visits Duke Leto and is introduced to Paul in Arrakeen, while the elaborately headdressed Mohiam is never hooded or associated with shadows. Although he wears a hood in neither version, Kynes does serve as a herald in both the film and the miniseries in that he does take Paul, Duke Leto, and Gurney Hallek into the desert to observe spice-mining. And the third herald in the film and miniseries is the worm that then comes to devour the spice harvester. Baron Harkonnen is not associated with shadows in either adaptation. And while Paul does save the Shadout Mapes from the hunter-seeker in both adaptations, Mapes is not so pointedly presented as a herald of the desert in either as she is in the novel. This diminishment of the number of blunders and number of heralds in the film and miniseries demonstrates how both are not as focused on Paul as a monomythic hero as is Herbert's version of the story.

The two conspirators most responsible for resurrecting Idaho-2 as a ghola and employing him in their scheme—Edric, the "monstrous" and "repellant" Guild Navigator, and Scytale, the shape-shifting Tleilaxu (a race that is universally despised)—are the loathly and evil heralds in Herbert's *Dune Messiah* (15). Rather than reveal the unknown world to the novel's monomythic hero, however, these heralds introduce Idaho-2 (who is actually its most significant unknown) into what is an unknown world only to him, Paul's court in Arrakeen; this initial inversion is appropriate because the monomyth itself is inverted in this novel, wherein the monomyth is not the primary plot and the main character is not the monomythic hero. Paul himself, in the guise of The Preacher, is the veiled and mysterious herald of the unknown world in Herbert's *Children of Dune*; emerging from Arrakis' desert, he wears a "mask" while interviewing Farad'n on Salusa Secundus, and it is his very existence that lures Leto II from the safety of Seitch Tabr to seek his father in the "unknown" world of Jacurutu, the legendary lost seitch of the water-stealers and The Preacher's secret, deep-desert base (85, 277). Early in *Children*, Farad'n's mother Princess Wensicia dispatches two Laza tigers from Salusa Secundus to Arrakis to assassinate Leto II and his twin sister Ghanima; as their attack is the immediate cause of Leto's flight from Seitch Tabr into the unknown regions of the desert, these terrifying predatory beasts also serve as this novel's heralds of the unknown world.

While Scytale does introduce the Idaho ghola to Paul's court on Arrakis in

Part I of the *Children of Dune* miniseries, this has less significance since Idaho-2 is not presented as a monomythic hero in the miniseries. Yet Paul as The Preacher is a herald of the deep desert to Leto II in the miniseries, much as he is in Herbert's novel. And, even though in the miniseries Leto II and Ghanima are attacked by them only after leaving Seitch Tabr, the Laza tigers are still beast-heralds of the deep desert in the miniseries as well. Moreover, there is more emphasis in the miniseries than in the original novel on the fact that the blunder that reveals the unknown world to Leto II is Alia's accepting from House Corrino the gift of that clothing (for the twins) that the Laza tigers have been trained to attack. In the miniseries, Alia accepts the clothing despite Irulan's misgivings and over her objections, yet this blunder is somewhat muddied by the fact that Leto II has decided to leave Seitch Tabr to seek Jacurutu before the tigers attack.

There is only one slim suggestion in the *Dune* novels that the hero ever refuses the initial call to adventure: When Idaho-2 asks Bijaz about the axlotl tanks in *Messiah*, the dwarf responds, "We had a terrific struggle with you. The flesh did not want to come back" (226). While Bijaz has almost identical lines in the miniseries, this has less significance there because Idaho-2 is not a monomythic hero in the adaptation. However, as the *Dune* miniseries' Paul is far less enthusiastic about the relocation to Arrakis than is the Paul of Herbert's novel or of Lynch's film, that Paul has the temperament to refuse the call to adventure—even though the decision is not his but Duke Leto's.

After receiving the call to adventure, the hero acquires supernatural aid from a figure who may personify his destiny. This might be a protective old man or crone who provides a talisman in a setting suggesting a womblike sense of peace; or it may be a guide, teacher, wizard, ferryman, hermit, or smith who offers aid in a context of danger or temptation. In Herbert's *Dune*, ironically, it is Dr. Yueh, Paul's "teacher" (4), whose treachery propels Paul towards his destiny but who nevertheless also provides Paul with talismans and aid in contexts that suggest both the safety of the womb and mortal danger. Yueh impulsively gives his dead wife's miniature Orange Catholic Bible to Paul (who later quotes its verses to the Fremen) while they are secure in Castle Caladan, and he subsequently hides Duke Leto's signet ring and a fremkit (which enables Paul and Jessica to survive in the desert) in the ornithopter that is meant to take them to their deaths. Still, Herbert's Paul has about as many supernatural helpers as his adventure in the unknown world has heralds, but these other "*companion-teachers*"—Thufir Hawat, Jessica, Duncan Idaho, Gurney Hallek, and Duke Leto— all offer aid solely in the context of the dangers awaiting them on Arrakis (28). There is no Orange Catholic Bible in either the film or miniseries versions of *Dune*, yet in both adaptations Yueh is Paul's teacher who does provide him with the ducal signet ring and with some (but not as much) desert survival equipment.

Although not so explicitly identified as such in the adaptations, Hawat, Jessica, Idaho, Hallek, and Duke Leto are still clearly Paul's teachers in them as well. Yet this is clearer in the more-elaborate miniseries than it is in the film. While Paul had received instruction in the Bene Gesserit way from Jessica and practices knife-fighting with Gurney in both versions, only in the miniseries does he later refer to Gurney as one of his "teachers," when they are reunited in the desert in Episode III. And only in the novel and the miniseries does Paul also receive academic instruction from Yueh, information about Arrakis from Hawat, and instruction in statecraft from Duke Leto.

Paul—who, as The Preacher, is both a hermit and a wizard in Herbert's and the SciFi Channel's *Children*—leaves to his son, Leto II, "that most powerful of all mystic talismans: the divine authenticity of Maud'Dib's religious bequest" (*Children* 2). Paul is most specifically Leto II's "guide" to his "Golden Path," his destiny, as the "Golden Path" is the content of Paul's "last vision," which is revealed to Leto II when Paul's persona temporarily possesses him early in *Children* (72). Edric, who is a type of ferryman as a Guild Navigator, brings Idaho-2 to Paul's court in *Messiah*. Idaho-2's metallic Tleilaxu eyes are a talisman intended to remind Paul of the ghola's origins. And the Tleilaxu also provide Idaho-2 with a guide, Bijaz, an older "brother ... from the same tank" whose task is to activate the subliminal compulsion that, when triggered at Chani's death, will be the catalyst that awakens the ghola's original persona (229). In the miniseries Idaho-2 has no metallic Tleilaxu eyes, is introduced to Paul's court by Scytale, not Edric, and is not a monomythic hero in any case, so his similar association with Bijaz has no monomythic significance. Leto II is the inheritor of Paul's religious bequest in the miniseries, as he is in the novel, but this divine authority is never referred to as a "talisman" in the adaptation. Paul's consciousness within Leto II is Leto II's guide to the "Golden Path" in the miniseries as well as in the novel, and Paul warns Leto II in the miniseries that the "Golden Path" is "dangerous." That Irulan has served as Leto II's and Ghanima's teacher, in Jessica's absence, is given more emphasis in the miniseries than it is in the novel.

Arrakis' deep desert is the unknown world to Paul and to Leto II in Herbert's *Dune* and *Children of Dune*, and the desert is a sphere of rebirth for Paul in several ways. As Yueh had planned, both their enemies and allies alike presume that Paul and Jessica have died there, killed by the "sandblast storm" through which they make their escape from Arrakeen; and, much as Jessica "felt reborn" on emerging unscathed from the storm, so too is Paul "like one come back from the dead" on recovering from his first prescient vision soon after they encounter Stilgar's troop (*Dune* 234, 242, 297). Moreover, Paul's newfound "*sense* of the future" gives him "the look ... *of someone forced to the knowledge of his own mor-*

tality," a premonition of death that is followed almost immediately by a symbol of rebirth, his foreseeing that the Fremen will rechristen him "Muad'Dib" (197, 199). While all of Arrakis is the unknown world in Lynch's *Dune*, Paul's arrival makes the planet a sphere of rebirth for the Fremen as well: the Fremen Reverend Mother Romallo states that the coming of Paul, "the voice from the outer world," will bring the Jihad and bring the Fremen "out of darkness." While there is no duel with Jamis in the film, Paul is renamed "Usul" and "Paul Muad'Dib" by Stilgar in the Cave or Ridges; and, as in the novel, the Harkonnens believe Paul and Jessica have been killed by a coriolis storm in attempting to escape from Arrakeen. While not as elaborate as in the novel (but more elaborate than in the film), Paul's and Jessica's escape from Arrakeen, finally, to Stilgar's Seitch Tabr is the threshold crossing in the miniseries. Paul dives his ornithopter into the storm at the conclusion of Episode I, and Episode II begins with Paul and Jessica having crashed in the desert after the storm has passed. In the miniseries Paul is renamed "Muad'dib" (but not "Usul") in the Cave of Ridges after his duel with Jamis and Jamis' funeral. In all three versions Paul's symbolic death and rebirth in escaping from Arrakeen—as everyone but the Fremen and Jessica think him dead—is echoed in the fact that almost everyone but Jessica thinks Paul dead when he later transmutes the Water of Life and succumbs to a three-week coma in which his vital signs are almost nonexistent.

Paul and Jessica encounter both destructive watchmen and protective guardians in crossing the threshold to the unknown world in all three versions of *Dune*. In the novel the destructive watchmen are the two Harkonnen guards who take them to the desert to die, Kinet and Czigo; "*the ones the Baron set to watch this pair*," whom Jessica sees following them; and those "*watchers for the watchers*" whom she assumes also exist (169). The protective guardians include Idaho, who is killed in an underground Ecological Testing Station while covering Paul's and Jessica's escape; Kynes, who offers them temporary shelter in the station and shields them after Idaho is killed; and Stilgar, who finds them in the desert and obeys Kynes' order to "*protect*" and "*save*" Paul (276). This is much like what happens in the miniseries, in which Idaho, Kynes, and Stilgar are similarly Paul's protective guardians. Yet the worm that then pursues them in the desert, more so than the two Harkonnen guards who take them there, is a destructive watchman in the miniseries. In the film there are many destructive watchmen who act during the Atreides' transition from Caladan to Arrakis, that version's threshold crossing. The Atreides know that "the Harkonnens would leave many suicide troops behind" on Arrakis; many "sabotage devices" are found by arriving Atreides troops; and Paul is threatened by a hunter-seeker controlled by a watcher hidden in the Arrakeen palace shortly after his arrival. Immediately thereafter the Shadout Mapes tells Paul that the Atreides have a traitor in their midst, and shortly after that Dr. Yueh disables the Atreides house shields—enabling the Harkonnen attack—and destroys the Atreides' army's weirding modules.

Paul's court in Arrakeen is the unknown world to Idaho-2 in *Messiah*. Its protective guardian is Stilgar, who—in yet another inversion of the monomyth—seeks to protect the court from the ghola, rather than to protect the monomythic hero from the unknown world. And Idaho-2's complete rebirth does not occur until his original persona is reawakened at the novel's climax and "he knew himself as Duncan Idaho" (259). The threshold to the unknown crossed by Leto II and Ghanima in Herbert's *Children of Dune* is Sietch Tabr's "qanat," the water-barrier that separates Stilgar's seitch from the desert proper (167), and the deep desert is a sphere of rebirth for Leto II in this volume in much the same way that the desert is for Paul in Herbert's *Dune*. After the twins kill the tigers, Ghanima returns to the seitch under the influence of a self-induced hypnotic suggestion that compels her to believe that Leto II has been slain; this forestalls any pursuit by convincing everyone (including Ghanima) that Leto II is dead as Leto II journeys to Jacurutu, "a perfect place for the dead to hide—among ... the dead of another age" (*Children* 213). After later sacrificing his humanity by merging with the sandtrout just prior to the novel's climax, yet another symbolic death, Leto II becomes known as the "Desert Demon," another rechristening that symbolizes rebirth (364). Stilgar, the official "guardian of the orphaned twins," is the threshold's protective guardian, while its destructive watchmen are Palimbash—the Fremen traitor whom Ghanima kills after discovering him standing in a "hidden entrance" to the seitch with "the transmitter which had released the Tigers"—and his "watching" accomplices (2, 198).

In the miniseries' Leto II and Ghanima live in Arrakeen, not in Seitch Tabr. Their threshold crossing into the desert occurs when Jessica warns Irulan that Alia is possessed by the memories of her ancestors and advises Irulan to flee with Ghanima and Leto II to Stilgar's Seitch Tabr. This threshold crossing leads to a sphere of rebirth when Leto II and Ghanima subsequently leave Seitch Tabr to seek out Jacurutu and find "answers." Much as in the novel, after the Laza Tigers are killed Ghanima appears to believe that Leto II has been slain while Leto II rides a worm to Jacurutu and is taken captive there. Wensicia then tells Jessica and Idaho-2, who have sought sanctuary on Salusa Secundus, that Leto II is dead. (Although Wensicia believes that Leto II has been killed through her own assassination plot involving the tigers, she accuses Alia of having planned this assassination attempt.) Leto II, who is visually associated with a butterfly repeatedly in the miniseries, is visually reborn in the desert after merging with the sandtrout: encrusted with sandtrout, he stands before a coriolis storm, is buried by it, but then emerges, resurrected as the "Desert Demon," from the sand. The protective guardians who defend the threshold crossing, then, include Irulan in the miniseries, as well as Stilgar. But the destructive watchman is still Palimbash, who controls the tigers from behind the rocks and is finally killed by Ghanima.

In the departure stage's final incident the hero is swallowed in the belly of the whale, an inward journey through which the hero is born again. This is often either a literal or a symbolic underground journey that depicts a literal or figurative descent into hades, and *memento mori* in the form of bones or skeletons are sometimes in evidence. The hero may be literally or symbolically mutilated, dismembered, or killed; or he may merely enter a temple or similar structure that is guarded by gargoyles. Idaho-2 must endure an inward journey, so that he can be born again, in that he must be brought to a crisis of internal conflict that will awaken his original persona. However, this is only explicitly clear in Herbert's *Dune Messiah*, not in Part I of the Sci Fi Channels' *Children of Dune*. Of particular interest in connection with the monomythic heroes who are protagonists, Paul and Leto II, is Campbell's assertion that the hero is the "incarnation of God" (41), for Paul is worshipped as a god in *Messiah*, and Leto II is worshipped as a God in *God Emperor of Dune*; in Herbert's novels the Bene Gesserit ultimately conclude that Paul and Leto II did not so much predict the future as create its specific path or shape with their prescient powers. Paul is worshipped as a god in the *Children of Dune* miniseries as well, and at the conclusion of the miniseries it is apparent that the powers Leto II acquires by merging with the sandtrout will make him a god to the freman also.

Arrakis in general and its desert in particular—the unknown worlds of all versions of the first three *Dune* novels—are repeatedly compared to "hell" in *Dune* (44–45, 124, 196, 209, 263, 284). The worms, which in each version of *Dune* literally threaten to swallow Paul and Jessica in the desert, also reinforce this reading of Arrakis as symbolic hell in that the Biblical Satan is cast into hades in the form of a serpent; and the Fremen word "Shaitan" means "Satan" as well as sandworm (529). In a series of figurative and literal underground journeys during their threshold crossing, in Herbert's *Dune* Paul and Jessica fly their ornithopter into a sandstorm to escape Harkonnen pursuers; are buried alive by another sandstorm during their first night in a stilltent in the open desert; are subsequently taken "down rock steps into" an underground desert "cave chamber," the Ecological Testing Station in which Idaho dies defending them; find temporary sanctuary in the subterranean Cave of Ridges to which Stilgar leads them; and finally find refuge in Sietch Tabr, a larger series of underground caverns (220, 288). After his duel with Jamis in the Cave of Ridges, Paul receives his Fremen troop name, Usul, from Stilgar and chooses Paul-Muad'Dib as his public name, a dual rechristening that signifies his rebirth as a member of Stilgar's troop. He later declares, "I am a Fremen born this day" when he subsequently performs the rite of riding a sandworm (404). Paul's most crucial death and rebirth experience occurs later still, however, when he transmutes the Water of Life and "*lay as one dead*" for three week before reviving (437). His symbolic mutilation is displaced, however, as it occurs when Mohiam tests him with the box in the first chapter, and "he could feel ... the flesh crisping and dropping away" from his hand (9).

This test with the box, Paul's symbolic mutilation, occurs at the beginning of both Lynch's and the SciFi Channel's versions of *Dune* as well. In the film version Paul and Jessica are taken to an underground water-storage facility on being found by Stilgar in the desert, but this is not part of their threshold crossing, which has already occurred. Paul and Jessica also seek refuge from the worms in a cave in the film, but do not fly through a coriolis storm, do not get buried in the sand in a stilltent, and enter no Cave of Ridges. Yet that Paul's sojourn in the desert is a symbolic death and rebirth is emphasized when Gurney exclaims, "Paul, they said you were dead" as the two are finally reunited. In the miniseries there are as many underground journeys associated with Paul's protracted threshold crossing from Arrakeen to Seitch Tabr as there are in the novel. Kynes and Idaho fly Paul and Jessica to a cavern Fremen seitch after picking them up in the desert, and Paul and Jessica then escape Harkonnen patrols by flying their ornithopter into a coriolis storm at the conclusion of Episode I. Early in Episode II they discover another Fremen cave in the deep desert, where they spend the night, and the next day they find refuge from a worm in another cave, where they are discovered by Stilgar's troop. They are then taken to Cave of Ridges (where Paul duels Jamis) before reaching Seitch Tabr.

In an initial inversion of an underground journey, Leto II emerges from Seitch Tabr, an underworld, into the open desert to fake his death at the claws of the Laza Tigers in Herbert's *Children of Dune*. Yet he avoids being slain by the tigers only by going underground again, diving several meters into a "narrow cut in the rocks ... until darkness enfolded him" (183). Like Paul, he also spends a night in a stilltent beneath the sand, to avoid detection after killing the tigers. His destination—Jacurutu, "the perfect place for the dead to hide" (213)—is yet another underground seitch, one in which he is first bludgeoned unconscious and then repeatedly threatened with death before being quizzed by Assan Tariq's father, Namri, who "saw himself as Mirzabah, the Iron Hammer with which the dead are beaten" (247). Jacurutu is guarded by a type of gargoyle, "a sinuous rock outcropping" that "lay like an immense worm atop the sand, flat and threatening" (234). After escaping Jacurutu, Leto II again buries himself alive beneath the sand in a stilltent, this time to escape a sandstorm; too deep beneath the surface to get air, he "sent himself into a dormancy trance where his lungs would move only once an hour" (302)—a deathlike state similar to the trance in which Paul lay for three weeks after drinking the Water of Life in *Dune*. Already symbolically killed, "dead to her" as a consequence of the hypnotic suggestion that Ghanima employs to convince herself that he has been slain by the tigers, Leto II is also mutilated in the desert when he finally allows the sand trout to penetrate his body: "He was no longer human. Cilia had crept into his flesh, forming a new creature" (*Children* 338–39). In the miniseries' Part II, Leto II and Ghanima go from Arrakeen to Seitch Tabr, a cave complex, and in Part III Leto II leaves Seitch Tabr to seek Jacurutu, another cave complex. Also in Part III, Leto II is mutilated by his symbiosis with the sandtrout, although his merging with them is not so complete in the miniseries, visually, as it is reported to be in the novel.

The Initiation Stage

The first incident in the monomyth's initiation stage is the road of trials, a series of tests in which the hero is aided by the supernatural helpers' advice or agents, by talismans given him, or by a benign power that protects him everywhere; in this episode the hero may also assimilate his shadow. Like Luke's facility with the Force, and equally problematical, in Herbert's *Dune* Paul's prescience is the benign power that protects him. And his three most critical trials are all explicit "tests" as well as explicit initiation rituals. The first is Mohiam's "test" involving the box, a Bene Gesserit rite intended "to determine if you're human"; the second is "the deadly test" of mounting and riding a sandworm, the Fremen "rite [of passage] to initiate a sandrider"; the third is *the test that the Reverend Mothers have survived*," transmuting the poisonous Water of Life (9, 386, 388, 437). Paul's duel with Jamis is a similar trial, another "test" that functions in the novel's plot as yet another initiation ritual: Jamis invokes "the amtal rule," the "test to destruction," in challenging Paul; Stilgar affirms that "death is the test of it"; and immediately after his victory Paul is accepted as a member of Stilgar's troop and twice rechristened.

Paul assimilates his shadow in his final trial in Herbert's *Dune*, his duel with Feyd. Not only are the Atreides presented as foils to the Harkonnens, "*the Light*" to the Harkonnen "*Darkness*," throughout the novel—although Paul realizes in the desert that "*he is Harkonnen*" through his mother Jessica, the Baron's daughter—but Paul and Feyd, cousins who are about the same age, are also meticulously developed as shadows (13, 205). Had Jessica obeyed them and given birth to a daughter, instead of to Paul, the Bene Gesserit would have mated that daughter to Feyd to produce their Kwisatz Haderach in the next generation.

The Baron's observation that Feyd "aspires to rule my Barony, yet he cannot rule himself" immediately follows Paul's test with the box, which demonstrates his supreme self-control (17). Similarly, Paul's duel with Jamis, a fair fight in which Paul is reluctant to kill his opponent, is juxtaposed to Feyd's hundredth gladiatorial match, a fixed fight in which Feyd demonstrates his bloodthirsty ruthlessness; afterwards, Count Fenring compares the two youths in wondering what Feyd "could've been with some other upbringing—with the Atreides code to guide him, for example" (339). Paul loves his father and strives to avenge his death, while Feyd despises the Baron and attempts to assassinate him. Moreover, while the Baron plots to have Feyd "go to Arrakis as [the Fremen] savior" and eventually "*gain the throne*," Paul does become both the Fremen "messiah" and, immediately after killing Feyd, the emperor (379, 235, 101).

Paul survives the ordeal with the box, which is termed a "test" in the miniseries, in both adaptations of *Dune*, and in both his prescient powers are given even more emphasis than they are given in the novel. In both adaptations he also succeeds in calling and mounting a worm (a feat that is also referred to as a "test" in the miniseries, although it is not so clear in the film that this is a Fremen rite of passage), in transmuting the Water of Life, which appears to give him power over the worms in the film, and in defeating Feyd. While there is no Jamis in the film, Jamis does challenge Paul to a duel to the death in the miniseries, and Paul's victory over Jamis in the miniseries is immediately followed by his being renamed "Muad'Dib." And while Feyd is not so emphatically Paul's shadow in the miniseries as in the novel, he is more Paul's shadow in the miniseries—in which he is compared and contrasted to Paul much more often—than he is in the film. In the miniseries only does Mohiam tell Jessica that, had Paul been born a girl, "he could have been wed to the Harkonnen heir." In the film the Baron does declare that when Rabban has "crushed" the Fremen sufficiently, driven them to "utter submission," he will send Feyd to them, but Feyd is never referred to as a "savior" or a "messiah." Yet in Episode II of the miniseries the Baron explains to Feyd that he will be hailed as "Feyd the savior" once he takes over Arrakis following Rabban's reign of oppression, and in Episode III the Emperor divines this Harkonnen plot to send Feyd to Arrakis as a "savior" after Rabban has brutalized the population. Also in Episode III does Feyd make an unsuccessful attempt to assassinate the Baron, does Feyd try to romance Princess Irulan as an avenue to the throne (something that does not happen in the novel), and does Paul reveal to Jessica that he has learned in taking the Water of Life (much later than in the novel) that the Baron is Jessica's father. Yet, after Paul succeeds in the test with the box, the Baron says of Rabban, not of Feyd, that "he aspires to rule House Harkonnen someday ... yet he can't even rule himself."

Idaho-2's crucial trial in *Messiah* is to overcome the Tleilaxu compulsion to kill Paul, once it is triggered, through recovering his original persona. Ironically, his supernatural helpers are the Tleilaxu themselves, who implant this compulsion as a mechanism for reviving Idaho's persona; Bijaz, who activates the compulsion at the appropriate time, is their agent. Idaho-2's unsuspected self is not only his original persona, which he literally assimilates by integrating it into his personality once it is resurrected, but also Bijaz, his shadow in that they "are like brothers" who "grew in the same tank"; the ghola is the dwarf's "target ... the instrument [he] was taught to play," and Idaho-2 finally kills Bijaz at Paul's command (228–29). In Part I of the *Children of Dune* miniseries Bijaz is similarly Idaho-2's shadow, and the ghola does kill the dwarf instead of Paul when Paul speaks the trigger words "She is gone." Yet, Idaho-2's internal conflict leading to the regaining of his original persona and refusal to kill Paul is not exhibited in the miniseries, as it is in *Messiah*, and it is primarily this omission that prevents Idaho-2 from being the monomythic hero as secondary character in Part I of the miniseries that he is in *Messiah*.

Early in Herbert's *Children of Dune* Leto II predicts that he and Ghanima will "be tested ... in the spice ... in the desert and in the Trial of Possession," and Jessica believes that "Leto had to be tested" to assure that he is not possessed by any of the personae inhabiting his "other memories" (80–81, 205). Following his ordeal with the Laza Tigers, his spice ordeal that is the test for possession conducted in Jacuturu, and his subsequently surviving a sandstorm in the desert, Leto II's final test is to accept the Golden Path—"this trial he and Ghanima had chosen"—and thus submit to losing his humanity by merging with the sandtrout (237). Leto II must then assimilate his opposite or unsuspected self twice—in his final confrontations with his shadow, Alia, and with his unsuspected double, Farad'n. Alia is Leto II's shadow, not only as the "Regent" ruling in his and Ghanima's names, but also in that she, too, is "born with a totality of genetic memory, a terrifying awareness that set their Aunt Alia and themselves apart from all other living humans"; possessed by the Baron's persona, Alia is the "abomination" that either twin may yet become (10, 4, 51). While Leto II is raised on Arrakis, Prince Farad'n is raised on Salusa Secundus, the prison planet that is "much like Arrakis" (*Dune* 32). Both have "doubts" about wanting "to become Emperor" (*Children* 82, 92); both have prescient dreams (see 34, 86, 113); and Jessica, who becomes Farad'n's teacher and surrogate mother, discovers that "he ... was consciously copying the Atreides" and that "he reminded her with heart-tugging abruptness of her own lost son," Leto II's father Paul (211, 252). Leto II's return to Arrakeen forces Alia to reveal that "she was possessed" and to commit suicide by leaping out a window; Leto II then takes control of Farad'n's troops, makes Farad'n his "Scribe" and the "secret father of [his] royal line" (as Ghanima's husband), and renames him Harq al–Ada (393, 407).

In the miniseries Leto II also survives the Laza Tigers, is also fed high concentrations of spice in Jacuturu in an attempt to make him "as mad as Alia" (but he assures his captors, "I have survived the crucible … I have silenced the voices who would possess me"), also survives a desert sandstorm, and also chooses the Golden Path. And Alia is also "Imperial Regent"—ruling in Paul's name until Leto II comes of age—who points out to the twins that they are all "preborn." In fact, Alia is at least as pointedly Leto II's shadow in Parts II and III of the miniseries as she is in Herbert's *Children of Dune*. Leto II protests early in Part II that he and Ghanima are "not like Alia," meaning that they are not possessed by the personae within them while Alia is possessed by the Baron. And Alia complains of being alone, while the twins have each other. After he denounces her as an "abomination" in Arrakeen at the miniseries' climax, Alia attacks Leto II with the crysknife with which she finally takes her own life. On Salusa Secundus Prince Farad'n doubts the wisdom of his mother Wensicia's plot, of which he is initially unaware, to regain the throne for House Corrino by assassinating the twins. As in the novel, in the miniseries, too, Farad'n is tutored in the Bene Gesserit way by Jessica and feels, when this training begins to show effects, that he is "being reborn." And Farad'n denounces and banishes his mother in Arrakeen just before Leto II denounces Alia and precipitates her death. Yet Leto II's assimilation of Farad'n is not so pronounced in the miniseries as it is in the novel. Leto II does not make Farad'n his scribe and does not change his name in the miniseries. And even though Ghanima and Farad'n are bethrothed in it as well, in the miniseries it is emphasized that, like Paul's and Irulan's, Farad'n's and Ghanima's marriage is to be a political union only, that they will not mate or produce children.

Three women in Herbert's *Dune* represent various aspects of the goddess. Chani, who appears repeatedly to Paul in his earliest prescient dreams, is the Lady of the House of Sleep with whom Paul has a mystical marriage in the desert. The complex and rebellious Jessica is the Universal Mother who combines all opposites. And Reverend Mother Mohiam is the bad mother, as the test with the box that she administers to Paul on Caladan is a symbolic castration. Paul also encounters three temptresses, although in each instance the temptation is a mild one. The first temptress, in Book One, is the Guild banker's daughter whom both Paul and Jessica realize is meant to seduce Paul during the formal banquet in Arrakeen. The second, in Book Two, is Harah, Jamis' widow, whom Paul must accept for a year as either wife or servant. The third, in Book Three, is Princess Irulan, the "patrician beauty" whom Paul will marry to secure the throne yet whom he swears to Chani "shall have no more of me than my name" (474, 489). For identical reasons, Chani, Jessica, and Mohiam are the Lady of the House of Sleep, the Universal Mother, and the bad mother, respectively, in both adaptations. Yet there is no woman as temptress in Lynch's film. And, while there is no Harah in the miniseries, Princess Irulan plays the role of temptress in it both at the banquet in Arrakeen, where she tries to seduce Paul, and at the conclusion, where she likewise becomes Paul's wife but not his mate.

The Fremen view Alia as a "*demi-god*," a "goddess," and "*the womb of heaven*" in *Dune Messiah* (91, 109, 209), where she assumes the roles of the Lady of the House of Sleep and the terrifying Universal Mother who combines all opposites. In "telling the story of the Far Places visited by the Priestess in her holy trance," Alia's acolytes chant that "she guards our dreaming souls," and "The Irulan Report" on St. Alia of the Knife notes that "*she represents ultimate tension*"; Bijaz expands on this in telling Idaho-2 that "she is the virgin-harlot.... She is vulgar, witty, knowledgeable to a depth that terrifies, cruel when she is most kind, unthinking when she thinks, and when she seeks to build she is as destructive as a coriolis storm" (180, 91, 227). Sabiha, Namri's daughter, is both the Lady of the House of Sleep and the temptress in Herbert's *Children of Dune*. She guards Leto II while he endures the spice ordeal in Jacurutu, and his visions of the two of them "entwined in love" (281) tempt him to renounce his Golden Path, whose necessary metamorphosis dictates celibacy. And Jessica becomes the bad mother in *Children*. Much like Mohiam vis-à-vis Paul on Caladan, she arrives on Arrakis after a decade's absence prepared to kill her grandchildren Leto II and Ghanima with a "poisoned needle ... the gom jabbar" (99) should they prove to be possessed. Alia and Farad'n's mother Wensicia, who plot independently to murder the twins, also assume the role of goddess as bad mother in *Children*.

Alia and Idaho-2 become lovers in Paul's palace in Arrakeen in Part I of the *Children of Dune* miniseries, and they are married by the time Part II begins. That Alia cheats on Idaho-2 with one of her priests, Javid, is emphasized in Parts II and III of the miniseries—in which Alia also plots to murder the twins, as does Wensicia—and Alia, with Wensicia, is primarily the goddess as bad mother in the miniseries. Yet Jessica becomes the goddess as bad mother in the miniseries as well. Alia warns the twins to be wary of Jessica, who as a Bene Gesserit is mistrustful of those who are "preborn," and Alia is justified in accusing Jessica of having "abandoned" her as a child in having returned to Caladan a decade earlier. It is Jessica, through Gurney, who has Leto II tested with the spice ordeal in Jacurutu—to determine if he is possessed, which she thinks is most likely, in which case he is to be killed, or to prove that he is not—and it is also Jessica who sends word to Stilgar to have the Fremen Naibs prepare to try her daughter Alia for possession. Sabiha is Leto II's guard and comforter in Jacurutu in the miniseries also, but she is not the temptation to Leto II in the miniseries that she is in Herbert's novel.

After encountering the goddess and temptress, the monomythic hero may experience atonement with the father or a father figure, who acts as his initiating priest, but this requires abandonment of the ego; and the initiation rites that enact atonement with the father may exhibit the violence each generation might wish to exact on the other. The father can be, and often appears to be, a tyrant or ogre, and the son cannot achieve atonement until he sees beyond this manifestation of the father; when he perceives the father's human face, the two are atoned. In all three versions of *Dune* Paul vows to avenge his father by overcoming the tyrant-ogre father figures personified in the Baron Harkonnen (his maternal grandfather) and the Emperor. As Emperor in *Dune Messiah* and the SciFi Channel's *Children of Dune* Part I, Paul is himself a father figure to Idaho-2; he is Idaho-2's initiating priest in that he is both the recipient of their gift as well as the catalyst that the Tleilaxu use to reawaken the ghola's original persona. The staged psychic drama that compels the Idaho-ego to supplant the ghola-ego when Paul says "She is gone"—at which time Idaho-2's compulsion to murder Paul conflicts with the original persona's loyalty to the Atreides and forces that original persona to emerge—combines wonderfully the idea that atonement with the father requires abandoning the ego with the notion that it may also contain elements of inter-generational violence.

Paul is also an initiating priest for Leto II in two quite different ways. First, Paul prevents Leto II from being assassinated moments after his birth by killing Scytale at the conclusions of *Dune Messiah* and of the SciFi Channel's *Children of Dune* Part I. Subsequently, in Herbert's *Children of Dune*, the Paul-persona within Leto II promises, "I will protect you in the trance. The others within will not take you" (225) when Leto II undergoes the spice ordeal in Jacurutu, an initiation ritual in which he must abandon his ego to establish a harmony with his other memories, any one of which might otherwise possess him. Thus, Leto II "let go of himself and became himself, his own person compassing the entirety of his past" (279). After escaping Jacurutu and merging with the sandtrout, Leto II finds Paul in the desert and sees finally his father's face: "Leto studied this face, seeing the lines of likeness as though they had been outlined in light. The lines formed an indefinable reconciliation" (341). Leto II then forces Paul into a "battle of the visions" from which he knows "*only one vision will emerge*" (343, 334)—an atonement that is also a contest "for mastery of the universe," for when Leto II's vision prevails, Paul acknowledges, "This is your universe now" and agrees to do Leto II's "bidding" (346, 372). Similarly, the Paul persona within him protects Leto II from being possessed by his other memories during his spice ordeal in Jacurutu in Part II of the miniseries. And it is clearer in the miniseries than in the novel that in embracing the Golden Path Leto II has done what "Muad'Dib was afraid" to do. Finally, after bonding with the sandtrout in Part III, Leto II meets The Preacher in the desert, recognizes he is Paul, and tries to give him Leto's signet ring. While The Preacher returns to Arrakeen with Gurney in the miniseries—and not, as in the novel, with Leto II—in the miniseries Paul dies in Leto II's arms while acknowledging Leto II as his "son" when he is slain by a Jacurutu assassin in Arrakeen while denouncing Alia.

The penultimate incident in the Initiation Stage is the hero's apotheosis. This is symbolized by an annihilation of consciousness that entails the merging of time and eternity and is characterized by a symbolic transcendence of duality—representing a return to the lost unity that preceded creation—signaled by the unification of such opposites as time and eternity, good and evil, male and female, or truth and illusion. In all three versions of *Dune* Paul's apotheosis occurs when he finally transmutes the Water of Life and enters the plane of apotheosis for the three weeks in which he lies in a deathlike trance, his consciousness annihilated, while exploring his visions. Paul's prescience is itself essentially a conflation of time and eternity, but in transmuting the Water of Life he also unites within himself the male-female polarity through becoming a male Bene Gesserit Reverend Mother. In *Dune Messiah* and Part I of the *Children of Dune* miniseries, Idaho-2 experiences an apotheosis in the annihilation of consciousness that accompanies the reawakening of his original persona; yet this is more significant in Herbert's novel than it is in the miniseries. Leto II experiences an apotheosis similar to Paul's, in both versions of *Children of Dune,* when he endures the spice ordeal at Jacurutu; and in both versions he literally transcends his humanity soon afterward when he merges with the sandtrout— a metamorphosis that makes him "*a living god*" (*Children of Dune* 400) to his Fremen followers but that is also a unification of the man-beast polarity. A nod to the concept of the unification of opposites, in Part III of the miniseries Wensicia beseeches Jessica on Salusa Secundus to "consider the union of opposites" (a Bene Gesserit teaching) and to join her in forging an alliance of Corrino and Atreides through the wedding of Farad'n and Ghanima.

Receiving the ultimate boon, which represents a way towards the regeneration of the hero's society, is the final incident in the initiation stage. The ultimate boon in its highest form is transcendent revelation, but the hero usually seeks such lesser gifts as immortality or extended life, power, or wealth. The transcendent revelation bestowed by their prescient visions at the moment of apotheosis is the greatest boon acquired by both Paul and Leto II, respectively, in all three versions of *Dune* and in both versions of *Children of Dune*, and for both characters this boon represents the regeneration of their societies. Paul uses his prescience to free the Fremen from Harkonnen oppression, and Leto II uses his to ensure the survival of humanity through the establishment of his Golden Path, which is to lead to humankind's regeneration in the distant future, ironically, through Leto II's repressive reign over the next 3,000 years. Paul's and Leto II's boons also entail the acquisition of supreme wealth and power, as they lead to both becoming Emperor, and Leto II's consequent metamorphosis greatly extends his lifespan as well, in addition to granting him the personal powers of super-strength, super-speed, and invulnerability. Idaho-2 achieves a more-limited revelation in the apotheosis that is the resurrection of his original persona, and this rebirth of personality that completes the resurrection of his body from the axlotl tanks is also a form of serial "immortality" (*Chapterhouse* 80).[3]

The Return Stage

While Leto II is tempted to "*just walk away into that desert*" rather than return to the known world in Herbert's *Children of Dune* (381), this is the only instance in any version of *Dune* or *Children of Dune* in which the monomythic hero even considers refusing to return. However, in both Herbert's and the SciFi Channel's *Dune*, but not in Lynch's film, Paul stalls his Fremen warriors and refuses to return to Arrakeen until his prescience tells him that the proper moment has arrived. Paul returns to Arrakeen to triumph over the Emperor and the Harkonnens in all three versions of *Dune*. In the novel and the miniseries this is a return to the known world, as the initial threshold crossing in both is from Arrakeen into the deep desert. However, as Caladan is presented as the known world in the film, the return to the known world is only symbolic in that version and occurs when the torrential rains of Caladan fall on Arrakis at the film's conclusion. In all three versions of *Dune* Paul's return to Arrakeen is opposed by "magic" means, the Guild fleet orbiting Arrakis and the five legions of Sardaukar camped on the Arrakeen plain, and furthered by "magic" means— Paul's prescience, his willingness to use the "Water of Death" to destroy the spice and thus to blackmail the Guild, the great sandstorm through which the Fremen attack astride giant worms, and the use of "atomics" to blast a way for storm and worms through the Shield Wall. Leto II's return from the desert to Arrakeen in both versions of *Children* is also furthered by "magic" means, the superhuman speed and strength he acquires through his metamorphosis. And in the miniseries this return to Arrakeen is more precisely a return to the known world than it is in the novel, for Leto II is raised in Arrakeen, not Seitch Tabr, in the miniseries. His invulnerable sandtrout skin is the "insulation" that protects Leto II from the danger of returning, Alia's treachery, in Herbert's novel.

Each monomythic hero also experiences a dilation of time in the unknown world, but this always occurs during his apotheosis, not during the return-threshold crossing. The three-week trance that Paul experiences after transmuting the Water of Life, while occupying an eternity of subjective time, seems to have occupied only a few minutes of real time in all three versions of *Dune*. Leto II experiences similar time dilations during his spice ordeal in both versions of *Children*. And Idaho-2 experiences his original persona's entire lifetime in the instant in which his original persona is awakened in *Dune Messiah*, if not so explicitly in the SciFi Channel's *Children of Dune* Part I. Paul and Leto II also bring a human talisman back with them from the unknown world: Paul brings Chani from the desert back to Arrakeen in all versions of *Dune*, and in Herbert's *Children of Dune* it is Leto II (not Gurney, as in the miniseries) who brings Paul, in the guise of The Preacher, from the deep desert back to Arrakeen. Idaho-2—who immediately echoes Paul's last words in *Messiah*, "Now I am free" (272)—had achieved his freedom to live in acquiring his original persona. And in both Herbert's and the SciFi Channel's *Children of Dune* it is clear that Leto II is aware that he is the vehicle of the cosmic cycle of change. Leto II, who calls himself "the first truly long-range planner in human history," vows "to create a new consciousness in all men" as he anticipates reigning for thousands of years in Herbert's novel (396, 406). And in the miniseries Ghanima tells Farad'n that Leto II will and must make "sacrifices for the future of us all."

5

The Terminator: Sarah Connor and Kyle Reese as a Composite Hero

While Jessica, his mother, accompanies Paul Atreides on his adventure in Herbert's *Dune* and its adaptations (the works that exhibit a dynamic most comparable to the sharing of the monomythic adventure between a male and female character seen in *The Terminator*), Paul himself possesses all of the traits of the monomythic hero and experiences nearly all of the episodes in the adventure's three stages. Thus, while Jessica exhibits a few of the hero's attributes and recapitulates several of these episodes as well, her characterization and experiences are unnecessary to completing the monomyth's pattern; Paul does it all on his own. But in *The Terminator* both Sarah Connor (Linda Hamilton) and Kyle Reese (Michael Biehn) are necessary to the completion of this pattern; the qualities and experiences of each fill in the many significant gaps in this pattern left by the other, so that neither, unlike Jessica, is superfluous in this respect. And Sarah is clearly the film's protagonist. She is the focus of all the action; Reese appears as her protector from the future, but Sarah ultimately saves herself; and she accomplishes this through transcending her initial self by changing dramatically from the beginning of the film to the end—due to Reese's intervention—while (like the Terminator's) Reese's characterization can be, and is, static throughout.

That Reese and Sarah "trade places" is literally articulated near the beginning of the last vehicle chase—in a film that is essentially one extended chase scene—when Reese orders Sarah to "trade places" with him, in the truck they have commandeered, so that he can hurl pipe bombs at the Terminator robot pursuing them on a motorcycle (Arnold Schwarzenegger) while she takes over as driver. One must strain to attribute any of the qualities of the hero to Sarah, yet Reese possesses most of them. However, Sarah alone experiences the Call to Adventure and the refusal of the call, while both (in different ways) experience elements of the departure stage's remaining episodes. Both also experience elements of the Road of Trials, yet Reese's execution of this episode is far more elaborate. Reese alone experiences the meeting with the mother-goddess and atonement with the father; both together, as the film's combined hero/heroine, symbolize apotheosis; and the boon—which is of the highest order, revelation—is actually experienced by the audience. Sarah alone experiences the return stage, as Reese dies before the film depicts it. Hence, while Reese seems to be the monomythic hero at the beginning, Sarah has become a monomythic heroine by the film's conclusion. And several of the monomythic heroes discussed by Campbell—such as the fairy-tale princess with the golden ball (49, 119), the Arapaho girl of the North American plains (53, 119), the Sumerian goddess Inanna (105), and Psyche (97–98, 120)—are women, just as many of the dreams Campbell analyzes are dreamt by women.

Qualities of the Hero

Aside from the fact that she is partially orphaned during the film when the Terminator slays her mother in her cabin at Big Bear, the one quality of the hero that Sarah comes closest to exhibiting is the possession of exceptional gifts; yet what is exceptional about her is her "destiny," that she will be the mother of humanity's savior, John Connor, and not any ability or anything intrinsic to her personality. Her "destiny" entails becoming a warrior to effect a change in the status quo—humanity's successful insurrection, led by John, against Skynet's machine rule—but she has not yet become a warrior, nor given birth to John, by the film's conclusion. As she is not only John's mother, but also "the legend" that Reese "volunteered" to go back in time to have the "chance to meet," she is somewhat like the mother who is assumed into heaven or crowned a queen; yet if Sarah's status as a "legend" is interpreted in this way, then her son John (who never appears in the film) would be the monomythic hero, not she.

Other qualities of the hero are similarly displaced. The special birth is neither Sarah's nor Reese's (about whose births we know nothing), but John's, as his is made possible only via time travel; the revelation of the film's last scene is that John had sent Reese back through time, not only to preserve Sarah's life, but also to impregnate her and thus to sire himself (i.e., John). And not only is Reese's role as John's father, ultimately, even more crucial than his role as Sarah's protector, it is also far more ironic; for Skynet thus makes the birth of its mortal enemy, John, possible—through devising and using the "time displacement equipment"—in its very attempt to prevent it, a desperate final effort to use time travel to thwart the already-successful insurrection. Moreover, while the hero can be the product of either a special or a virgin birth, it is not Sarah, John's mother, but Reese, his father, who is the "virgin" parent; Reese confesses to Sarah that he has never made love; thus their coupling in the Tiki Motel immediately afterwards, which neither knows at the time will produce John, is Reese's sole sexual experience.

In addition to being the virgin father, Reese is also an exile and an orphan who does not fear death. That he is an orphan is implicit in his testimony that he "grew up after [the nuclear Armageddon unleashed by Skynet], in the ruins, starving, hiding from ... hunter-killer ... patrol machines ... rounded up, put in camps for orderly disposal." He is an exile in 1984 because he has no way to return to the bleak world of 2029 from which he came; as he explains to police psychologist Silberman, since Skynet's time machine is to be destroyed immediately after Reese uses it, "I can't [get back]. Nobody goes home. Nobody else comes through. It's just him [the Terminator robot, which ostensibly cannot be stopped] and me." Thus, the one-way trip to 1984 for which Reese "volunteered" is a suicide mission; he later tells Sarah, "I'd die for John Connor," and he does. Also, while Reese in no way seeks his father, he does become his surrogate father's father, and thus creates his "father," as John is clearly a father-figure to Reese and is the appropriate age to be his biological father: Reese appears to be in his mid-twenties, and, as John must be born in 1985, he would be 44 years old, a generation older, when he sends Reese back in time in 2029.

Reese's exceptional gift is his sacrificial love for a woman he has never met, Sarah, which prompts him to volunteer for this suicide mission. Immediately before they make love he tells her, "I came across time for you, Sarah. I love you. I always have." This is even more remarkable in that such romantic love is the symbolic deficiency from which Reese's world of 2029 suffers. While this post-apocalyptic future is comprehensively deficient, all its monumental shortcomings are epitomized in the fact that it is so irredeemably bleak, and humanity so desperately focused on survival alone, that love is an unattainable (and perhaps unimaginable) luxury. When Sarah asks what the women of his time are like, Reese responds, "Good fighters." When he then reveals that he has "never" had "someone special ... a girl," and observes in this context, "Pain can be controlled. You just disconnect it," Sarah replies, with an eloquent sadness that assesses Reese's emotional life as well, "So you feel nothing."

Reese is, and has the appropriate conditional qualities of, the warrior, the lover, and the world-redeemer. He is a warrior by occupation, "a soldier ... with the 132nd under Perry from [20]21 to [20]27 ... assigned to recon ... the last two years [2028–29] under John Connor"; and he changes the future's status quo, not only by preserving Sarah's life in 1984, but also by siring John, who will lead the revolt that defeats Skynet twenty-five years later. Reese is a world-redeemer by virtue of having sired another world-redeemer; and it is in their roles as world-redeemers that Reese and John, who is also Reese's surrogate father as well as his son, are one. Thus, the triumph of man over machine in 2029, a macrocosmic triumph that is epitomized in Reese's and Sarah's successful microcosmic struggle against the Terminator robot in 1984, is made possible only because Reese is Sarah's lover; and traveling through time to save her from this relentless, unstoppable machine is the impossible task that leads Reese to their "bridal bed" in the Tiki Motel. Reese had fallen in love with a photo of Sarah, which John had given to him, that is destroyed before Reese travels back in time; and he tells Sarah that he "used to always wonder what [she was] thinking" when that photo was taken. Ironically, in the film's final scene she reveals that in that moment she is thinking of Reese and of their love, for she says into her tape recorder as the photo is being taken, "In the few hours that we had together, we loved a lifetime's worth."

The Departure Stage

The blunder that reveals the unknown world of 2029, and her destiny, to Sarah is not only Skynet's mistake in creating the time machine that enables John's father Reese, as well as the Terminator, to travel back to 1984, but is also the Terminator's "systematic" error in initially killing the two other Sarah Connors whose names precede Sarah's in the phone book—which alerts Sarah that her life is in danger, when she hears the consequent news reports—because it does not know which Sarah Connor is its intended victim. The robot also kills Sarah's roommate Ginger, whom it thinks is Sarah, as she listens to the lyrics "It's a mistake, die, die, die" on her walkman. Reese, who she believes is stalking her, is the first herald from the year 2029 that Sarah notices, but she soon encounters a second—a more mysterious, dark, loathly, terrifying, and evil—herald when the Terminator first tries to kill her in Tech Noir. As it is a "cybernetic organism," not a true human being, the Terminator is also a species of beast. Reese emphasizes that Sarah's call to adventure is a call to live or to die in telling her as he rescues her in Tech Noir, "Come with me if you want to live." Later, after dressing his superficial bullet wound, Sarah announces that she would refuse the call, if she could, in telling Reese, "I didn't ask for this 'honor,' and I don't want it, any of it." Reese, who teaches Sarah how to be a hero as well as how to fight and survive, is the teacher who offers to aid her against the mortal danger posed by the Terminator. Yet John Connor is, in turn, Reese's guide, teacher, and ferryman—in that he is the mentor who sends Reese back to 1984—as well as the older man who provides Reese with a talisman in the form of the photo of Sarah, while Skynet fills the role of smith vis-à-vis Reese as hero in constructing the time machine.

The hero next crosses the threshold to an unknown world that leads to a sphere of rebirth and may be defended by a protective guardian and/or a destructive watchman. Reese's crossing to 1984, an unknown world to him, is both implicitly and explicitly a symbolic rebirth. He materializes in a fetal position, naked, and steaming—like a newborn animal—and later tells Sarah that traveling through time is like "white light ... pain. It's like being born, maybe." The protective guardian who ushers him across this threshold from 2029 is John Connor, and the destructive watchmen are the Skynet defenses that John's forces must overcome to commandeer the time machine. (Sarah's threshold crossing occurs at the very end of the film and, the counterpart to Reese's, is the re-crossing of the threshold that occurs in the monomyth's return stage—which she performs in lieu of Reese, who is dead, by driving into the gathering "storm" that symbolizes the apocalyptic future from which Reese had come. Yet this future will eventually be a sphere of rebirth for humanity due to her son John's triumph over the machines. Still, her journey towards this future also features a destructive watchman, the Terminator, whose sole objective is to kill her, and a protective guardian, Reese, whose explicit mission is to keep her alive.)

In the departure stage's final episode the hero is swallowed in the belly of the whale. The closest Sarah comes to an underground journey is her attempt to seek refuge in Tech Noir, the "underground" club in which the Terminator first assaults her. Somewhat displaced, the film's symbolic hell is the future towards which Sarah is headed at its conclusion, and from which Reese had come at its beginning. The opening and subsequent scenes set in 2029 feature as a recurring image improbably vast beds of human skulls, *memento mori*, being crushed by tank-like machines. That this future is a symbolic hell is also suggested by the film's opening crawl, which informs the audience that "The machines rose from the ashes of the nuclear fire," and Sarah later acknowledges that Reese's "world is pretty terrifying."

Sarah is symbolically killed, twice, when the Terminator executes her two namesakes; another waitress at the restaurant emphasizes this in telling her, as they watch news coverage of the first murder, "You're dead, honey." And Reese is literally killed in the explosion that dismembers the Terminator in the automated factory, while Sarah is crippled when a large hunk of shrapnel from the partially demolished robot then pierces her thigh. Moreover, the Terminator—which is meticulously portrayed as Reese's shadow—is systematically mutilated, and entirely stripped of its initial human appearance, throughout the course of the film. It is repeatedly shot by Reese and the police, is immolated and loses its eyebrows and left eye in a car crash, and its organic epidermis is finally so damaged that it begins to putrefy—and then (often comically) attracts flies, repels passersby, and smells like "a dead cat"; the robot finally falls from a speeding motorcycle only to be run over by an oil-transporting semi, is consumed in flames and reduced to a metal skeleton when the semi's cargo explodes, and is blown apart by the last of Reese's pipe bombs before Sarah finally crushes what remains in a hydraulic press. (The only suggestion of a gargoyle is the pair of Gargoyle sunglasses the Terminator wears to disguise his missing left eye.)

The Initiation Stage

Sarah's road of trials entails surviving the Terminator's assaults, finally destroying it, and accepting her destiny. Reese, her helper, aids her in accomplishing each of these objectives. And in finally crushing the robot she assimilates her opposite self—as she represents the forces of life throughout the film, especially in her role as John's mother, while the Terminator obviously represents death, most pointedly in its final manifestation as the animated metal skeleton that Sarah destroys. Reese's road of trials is more elaborate. He must locate and save Sarah, identify and attempt to destroy the Terminator, and in the process repeatedly evade and escape from both the killer robot and the police. John, his helper, provides aid by defining Reese's mission and giving him a talisman, the photo of Sarah, which affords Reese his only advantage over the Terminator by enabling him to know what Sarah looks like and thus to identify her first. While Reese is a human whose mission is to save Sarah, and the Terminator is a robot whose mission is to kill her, they are shadows rather than foils because, even though their differences are crucial, they have a far greater number of similarities. Both use Skynet's "time displacement equipment" to materialize in 1984, naked and in a nimbus of lightening; and both must then acquire clothes, firearms, and transportation, as well as locate Sarah.

The Terminator steals clothes from a street punk after killing his two companions, while Reese steals pants from a bum in an alley and a trench coat and sneakers from a closed department store into which he ducks to evade the police. He steals a shotgun from a police car, while the robot steals a shotgun, a forty-five with a laser sight, and an Uzi from the Alamo Sport Shop, and in the process kills the proprietor. Reese hotwires a car near a construction site, while the Terminator steals one by bashing in the window and dismantling the ignition. Both look up Sarah Connor's address in the phone book and eventually pursue her to Tech Noir, where both draw their weapons almost simultaneously. Even though Reese complains, when Sarah bites his hand, "Cyborgs don't feel pain; I do," he later likens himself to the robot in telling her, "Pain can be controlled. You just disconnect it." And Reese initially follows Sarah, which she notices, so that he can both identify the Terminator and save her from its assault when it inevitably makes its first attempt on her life; thus, Sarah at first mistakes Reese for the Terminator—further reinforcing their depiction as shadows—in erroneously concluding that she is being stalked by the man who had already killed two other Sarah Connors. Each assimilates the other when Reese is killed while blowing the Terminator apart, enabling Sarah to evade and finally to destroy its still-animate torso.

The hero might also encounter a goddess, a temptress, or both. This episode applies only to Reese, who finds in Sarah the goddess with whom he has a mystical marriage, his sole sexual experience, in a droll inversion of a special location, the Tiki Motel. Sarah is both the Lady of the House of Sleep and the Universal Mother: she is literally the goal of Reese's quest (which is to sire her son, as well as to preserve her life) in becoming, blissfully, the reply to his only desire (which is to venerate and protect her) when they make love; and, while she personifies perfection to Reese, who passionately avers that he is not "disappointed" in her, she also pointedly combines opposites by transforming herself throughout the course of the film from a ditsy, incompetent waitress who doesn't have a date for Friday night into "a legend," a committed survivalist who is completely dedicated to, and capable of, raising her unborn son to be humanity's future savior. After encountering a goddess or temptress the hero may experience atonement with the father or a father figure, through whom the hero enters the world, but this requires that the hero abandon his ego. John Connor, already Reese's father figure, propels Reese into the world by sending him through Skynet's time machine to 1984. Reese abandons his ego in the selfless act of volunteering for this suicide mission. And he achieves "at-one-ment" with John—not, as is customary, through a face-to-face reconciliation involving mutual recognition—but, more literally, through siring him and thus becoming, like John, another world-redeemer.

The penultimate incident in the initiation stage is the hero's apotheosis, which is symbolized by an annihilation of consciousness that entails the merging of time and eternity and is characterized by a symbolic transcendence of duality—representing a return to the lost unity that preceded creation—signaled by the unification of such opposites as time and eternity or male and female. Reese merges or unifies time (the Western perception that only the transient, present moment exists) and eternity (the Eastern notion that all moments exist and persist equally, and that our moment-by-moment perception of time is only an illusion) through the very act of traveling through time *per se*—which, as he describes it, is also as close as he comes to experiencing an annihilation of consciousness. Apotheosis is literally a transcendence of one's humanity to become godlike; thus, there is at least the suggestion of apotheosis in the appearance of the transformed Sarah of the film's last scene as well as in the fact that the Sarah depicted in this scene is the manifestation that will become a "legend" by the year 2029. And the film collapses the male/female polarity through its unique interpretation of the monomyth itself, by presenting only the conflation of Reese and Sarah as its variation on the monomythic hero—as they experience the hero's adventure only jointly, but neither does so alone—as well as by uniting them biologically in their crucial, mutual conception of John.

Receiving the ultimate boon, which is the means for the regeneration of the hero's society and in its highest form is transcendent revelation, is the initiation stage's final incident. In 2029 John Connor, the product of the film's unification of the male/female polarity, is literally the means for humanity's regeneration; and the fact that his leadership alone preserves the human race, which Reese notes was "that close to going out, forever," constitutes a gifting of humanity, of his entire species, with immortality or extended life. Yet revelation, the highest boon, is finally reserved for the audience, which is gifted in viewing the film's last scene with an elegantly multi-layered, startling revelation: first, that Reese is John's father; then, on reflection, that John must have knowingly sent Reese back in time primarily to orchestrate his own conception as well as to preserve his mother's life (which the audience now realizes is a secondary objective masking the primary objective); and finally, on further reflection, that John's birth and entire existence is made possible only through Skynet's desperate attempt to use time travel to erase his existence by assassinating his mother before he is born—that Skynet orchestrates its own defeat in trying to prevent it. (This irony is compounded in *Terminator II*, which reveals that the technology that evolves into Skynet is developed through analysis of the remains of the Terminator's innovative circuitry. Thus, Skynet enables its own conception—as well as John Connor's, who will defeat it—by sending the robot, which will be followed by Reese, back in time; it both creates and destroys itself in the same act of attempting to prevent its enemy's birth.)

The Return Stage

Just as the encounter with a goddess and atonement with the father involve only Reese, so too does the return stage, like the call to adventure and refusal of the call, involve only Sarah—as it, too, is compressed into this final scene, which occurs after Reese's death. And Sarah can return to the future in Reese's stead precisely because they share the adventure of the hero between them, are in this sense the female and male manifestations of the same character. While Reese uses Skynet's time machine to go to the past, Sarah returns to the future in the same pedestrian way in which we all get there, by inexorably moving towards it along the arrow of time moment by moment. Death is the only way to prevent this return, and the visibly pregnant Sarah has clearly chosen life, to accept her transcendence and embrace her destiny, and thus to give the boon to humanity, by the film's last scene. Her magic flight is her flight from the impending nuclear Armageddon into the remote mountains of Mexico, the haven she is driving towards at the film's conclusion; this flight into the future is furthered by her knowledge of the future and of her role in it provided earlier by Reese, and is magic in that she acquires this knowledge as a result of time travel. The film concludes with Sarah symbolically crossing the return threshold in finally driving into "la tormenta," "the storm" on the horizon that symbolizes to her the coming apocalypse; in the film's last exchange of dialogue, the proprietor of the Mexican gas station tells her, "There's a storm coming," and she replies, "I know."

Sarah has accepted the world into which she is crossing; she has a dog, as Reese had told her that dogs can detect terminators, as well as a pistol in her jeep to provide protection—insulation—against the dangers this future may pose. And she crosses the return threshold with two talismans: the fetus of John Connor that she carries within her and the photo taken at the gas station. While she stops to fill up her tank, a boy takes her photo and sells it to her; this is the second talisman of her quest, acquired at the return threshold, but the audience recognizes that it is also the photo John will later give to Reese. Elegantly and ironically, as this is a time travel film, the very same object that is the talisman Reese receives prior to his initial threshold crossing is also the talisman that Sarah, now his surrogate, receives—that is, in fact, created—as she later crosses the return threshold in his stead. In dictating her memoirs for her unborn son into her tape recorder—as well as through her appearance, location, and accessories—Sarah indicates that she has accepted her destiny as, and has become, the "legend" who will teach her son how to fight and defeat the machine. Through accepting her transcendence Sarah masters the worlds of the present and the future; in accepting her destiny she becomes conscious that she is the vehicle of cosmic change, and thus attains the freedom to live.

6

Back to the Future: Science Fiction Film Comedy as Adolescent Wish Fulfillment Fantasy

The first line in *Back to the Future* is a radio ad voiceover announcing that "Statler Toyota is making the best deals of the year on all 1985 models"; when he sees a Statler Toyota 4 × 4 displayed in Hill Valley's town square later that day, protagonist Marty McFly muses to his girlfriend, "Jennifer, some day ... wouldn't it be great ... [to] take that truck up to the lake." Earlier, Vice Principal Strickland had warned Marty that his band, the Pinheads, doesn't "have a chance" of being selected to play at the high school dance; when the band is summarily dismissed from the audition for being "just too darned loud," Marty complains, "I'm never gonna get a chance to play in front of anybody." Comparing Marty to his father, George, who "was a slacker, too," Strickland also observes that "no McFly has ever amounted to anything in the history of Hill Valley"; Marty's reply, that "history is going to change," foreshadows his time travel adventure's conclusion, which entails the fulfillment of all his teen-age aspirations.

Not only does he play guitar at his high school's "Enchantment Under the Sea" dance in 1955, and not only does he discover, in the alternate 1985 at the end of the film, that he owns the 4 × 4 he had coveted earlier, which is washed and waxed and ready for his trip to the lake with Jennifer, but he also finds on his return to 1985 that his family's history of failure is reversed. Initially, Marty is embarrassed by his father's spineless deference to antagonist Biff—which George acknowledges in confessing, "I'm afraid I'm just not very good at confrontations"—as well as by the other members of his pervasively dysfunctional family: his disaffected, puffy, alcoholic, prudish mother, Loraine; his brother, David, who must take the bus to his dead-end job in a fast-food restaurant; his sister, Linda, who can't get a date; and even his uncle, "Jail-bird" Joey, who has again been denied parole. Yet, while Joey may still be incarcerated, in the alternate 1985 created through Marty's time travel mishaps Linda has more suitors than she can keep track of; David wears a suit and drives a car to his office job; Loraine is affectionate, trim, athletic, and permissive; and George has become a father Marty can respect. Not only is Biff, who has readied the 4×4, now slavishly subservient to George—their roles reversed as a consequence of Marty having inspired his father in 1955 to stand up to Biff, his high-school tormentor, in order to win Loraine—but George also demonstrates that he has "amounted to" something in Hill Valley through having just publishing a novel, *A Match Made in Heaven*, that is based on Marty's (re)instigation of their romance.

Similarly, at the beginning of *Star Wars Episode IV—A New Hope*, young Luke Skywalker yearns to be freed from Uncle Owen's moisture farm on Tatooine, to go to "the Academy" to become a pilot, to know something about the Rebellion, to learn about his mysterious father, and to follow in his father's footsteps to become a Jedi Knight. By the end of *Episode IV* he has throw off the yoke of the farm, become a crack pilot in the Rebellion, and saved the freedom-loving peoples of the galaxy from the horror of the Death Star; by the end of the initial trilogy he has learned more about his father than he had wanted to know, achieved a death-throes reconciliation with him while returning freedom to the galaxy by overthrowing Emperor Palpatine, and become a Jedi Knight. *Back to the Future*, like *Star Wars*, is a specific type of fantasy—the adolescent wish-fulfillment comedy—that is particularly compatible with Campbell's monomyth. Campbell not only demonstrates that the monomyth, the adventure of the hero, is essentially an elaborate recapitulation of an archetypal adolescent experience, the primitive initiation ritual, but he also argues that comedy is a touchstone of the mythological. *Back to the Future* is another first installment in another highly successful SF film trilogy that, in 1985, was the final film released during the second great science-fiction film boom of 1977–85, which was inaugurated by the 1977 release of *Star Wars*. Another fantasy superficially disguised as science fiction (but as a time travel tale, not a space opera) that is likewise an adolescent wish-fulfillment comedy, *Back to the Future* also utilizes Campbell's monomyth as its underlying plot structure. The monomyth's systematic deployment in *Back to the Future* reinforces profoundly that film's similarity to *Star Wars* as another adolescent wish fulfillment fantasy disguised as science fiction through the consequent generation of an overwhelming number of additional mutual correspondences; reveals as well *Back to the Future*'s more general kinship, via this shared mythological plot structure alone, to a great many other late twentieth-century science fiction novels and films to which it likewise bears little superficial resemblance; and also situates *Back to the Future* within the grandest and most extensive of literary traditions, one that contains the national epic and stretches back beyond Homer's *Odyssey* to the primordial beginnings of myth, ritual, and culture.

Qualities of the Hero

Marty McFly exhibits most of the qualities of the monomythic hero and experiences nearly all of the episodes that constitute his adventure. Referring early in the film to Loraine's prudish dismissal of her dating problems, Marty's sister Linda marvels, "It's a wonder I was ever born"; Marty says the very same thing again, in 1955, on observing his future father's inept, romance-challenged approach to wooing Loraine. While also comic in numerous other ways, the high-concept humor of *Back to the Future* hinges on the film's central conceit that, on traveling to the past, Marty encounters his parents as teenagers, interferes with their first meeting (by saving George from being hit by Loraine's father's car, an accident that would have resulted in the two falling in love, only to be struck by the car himself, so that Loraine develops a crush on him instead), and then discovers that he must fix—and "fix up"—his parents, to assure that they fall in love and marry after all, in order to insure that he and his siblings will be born. Thus, Marty's birth—or, more precisely, his re-birth in the alternate timeline he creates through his adventure—is special in that he must arrange it himself, must facilitate his own conception by playing "cupid" to his own parents. In this respect Marty is not only generally like Luke in the *Star Wars* trilogy but is also most specifically like the unseen John Connor in *The Terminator*, who orchestrates his own conception by sending his father Kyle Reese back in time to impregnate his mother Sarah Connor.

Marty is a social exile in the film's initial 1985 and becomes a more thorough exile, as well as technically an orphan, in 1955. Strickland quickly establishes that Marty is Hill Valley High's social outcast: He calls Marty a "slacker" and a "loser," gloatingly underscores that Marty is habitually out of step with his peers and their social conditioning in giving him his fourth "tardy" slip of the week, accurately predicts that he has no chance of performing at the school dance, and reprimands him for associating with Hill Valley's most prominent recluse, Doc Brown. Yet Marty is literally an exile from his own era in 1955; he laments to Brown, "I've got a life back in 1985," and he experiences frequent comic difficulties in relating to people, and even to common objects, due to the defamiliarization of his 1985 vocabulary and expectations in this time period. As he is wearing a down vest that is repeatedly mistaken for a "life-preserver," almost everyone he meets in 1955 thinks he is a "sailor." Lou has no idea what Marty is talking about when he orders a "Tab" and then a "Pepsi Free" at Lou's Café's, and has only black coffee to offer when Marty then requests something without sugar in it; later, George has to show Marty how to open a soda's non-twist-off cap. Similarly, Loraine's family has never heard of either "reruns" or "John F. Kennedy," and Brown, who scoffs at Marty's assertion that Ronald Reagan will become president, is so perplexed by Marty's slang use of the word "heavy" that he muses, "Why is everything so 'heavy' in the future? Is something wrong with the Earth's gravitational pull?" While stranded in 1955 Marty is technically an orphan, as well as literally in exile, because, while they are alive, George and Loraine are not yet his mother and father; thus, when Loraine's mother offers to contact his parents, Marty informs her that "nobody's home."

Marty spends much of his time in 1955 seeking his father and triumphing over a pretender. After first meeting him in Lou's Café, curiosity prompts Marty to follow George to Loraine's house, where Marty is struck by the car that would otherwise have injured his father. Subsequently, Brown deduces that this "inter-action" between Marty and his parents has transferred Loraine's destined infat-uation with George—a consequence of "the Florence Nightingale effect" that would have culminated in their marriage—to Marty, and that Marty and his siblings will be "erased from existence" unless Marty can reverse such "serious repercussions on future events" by getting George and Loraine to kiss at the Enchantment Under the Sea dance, as Loraine's version of family folklore main-tains that "if your father hadn't kissed me at that dance, none of you would have been born." Thus, Brown instructs Marty to "stick to your father like glue and make sure he takes her to that dance," which prompts Marty to pursue George with such single-minded persistence that George at one point asks him, "Why do you keep following me around?"

Yet, when Marty tells him in the school cafeteria that Loraine wants him to ask her out, George mistakenly believes she wants to go with Biff, who is at that moment forcing himself on her as she indignantly resists his unwanted advances. Loraine really wants to date Marty; yet "destiny" has decreed that George is the rightful claimant to Loraine's girlish affections; and Biff—who wistfully instructs Marty, in 1985, to "Say 'hi' to your mom for me"—is, in 1955, the boorishly insistent pretender to that claim. Although Marty triumphs over Biff first, by tripping and sucker punching him in Lou's Café and then leading him on the chase that culminates in his car being buried in manure, George finally and irrevocably overcomes Biff—in a more pertinent context, and as a direct but unanticipated result of Marty's plotting and coaching—by knocking him unconscious as he tries to rape Loraine in a parked car at the dance. Thus,

Marty still triumphs (both personally and through a surrogate, George) over a pretender as his parents' "true son," even though the rightful place that Biff attempts to usurp is George's (not Marty's) place in Loraine's affections.

The notion that Marty doesn't fear death is problematic. Although he is courageous in each of his 1955 encounters with Biff as well as in agreeing to follow Brown's absurdly improbable plan to harness the lightning bolt (and despite the fact that the model car in Brown's demonstration bursts into flames), Marty's primary motivation is his fear of being "erased from existence." Yet he succeeds in fixing—and "fixing up"—his parents because he does exhibit "exceptional gifts." While he could neither unite his parents nor return to 1985 without the knowledge of the future he possesses as a time traveler, Marty's true exceptional gifts are his innate talents and personality traits. Not only is he an expert skateboarder, which enables him to triumph over Biff in the car chase, and not only is he an excellent guitarist, which enables him to replace Marvin Berry and thus keep the dance going until his parents can consummate their fateful kiss, but he is also, most importantly, remarkably hip, glib, and creative. Far more adept and experienced at relating to women than is George—although this is also a running comic commentary on teen-aged socialization in the 1950s as contrasted to the 1980s—Marty has a deeper understanding of human motivation in general and of female psychology in particular than does his father; he knows what a woman wants to hear. Not only does he manipulate George into pursuing Loraine, finally, by posing as Darth Vader from the planet Vulcan and threatening to melt SF fan George's brain with Van Halen power chords if he doesn't, but Marty also offers George some sound (if, ultimately, useless) advice on how "to ask Loraine out"—showcasing his impressive repertoire of pick-up lines as well as his awareness that "girls just love that kind of stuff"—and ultimately provides George with the crucial insight that Loraine can be won by the man who is "strong enough to stand up for the woman he loves."

Marty's world is a small one, and the deficiencies it suffers are those very flaws in his parents and siblings—the culmination and epitome of the McFly family's history of failure in Hill Valley—that the film's wish-fulfillment conclusion corrects. Thus, Marty exhibits the conditional quality of the warrior, which is to change the status quo, in having inadvertently created through his time travel adventure the new and improved 1985 revealed at the end of the film. While the original 1985's Loraine, for example, is an overweight, depressed, hypocritically prudish, unhappily married alcoholic—who fills her water glass with vodka at dinner, glares at George while observing that "We all make mistakes in life," and believes that Marty is "goin' camping with the guys" because she would "freak out" if she knew that he really intends to spend the weekend at the lake with Jennifer—the revised 1985's Loraine is trim and athletic, flirts with a similarly improved George, with whom she is clearly still in love, and teasingly approves of Marty's impending "big date" with Jennifer, which she knows he has "been planning all week." Of course, Marty evinces characteristics of a warrior not only in that he satisfies the relevant conditional quality of changing the status quo, fantastically, via time travel, but also, more mundanely, because he confronts school bully Biff himself—in the cafeteria and at the dance, as well as in Lou's Café—and even teaches George to box in concocting the scheme that would have had George attract Loraine by winning a staged fight with Marty, but which gloriously misfires when George inadvertently but successfully confronts Biff instead, the event that is the immediate cause of the positive changes affecting 1985.

Marty is also the hero as lover, but in a similarly convoluted manner that likewise involves Marty sharing elements of this conditional quality of the hero, too, with George. While accomplishing the impossible task of "fixing up" his parents does lead to a bridal bed, it leads to their bridal bed, as intended, not to Marty's. Yet accomplishing the even more impossible (in fact, the ridiculously unlikely) task of getting "back to the future" by harnessing a lightning bolt leads Marty to his own bridal bed as well. Only by returning to 1985 can Marty keep his date with Jennifer, which the film repeatedly implies is "special" because they plan to become lovers during their much-anticipated weekend at the lake, and this implication is reinforced at the film's conclusion when Brown tells Marty and Jennifer that they are married and have children in 2015. Thus, while Marty's triumph over Biff as pretender is symbolized by Loraine, who marries George as a consequence, Marty's triumph in returning successfully to 1985 is symbolized by Jennifer, with whom he is reunited just before Brown returns from 2015 and whisks them both off to a new time travel adventure in the sequel.

Yet Marty is primarily the hero as world redeemer, in that he ultimately saves the small world of his family by redressing the deficiencies that small world suffers; and the film is relentless in pointedly demonstrating that Marty learns through his visit to 1955 that he is a lot like his father, the conditional quality of a world redeemer. However, the fact that George, too, exhibits the first two conditional qualities of the hero (as warrior and lover) is a far more subtle and elegant indication that he and Marty are surprisingly similar, and their many similarities are emphasized even before Marty travels to the past. Strickland tells him in 1985, "You're a slacker. You remind me of your father when he went here. He was a slacker, too.... You're too much like your old man." And when Jennifer urges Marty to send his "audition tape" to a record company after his band is eliminated at the school dance try-outs, he answers, "What if they say I'm no good? ... I just don't think I can take that kind of rejection. Jesus, I'm starting to sound like my old man."

Indeed, when Marty discovers in 1955 that George writes science fiction stories and asks to read one, George replies, "I never let anybody read my stories.... What if they didn't like them? What if they told me I was no good?" And when, in the same conversation, Marty then suggests that he ask Loraine to the dance, George responds, "What if she said 'no?' I don't think I could take that kind of a rejection." That Marty is much like his father as a teenager is visually established when we first see the 1955 incarnation of George sitting beside Marty in Lou's Café: Both father and son exhibit the same posture, with hand on back of head, before they even notice one another, and both then exhibit precisely the same goofy awkwardness while turning, in perfect synchrony, to respond to Biff's call of "Hey, McFly." Moreover, in the alternate 1985 of the film's conclusion George gives Marty the same advice that Marty (who had first heard it from Brown) had given him in 1955: "When you set your mind to it, you can accomplish anything." Of course, this emphasis on the similarities between Marty and George is finally reinforced one last time when Brown returns from 2015 in the film's last scene and informs Marty that he, too, is destined to become a father, like George, and that—after having just spent most of this film fixing his parents—Marty must go "back to the future" with Brown in the sequel to "do something about your kids."

The Departure Stage

Marty receives a literal call to adventure when Brown phones him at 8:25 a.m., October 25, 1985, and arranges to meet him at 1:15 that night at Twin Pines Mall; he subsequently receives a second (a wake-up) call to adventure, at 12:28 that night, when Brown phones him again to ask that he bring along a video camera. Marty's call to adventure also entails a herald character and two blunders that reveal the unknown world of time travel. Sometimes the herald is a beast, and the herald in *Back to the Future* is Brown's dog Einstein, who introduces Marty to this unknown world by becoming "the world's first time traveler" when Brown sends him one minute into the future in the time machine he has built into a Delorean, the experiment Marty had been summoned to the mall to witness.

As a camera pan reveals the nuclear materials container under Doc's lab cot, the second line of the film is a TV news bulletin voiceover reporting that "officials at the Pacific Nuclear Research Facility have denied the rumor that the case of missing plutonium was ... stolen from their vault.... A Libyan terrorist group had claimed responsibility.... Officials now attribute the discrepancy to a simple clerical error." Brown later informs Marty that he had "ripped off ... a group of Libyan nationalists. They wanted me to build them a bomb, so I took their plutonium and gave them a shoddy bomb casing full of used pinball machine parts." Brown needs the plutonium to fuel his time machine, but his having "ripped off" the Libyans to get it is the first blunder, as the terrorists follow him to the mall and gun him down in revenge just before he can embark on his own excursion into time. The second blunder, which effects the threshold crossing in combination with the first, is Marty's attempt to escape the Libyans by out-racing them in Brown's Delorean, which, when fueled and programmed, becomes a time machine on attaining a speed of 88 mph. As the car is already fueled for Brown's aborted trip to the future, but whimsically programmed to go to 1955 instead, Marty inadvertently transports himself to the past when he engages its overdrive, to "see if you bastards can do 90," while running from the Libyans.

Marty tacitly refuses the call to adventure by falling asleep; only Brown's second call, which awakens him, enables him to keep their appointment to rendezvous at the mall. Yet Marty also symbolically refuses the call to adventure, later, by repeatedly refusing to believe that he has been transported to 1955 at all. He first decides that it is "all a dream, just a very intense dream," a notion reinforced by the film's soundtrack, which plays the contemporaneous "Mr. Sandman" as Marty wanders into the Hill Valley of 1955. He subsequently reasserts that "this has got to be a dream" when he sees the date, "November 5, 1955," on a discarded newspaper; concludes, at first, that he has had "a horrible nightmare ... dreamed that I went back in time" when he awakens the following morning in his teenaged mother's bedroom; and finally believes, at first, that his entire experience in 1955 had merely been a "nightmare" when he awakens in his own bed the "next" morning (October 26) in the alternate 1985 of the film's conclusion.

After accepting the call, the monomythic hero receives supernatural aid from an old man or crone, who provides a talisman in a setting suggesting a womblike sense of peace, or from a guide, teacher, wizard, ferryman, hermit, or smith, who offers aid in a context of danger or temptation. Brown, of course, is the old man who provides Marty with the talisman of a time-traveling Delorean. *Back to the Future*'s crone is the dotty middle-aged woman collecting money to save the clock tower in Hill Valley's town square; she gives Marty a "Save the Clock Tower" flyer, another talisman, which enables 1955's Brown to know exactly when and where the lightning bolt that he hopes to harness to return Marty to 1985 will strike. Brown is also Marty's guide and teacher, in 1955; a hermit, as Hill Valley's prominent recluse, in 1985; and a wizard, ferryman, and smith in both time periods, as he is the inventor who constructs or retrofits the time-traveling Delorean in both 1985 and 1955.

Clearly, the threshold crossing that leads to a sphere of rebirth is Marty's visually spectacular relocation from 1985 to 1955 via Brown's time machine. And 1955 is Marty's sphere of rebirth in an oddly literal way that is realized only through *Back to the Future*'s time-travel premise, for Marty's primary objective during his week's stay in 1955 is to insure that he will be born (again) by setting his parents' romance on the right course (again) through maneuvering them into kissing for the first time (again) at the Enchantment Under the Sea dance. A protective guardian, a destructive watchman, or both may defend the threshold to the unknown world. Marty's protective guardian is Brown, whose comically gallant attempt to "draw their fire" when the Libyans appear provides Marty with his opportunity to escape them in 1985 by crossing the threshold to 1955. Of course, the Libyans are the destructive watchmen who demolish a Photo Hut stand in unwittingly defending the threshold to 1955 by firing machine guns and an anti-tank grenade at Marty as he flees across it, equally unwittingly, in the Delorean. But destructive watchmen occupy both sides of this threshold; immediately after arriving in 1955 Marty encounters Mr. Peabody—a farmer who demolishes his barn door and mailbox in repeatedly firing a shotgun at Marty, whom he mistakes for an extraterrestrial "mutate son of a bitch ... space bastard" when Marty emerges from the futuristic Delorean in Peabody's barn while wearing an equally futuristic hazmat suit.

While being swallowed in the belly of the whale is the single episode of the monomyth that is most frequently and extensively elaborated in science fiction novels and films employing this plot structure, *Back to the Future*'s treatment of it is uncharacteristically muted. Surely, the theme of the "Enchantment Under the Sea" dance is a subtle reference to the concept of being swallowed in the belly of the whale, yet the closest Marty ever comes to experiencing anything like an underground journey in this film—although it occurs, appropriately, during the dance—is when he is temporarily locked in the trunk of the Starlighters' car. Also, Brown (but not Marty) clings for his life to the pair of prominent gargoyles embellishing the clock tower while later reconnecting it to the electric cable that will channel the lightning bolt into the Delorean, and Marty is symbolically dismembered at the dance when his hand begins to fade— both in reality and in the family photo he had earlier shown Brown—as he struggles to play the guitar. Yet any hint of a descent into hell is displaced to the sequel, *Back to the Future Part II*—in which the symbolic "hell" is the bonfire-lit, biker-infested Hill Valley of an alternate-alternate 1985 that is ruled by Biff, "the luckiest man in the world," after he uses the *1950–2000 Sports Almanac* Marty acquires in 2015 to amass a fortune—and any literal underground journey is displaced to the next sequel, *Back to the Future Part III*, in which the Delorean is hidden in a cave in 1885.

The Initiation Stage

The first incident in the monomyth's initiation stage is the road of trials, a series of tests in which the hero is assisted by the advice or agents of those who had offered supernatural aid, by the talismans given him, or by a benign power that protects him everywhere; it may also require that the hero assimilate his shadow or unsuspected self. In addition to insuring that he will be born, Marty must also get "back to the future" as well as somehow prevent Brown from being killed by the Libyans once he returns; these three objectives are his tests. Brown's advice is instrumental in enabling Marty to accomplish the first two tasks, and he is also aided in returning to 1985 by the two talismans, the clock-tower flyer and the Delorean. Ironically, however, while Marty attempts to use the Delorean to save Brown, too, by returning to 1985 ten minutes before he left, only Brown's failure to follow his own advice preserves his life. The Delorean stalls after arriving in 1985, and Marty runs to the mall just in time to see Brown gunned down (again); yet Brown saves himself by wearing a bullet-proof vest he had donned as a consequence of having taped together and read, later, the warning note Marty had given him in 1955, which he had then immediately torn up due to his conviction that "no one should know too much about his own future." However, Brown's advice is ultimately triumphant. He tells Marty in 1985, "If you put your mind to it, you can accomplish anything"; and Marty conveys this advice to George in 1955 (in addition to repeating it to Jennifer in 1985), only to hear the adult George, on receiving copies of his first novel, repeat it back to him in the alternate 1985 of the film's conclusion.

Marty assimilates his shadow by transforming his teenaged father, George, not only into someone he can more readily respect, but also into someone a lot more like himself—someone who will, quite uncharacteristically, stand up to Biff in order to protect, and thus win, Loraine. As the many details of characterization through which Marty fulfills the conditional quality of the world redeemer—learning that he and the father are one—suggest, George is already Marty's shadow. This is further reinforced by the fact that Marty takes George's place in Loraine's affections as a direct result of having taken George's place as the victim who is hit by her father's car. Despite their many similarities, the crucial difference between them is Marty's glibness, his ability to persuade others—including George—and most specifically his ability to talk to women. And this verbal facility is symbolically transferred from Marty to George at the film's conclusion when it is discovered that the improved George of the alternate 1985 Marty creates has become a successful novelist.

The hero might also encounter a goddess, a temptress, or both. While Jennifer is the goddess with whom Marty will have a mystical marriage in a special location—the much-anticipated weekend trip to the lake—the teenaged Loraine whom Marty encounters in 1955 is both the Lady of the House of Sleep, as he first sees her when he awakens in her bedroom, and the bad mother, as she both threatens symbolic castration (when Marty's hand begins to fade because she has not yet kissed George at the dance) and is potentially a locus of forbidden desire (as she "has the hots" for Marty even though she is his mother). Of course, just as the new, alternate Loraine at the film's conclusion is a "good" mother in the most conventional sense, so too is the original Loraine at the beginning of the film a "bad" mother in the most conventional sense. Yet the juxtaposition of the original Loraine to both the final Loraine and the teenaged Loraine, as she is a foil to both, suggests that this composite Loraine (in all of her manifestations taken together) is primarily the Universal Mother as a combination of opposites. The original Loraine—who is so prudish that Marty jokes to Jennifer, "I think she was a nun"—tells Linda, "When I was your age I never chased a boy or called a boy or sat in a parked car with a boy." Yet 1955's Loraine has taken off Marty's pants and put them on her "hope chest" to tend to the bump on his head, squeezes his thigh under the table while they dine with her family, and suggests that he "spend the night ... in my room." Later, after having followed him to Brown's lab and asked him to the dance, she further astonishes Marty by telling him, when they arrive there, that she would "love to park.... It's not like I've never parked before."

Oedipus is one of the many embodiments of the monomythic hero discussed extensively by Campbell (4, 7, 79n, 111, 122–23, 139, 154, 353, 355), and much of the humor of *Back to the Future* derives from the film's comic reversal of the Oedipus complex. Oedipus, who is ignorant of their identities, is cursed because he kills his father, Laius, and weds his mother, Jocasta, who may or may not be aware that he is her son. Marty, who knows their identities, is rewarded for transforming his father, George, so that George can wed his mother, Loraine, who pursues and is "romantically infatuated" with Marty but is not aware that she is his mother. Thus, 1955's Loraine is also Marty's woman as temptress, yet this temptation is easy for him to resist, for not only is it Marty's goal to transfer the affection Loraine feels for him to George, but when the moment in Marty's plan that requires him to make out with Loraine while they "park" arrives, Marty also discovers that he "can't do it," and he is then clearly terrified when she makes a pass at him instead.

After encountering the goddess and temptress, the hero may experience atonement with the father or a father figure. Perhaps because George is such an unsatisfactory biological father, Brown is Marty's surrogate father. Strickland chides Marty for "still hanging around with Dr. Emmet Brown" in 1985, Marty cries out in anguish when Brown is shot by the Libyans, and Brown is the first and only person whom Marty attempts to locate and then turns to for help in 1955. Of course, Brown is the initiating priest through whom Marty passes into the other world of 1955 in that Marty uses Brown's time machine to travel to that year; and their moment of atonement occurs when Marty sees that Brown has saved himself from the Libyans through having taped back together and read the warning note he had initially torn up when Marty had given it to him in 1955. Still, Marty must transform George into someone with whom Loraine could fall in love so that George, too, can become the initiating priest who, by siring Marty, will enable him to be born at all. (To some extent, then, Marty must serve as his own initiating priest.) And they are atoned when Marty sees that the father he could not respect in the original 1985 has, in the alternate 1985 of the film's conclusion, both become a successful author and reversed his formerly servile relationship to Biff.

The penultimate incident in the initiation stage is the hero's apotheosis. Even though this is the monomyth's climactic episode, the hero's apotheosis is muted to the point of extinction in *Back to the Future*, perhaps due to the film's comic tone, much as it is in *Star Wars*. While he does perform the god-like act of transforming reality, Marty, like Luke Skywalker, experiences no dramatic annihilation of consciousness or conjunction of opposites. (Unlike Luke, Marty does not even get a medal.) And, while engineering one's own existence may be seen as a boon that is at least distantly related to acquiring immortality, the rewards Marty receives at his adventure's conclusion—a Toyota 4x4 and other material signs that his is now a more successful and affluent family—are all on the lowest level of those least valuable and merely symbolic boons, wealth and power.

The Return Stage

As is usually the case in science fiction films that utilize the monomyth as a plot structure, this Return Stage of the adventure is given a far more cursory treatment in *Back to the Future* than are the two earlier stages. While Marty desperately wants to return to 1985, he is late in meeting Brown at the clock tower because he refuses to return until he has changed out of the 1955 "zoot suit" he had worn to the dance; he then refuses to use the time machine without first taking steps to save Brown from the Libyans; and after Brown rebuffs these attempts, Marty finally sets the time machine to return to 1985 ten minutes before he had left it, so that he can warn Brown before the Libyans arrive at the mall. While Marty's return is furthered by his knowledge of when and where the lightning bolt will strike—and while Brown's scheme to harness the lightning bolt may also be considered a magic means of return solely because its chance of succeeding is infinitesimal even under the best of circumstances—this already improbable scheme is also opposed by the falling tree limb that disconnects the electric cable intended to channel the lightening into the Delorean, by Brown's slapstick difficulties in reconnecting it, and by the fact that Marty actually misses the moment at which he should begin his acceleration to 88 miles per hour because the Delorean stalls.

After miraculously returning to 1985 anyway, Marty easily accepts the new reality he discovers there because it is such an improvement over his previous reality. His returning to 1985 ten minutes before he left it, even though he spends a week in 1955, constitutes a dilation of time in that unknown world. The Libyans, of course, are the danger Marty anticipates encountering again in 1985; and the insulation against danger that Marty provides himself is that extra ten minutes he intends to use to save Brown's life. The talisman of his quest, an object that proves that Marty had traveled to the unknown world, is the note he had written to Brown in 1955 that Brown unexpectedly displays in 1985 to explain his life-saving decision to wear a bulletproof vest—even though it is Brown, not Marty, who conveys the note from 1955 to 1985. Technically, Marty becomes master of the two worlds when Brown returns from 2015 the next morning and insists on taking him "back to the future" in a modified Delorean that can now cross the threshold of time freely because, having been outfitted with a "Mr. Fusion," it no longer needs plutonium as fuel. And Marty attains the freedom to live, is freed from anxiety, not only because the version of 1985 he now finds himself in is such an improvement over his original 1985, but also because Brown assures him (albeit inaccurately, given the events of the sequel) that "both you and Jennifer turn out fine" in 2015 even though "something has got to be done about your kids."

The monomyth can be as easily appropriated by the time travel tale—in George Pal's *The Time Machine*, *Time After Time*, *The Terminator*, *Star Trek IV: The Voyage Home*, and *Star Trek Generations* for example, in addition to *Back to the Future*—as it is by space opera, for the transition from one time period to another can provide an other world (as well as the potential for equally dramatic threshold crossings to and from it) as readily as does travel from one planet to another. However, as it is quintessentially a mythological plot structure that would seem to lend itself most naturally to fantasy—in addition to being intrinsically compatible with adolescent wish-fulfillment fantasy in particular—this frequent deployment of the monomyth in what appears to be science fiction films might seem anomalous. Thus does it often appear in films, like *Back to the Future* and *Star Wars*, that are really fantasy only thinly disguised as SF—old wine in a new bottle—in which the tropes of science fiction are merely a fantastic veneer. Indeed, *Back to the Future* self-consciously mocks its pretense to being science fiction, which is part of the comedy, not only in making the mechanism of Marty's return to 1985 so wildly improbable, but also by insisting on calling attention in its last scene to a pointed inconsistency involving its time-travel premise. When Brown is about to transport Marty and Jennifer from Marty's driveway (in 1985) to 2015, Marty notes that they "don't have enough road" to attain a speed of 88 miles per hour. While this prompts the last line of the film ("Roads ... Where we're going, we don't need roads") as well as the revelation that the Delorean can now fly, it should also prompt the alert viewer to remember that Brown had successfully used that very road to travel to 2015, for the first time, on the previous evening, before the Delorean could fly. In a film in which much of the comedy derives from meticulous attention paid to small details, such a glaring final inconsistency is probably not accidental.

7

Red Pills, Problematical Realities, Metaphorical Dreams and the Monomyth in *Total Recall* and *The Matrix*

Soon after *Total Recall*'s protagonist Doug Quaid (Arnold Schwarzenegger) arrives on Mars, ReKall's pitchman Dr. Edgemar seems to visit Quaid in his Martian hotel room in an attempt to convince him to swallow a red capsule that Edgemar asserts is a "symbol" of Quaid's "desire to return to reality ... back on Earth," and his "last chance" to reject his "free-form delusion" of being a secret agent on Mars, before he is lobotomized. ReKall sells clients implanted memories of interplanetary vacations; and Edgemar claims that Quaid's ostensible "delusion" is a "dream started in the middle of the implant procedure"—the manifestation of a "schizoid embolism" suffered while receiving a Martian-vacation memory implant with the "ego-trip" option of assuming the persona of a secret agent—and that Edgemar himself, while he seems corporeal to Quaid, is an insubstantial phantasm ReKall has projected into Quaid's "delusion," back on Earth, to "talk him down." But when he sees Edgemar sweat, Quaid kills him, as this convinces Quaid that Edgemar is a physical reality subject to the dangers of the situation—not incorporeal and thus unassailable—and, therefore, that Quaid really is a secret agent on Mars and that the red capsule is probably a sedative intended to facilitate his capture.

Soon after Agent Smith (Hugo Weaving) interrogates *The Matrix*'s protagonist Neo (Keanu Reeves) in what seems to be 1999, legendary hacker Trinity (Carrie Ann Moss) takes Neo to her mentor Morpheus (Laurence Fishburne), who offers Neo the choice of swallowing either a blue or a red capsule as his "last chance" to choose between continuing to inhabit, respectively, "a computer-generated dream world"—the Matrix, a "neural interactive simulation" of 1999—or the post-apocalyptic "desert of the real" of 2199 (or so) in which a deluded humanity does not know it is a captive heat and energy source for an "artificial intelligence." When Neo chooses the red capsule, Morpheus explains that it is "part of a trace program ... [to] pinpoint [his] location [in] the real world" in order to unplug Neo's body, literally, from the pod through which he is connected to the Matrix. Here, the blue pill is the sedative, as Morpheus also tells Neo that if he chooses that one he will merely "wake up in ... bed."

Each film's protagonist is told that he inhabits a false reality, metaphorically a "dream," and is given one last chance to choose to inhabit "true" reality by swallowing a red pill, yet both films are intentionally ambiguous, and neither conclusively establishes what its "true" reality is. However, as Morpheus appears to be telling the truth, while Edgemar appears to be lying, swallowing the red pill appears to constitute choosing reality only in *The Matrix*, while doing the same thing in *Total Recall* would appear, without further consideration, to be choosing delusion over reality unwittingly. But a closer analysis reveals that the apparent axis of Quaid's choice in *Total Recall* may itself be illusory—that in choosing to swallow or not to swallow the red pill he may not be choosing between delusion and reality, after all, but might merely be choosing between one delusion and a different delusion—or, if he truly is choosing between delusion and reality, that he must be making the wrong choice: While *Total Recall*'s internal logic suggests it may be possible that Edgemar is telling the truth, that Quaid might be experiencing a "free-form delusion" (even though the film seems to dismiss this possibility in the same scene in which it is raised), the same internal logic dictates that it is not possible for Quaid be the secret agent on Mars he believes himself to be, that his adventure as it unfolds on the screen cannot be the film's reality; thus, while Quaid might possibly return to reality if he swallows the red pill, he will surely remain in some kind of delusion if he does not. In any case, however, both Neo and Quaid believe they are choosing reality and rejecting a "dream" by refusing to swallow a pill (blue and red, respectively), and each rejects the "dream" literally as well as metaphorically in that the pill each refuses to swallow is probably a sedative. That such ontologically convoluted yet strikingly similar tropes are pivotal moments in both these films is not merely a coincidence, however; the trope itself—most simply, that swallowing a red pill ostensibly gives the hero one last chance to escape a metaphorical "dream" and return to reality—is in each film a densely packed confluence of significant, interrelated, and sometimes enigmatic elements of setting, plot, character, metaphor, and allusion that both films also have in common and that under still closer examination reveals, in turn, many additional but less apparent similarities of plot structure and characterization.

When they first meet Morpheus tells Neo, "You have the look of a man who accepts what he sees because he expects to wake up. Ironically, this is not far from the truth." And after Neo swallows the red pill, Morpheus seems to emphasize his earlier assertion that this act is a rejection of a thoroughly convincing "dream world" in asking, "Have you ever had a dream ... that you were so sure was real? What if you were unable to wake from that dream? How would you know the difference between the dream world and the real world? ... What is 'real?'" Morpheus' questions in themselves, and that Neo's choice is to swallow one pill or an identical pill of an arbitrarily different color, each suggest independently that there is no way Neo can conclusively determine which of the realities he experiences is a delusion and which, if any, is real. As with the two pills, it's six of one and a half-dozen of the other: If the film's apparent premise that Neo has lived all his life so far in a perfect illusion is true, then logically he can never thereafter determine if any apparently real experience he has is illusory or not—despite the fact that every literal (but no relevant figurative) detail of the film reinforces Morpheus' assertion that 1999 is the "dream" and the post-apocalyptic world of 2199 is reality, as every aspect of Neo's existence in the ostensibly illusory "1999" (despite his suspicion that something is amiss) had likewise reinforced his belief that 1999 is reality. While the film's internal consistency compels the audience and a reluctant Neo to accept Morpheus' explication, ultimately Neo must accept it on faith alone. That the mythological Morpheus is the Greek god of dreams could imply that Morpheus' ontological questions actually reinforce the film's inherent ambiguity, that perhaps Morpheus' world of 2199 is really the (or a) "dream"; but, in any case, this mythological allusion unequivocally reinforces the extended metaphor that Morpheus' questions incorporate, the relentless comparison of ostensibly delusional reality to a "dream" (just as it also reinforces, merely by being mythological, *The Matrix*'s even-more-relentless deployment of the monomyth as its plot structure).

We first see Neo asleep before a computer monitor on which a news story headlined "Morpheus Eludes Police at Heathrow Airport" is replaced by the text message, "Wake up, Neo." When he does awaken, his cursor informs him, "The matrix has you. Follow the white rabbit"; he immediately discovers Choy and Dujour, a woman with a white rabbit tattoo on her shoulder, at his door; and he asks Choy, "Do you ever have that feeling where you're not sure if you're awake or still dreaming?" When Neo then sells him an illicit computer disk and warns him not to "get caught using" it, Choy responds, both pertinently and prophetically, "I know.... You don't exist. This never happened," and, even more presciently, "You need to unplug, man." At the conclusion of the subsequent scene in which Agent Smith interrogates him—right after Neo's mouth horrifically disappears and a surveillance device that looks, appropriately, like a hideous mechanical "bug" burrows into his navel—Neo awakens in bed as if from a nightmare. And, much later, Agent Smith tells a captive Morpheus that the Matrix was originally designed to be a utopia, a "perfect world" without suffering, but that humanity could not accept the illusion of a world without suffering and rejected "the perfect world [as] a dream your primitive cerebrum kept trying to wake up from."

The text-message instructions to "follow the white rabbit" is one of the film's numerous but always counterintuitive references to *Alice in Wonderland*— to which Morpheus alludes even more clearly when he later asks Neo to choose the red or blue pill and notes that selecting the red pill is electing to "stay in Wonderland" and see "how deep the rabbit hole goes." Significantly, Neo's choice of pills and, consequently, his choice of realities are still six of one and a half-dozen of the other in this allusive context, too. Neo can either take the red pill to go down "the rabbit hole" to "Wonderland," or take the blue pill to "wake up in ... bed," but he will have chosen to remain in a "dream" in either case, as Wonderland is Alice's dream, not her reality. That is, in the context of Morpheus' allusion Neo chooses a "dream" no matter which pill he swallows: If he takes the blue pill, he will remain in the metaphorical "dream" of 1999; yet choosing the red pill will take him "down the rabbit hole" to "Wonderland," the locus of Alice's dream.

Immediately after Neo swallows the red pill in 1999, one of the crew aboard Morpheus' hovercraft the *Nebuchadnezzar*, Cypher, notes in 2199 that "It means, 'Buckle your seatbelt, Dorothy, 'cause Kansas is goin' bye-bye.'" This allusion to the 1939 film version of *The Wizard of Oz*, another fantasy in which a young woman's adventure is a dream, assigns the status of reality to 1999 and the status of "dream" to 2199 by associating Kansas, Dorothy's reality, with Neo's world, and Oz, Dorothy's dream, with Cypher's and Morpheus' world—contrary to their explicit designations in the film and yet oddly consistent with Morpheus being, allusively, the god of sleep—just as Morpheus, even more inexplicably, had only moments earlier assigned the status of "dream" to his world of 2199 in referring to it as "Wonderland." Almost simultaneously, Neo sees a fractured wall mirror mend itself and tentatively pokes his finger through the looking glass—another, visual allusion to the Alice stories that yet again associates 1999 with reality and 2199 with a "dream" world, for Neo in 1999 is analogous to Alice on reality's side of the looking glass, Cypher's and Morpheus' 2199 is analogous to the other side of the looking glass, and Neo soon finds himself there with Morpheus in "the construct" (the initially featureless "loading area" computer program in which Morpheus and his crew equip themselves to venture into the Matrix), where Morpheus again tells Neo, "You've been living in a dream world."

While *The Matrix* consistently portrays 1999 as the delusion and 2199 as reality—even though Neo cannot conclusively determine which is which, and all the film's allusions to fantasy dreamlands metaphorically contradict this reading—*Total Recall* explicitly leaves open to conjecture the question "What is real?" And in *Total Recall* this is a question about the status of what is being depicted on the screen. From the moment Quaid seems to awaken from its opening dream sequence, the film is delightfully ambiguous as to whether the events on the screen are reality, an illusion (the intended but unexpectedly convoluted memory implant/ego trip), a "delusion" (the memory implant/ego trip gone awry due to a "schizoid embolism"), or an uninterrupted continuation of the initial dream sequence in which Quaid only dreams that he wakes up. Finally, if still tentatively, this film literalizes and thus conflates its more-insistent and more-complex metaphorical comparisons of dreams to delusion, illusion, and reality. A plethora of clues and hints throughout the film first suggest and then call into question each of these four possibilities, even though two of them are invalidated by the film's internal logic. Yet the film generates much of its disorienting but exhilarating ontological ambiguity by encouraging the viewer to vacillate between these two invalidated interpretations only, while quickly dismissing or suggesting only obliquely the only two proffered interpretations that are logically possible. The events depicted cannot be either reality or the intended "ego-trip" memory implant—even though the story is presented almost exclusively from within these internally flawed frames of reference—but must be either a free-form delusion or a dream.

Reading the events depicted as reality cannot accommodate crucial details of Quaid's visit to Rekall, among a great many other specific details. Quaid is shown precisely accurate images of the alien installation he will later visit on Mars, but all information about "alien artifacts" is being withheld from the public, so there is no plausible way Rekall could have obtained these images. He also is shown a visualization of the "exotic woman" to be incorporated into his illusory adventure, girl 41A, but she looks exactly like a woman he encounters in "reality," Melina (Rachel Ticotin), the love interest/hooker/revolutionary he subsequently encounters on Mars. And in retrieving Quaid's intended implant, 62B-37, Ernie the technician mutters, "That's a new one ... blue skies on Mars," indicating that the climax of the intended ego-trip implant is, likewise, identical to the preposterous conclusion of Quaid's "real" adventure—the nearly instantaneous terraforming of Mars. Even if he is fixated on Mars and enticed by the secret-agent "ego-trip" option because he really had been a secret agent on Mars, it is still just too outrageously improbable that Quaid could subsequently experience in "reality" every promised feature of the same improbable, illusory adventure—with the identical exotic woman, involving the same secret location and artifacts, and culminating in the same wildly unlikely finale—that was to have been the contents of his implant.

All these details that undermine the possibility that the depicted events really occur also, of course, reinforce the alternative interpretation that these events are merely the details of the promised ego-trip implant. Yet many different elements of Quaid's adventure are inconsistent with this second reading. For example, Quaid eventually kills both Harry, his ostensible co-worker, and Lori (Sharon Stone), his ostensible wife. But, as Quaid is promised that his "brain will not know the difference" between implanted and real memories, the implant should not contain any details that will contradict the reality to which Quaid will return on leaving Rekall—a reality that would still contain Harry and Lori as co-worker and wife. Also, even after Quaid leaves ReKall, the film still depicts numerous scenes he cannot be witnessing because he isn't there—such as several involving conversations between Cohagen, who rules Mars for "the Agency," and his chief henchman Richter (Michael Ironsides)—and that, therefore, would be inconsistent with a memory implant's first-person point of view (except, possibly, as some narrative conceit). More conclusively, although the woman whose image Quaid sees at Rekall should be the same woman he meets on Mars if all subsequent events are the contents of his memory implant, this interpretation does not explain how this woman can also be the same woman he dreams about in the film's opening sequence. The improbability of the woman in Quaid's dream being identical to Rekall's girl 41A invalidates this second interpretation much as the improbability of Rekall's girl 41A being identical to Melina invalidates the first.

While both would be unmotivated and apparently pointless elaborations, it is nonetheless possible that the intended memory implant could include Edgemar's appearance on Mars *per se* as well as his irrational reason, given even this premise, for being there—that he plays a small and totally superfluous role in Cohagen's absurdly convoluted, disastrously unwieldy, pathologically psychotic plot to use Quaid to infiltrate revolutionary leader Kuato's headquarters. However, if this is reality, there is no sufficient or even remotely plausible justification for Edgemar, a spokesman in ReKall's Metro video ads who has no known ties to the Agency, to turn up in Quaid's Martian hotel on such a potentially suicidal and absolutely unnecessary mission—that is, to convince Quaid to swallow a sedative so that Richter can capture him more easily—since Cohagen has deliberately derailed several much-more-promising opportunities Richter has had to capture Quaid, earlier in the film, precisely because Cohagen does not want Quaid to be captured; Cohagen wants Quaid to remain under pursuit but free so that Melina and the other rebels will believe his story—that he has betrayed Cohagen and sided with the rebels—and take him to Kuato. By far the best rationale for Edgemar's appearance on Mars is the explanation he offers—that Quaid is still on Earth experiencing a "free-form delusion" caused by a botched memory implant, and that Edgemar is a phantasm ReKall has projected into Quaid's mind to "talk him down." Even though Quaid discounts Edgemar's explanation on seeing him sweat, the sweat itself could easily be an element of Quaid's delusion generated to maintain the delusion.

While it means that Quaid will ultimately be lobotomized because he did not swallow the red pill, this interpretation (that Quaid's experience is a "free-form delusion" caused by a "schizoid embolism") involves no insurmountable logical inconsistencies. As all the delusional events that occur after the botched implant procedure begins would be based on what Quaid is told at ReKall as well as on the contents of the implant itself, this interpretation accounts for all but one of the highly improbable coincidences that invalidate the first two interpretations, leaving unexplained only the fact that the woman in Quaid's dream is identical both to Rekall's girl 41A and to Melina. Yet this can be accounted for in a number of ways: The most plausible explanation is that the scene in which Quaid chooses girl 41A occurs after the implant procedure begins and is itself part of the delusion—a possibility suggested by the fact that Dr. Luft asks "Ready for dreamland?" just prior to this scene, while injecting Quaid with "narcodine," which might signal the film's indeterminate demarcation between reality and delusion. And many additional details support this interpretation. For instance, Harry warns Quaid that a friend "tried one of [Rekall's] special offers—nearly got himself lobotomized," and a Dr. Edgemar is listed in the directory Quaid consults on entering the ReKall building's lobby, although these particulars are also consistent with the interpretation that all events are real. More conclusively, the first video image shown Quaid at ReKall depicts a dragon-like "two-headed monster"; while no identical monster appears on Mars, Quaid's delusion may have recycled the concept, if not the image itself, in generating the rebel leader Kuato, a two-headed mutant. And Edgemar on Mars accurately predicts, "One minute you'll be the savior of the rebel cause, and the next thing you know you'll be Cohagen's bosom buddy. You'll even have fantasies about alien artifacts." Such accuracy in predicting such unlikely turns of events coming from someone who cannot foresee a far more likely and immediate outcome, that he will be dead in less than a minute, can be explained by the justification for his appearance that Edgemar provides: These items are later incorporated into Quaid's delusion because absolutely anything Edgemar's phantasm says can plant the seeds of later events in his mind.

In fact, Edgemar argues quite convincingly that Quaid's experience must be a delusion precisely because Melina had appeared to him in a dream prior to his visit to Rekall: "Can you hear yourself?" he asks Quaid, "The girl is real because you dreamed her!" When Quaid counters by saying, "Ah, I get it. I'm dreaming. And all this is part of the delightful vacation your company has sold me," Edgemar replies, "Your dream started in the middle of the implant procedure." Here the term "dream" is used ambiguously to refer, by turns, to an actual dream, to the intended memory implant, and to the "free-form delusion" it may have produced. Yet the fourth, implicit interpretation of the film's depicted events is that the entire film is a continuation of the dream Quaid only appears to awaken from at its beginning. Of course, it is impossible to prove that the depicted events are *not* the contents of a dream, although any significantly inexplicable inconsistency that would invalidate all three alternative interpretations—which the film finally does not provide—could suggest that all depicted events must be the contents of a dream.

And the possibility that the entire film might be Quaid's dream is suggested repeatedly, as if Quaid were trying to tell himself in his dream that he is only dreaming. The film's first lines of dialogue, Lori's first words to Quaid after he appears to awaken, are, "Doug... Honey, are you all right? ... You*'re* dreaming." Significantly, she uses the present rather than the past tense. She tells him later, "Sorry, Quaid, your whole life is just a dream." Quaid's alter-ego, Howser, jokes, "Maybe we'll meet you in our dreams. You never know," in the videotape Cohagen shows Quaid near the film's conclusion. Cohagen subsequently tells Quaid at the alien reactor site, "You're nothing! You're nobody! You're a stupid dream! Well, all dreams come to an end." The film's climax repeats the contents of the initial dream (or, perhaps, dream-within-a-dream) sequence: Quaid is again with Melina and is again suffocating due to exposure in the thin Martian atmosphere. And in the film's last lines of dialogue—after the alien reactor produces the breathable air that miraculously saves them both—Melina marvels, "It's just like a dream"; Quaid replies, "I just had a terrible thought. Perhaps it is a dream"; and Melina responds, "Then kiss me before *you* wake up!" Significantly, Melina uses the second-person singular pronoun, "you," not the plural, "we," or even the more reasonable, first-person singular pronoun, "I."

Total Recall tricks its audience into believing that the two most likely interpretations of its plot are that the events depicted are either reality or the memory implant Quaid has purchased, but closer attention to the film's details indicates that neither of these interpretations is plausible and that these events must actually be one of two other suggested possibilities: They are either Quaid's delusion, based on the intended memory implant, or Quaid's dream. This ambiguity is reinforced by the motifs of deception and illusion that suffuse the film (Palumbo, "Inspired"). But, regardless of whether Quaid's experience is a delusion or a dream, it occurs in two worlds: the world Quaid is familiar with, Earth, and the world with which he is unfamiliar, Mars. *The Matrix* likewise occurs in two worlds: the illusory world of 1999, with which Neo is familiar, and the unfamiliar but ostensibly real world of 2199. Such a transposition of the protagonist from a known and mundane world to an unknown world in which he experiences a quest-like adventure is the fundamental characteristic of Joseph Campbell's monomyth; and these two films are most deeply similar in that in each the protagonist embodies the qualities of the hero and enacts the hero's adventure as described in Campbell's *The Hero with a Thousand Faces*. This is more apparent in *The Matrix*, the "plot" of which, Kimball notes in passing, "enacts a variation of the myth of the hero" (176).

Qualities of the Hero

Almost every science fiction film that utilizes this plot structure, while incorporating many qualities of the hero into its protagonist, strongly emphasizes the departure stage, omits one or more key elements of the initiation stage, and radically downplays the return stage; these films are no exception. Both Quaid and Neo are the victims of a special, virgin birth into a form of exile. Cohagen and Hauser created the Quaid persona to enable Hauser, as Quaid, to infiltrate Kuato's Martian insurgency; this invention of an artificial personality loyal to Kuato's rebellion is necessary because many of the rebels, like Kuato, are mutants with psychic powers that would enable them to detect an ordinary double-agent. Thus, Hauser himself is exiled to the Quaid identity, as well as to the "dead-end job" as a "lowly construction worker" on Earth to which Quaid himself feels exiled.

Like most humans in 2199, Neo is gestated and birthed by machine, "born into bondage, born into a prison for your mind," the Matrix. Shortly after he ingests the red pill, Neo's body is freed from the pod in which he had served as a human battery to the artificial intelligences who rule the Earth. This is another virgin birth—visually and symbolically, if not literally—in that Neo's naked body emerges from a thick amniotic fluid, numerous umbilical cords disengage explosively from him, and he is flushed down a tube that serves as a symbolic birth canal into the stagnant waters from which Morpheus' crew recovers him. While exiled from the real world of 2199 in his pod, Neo is also an exile of sorts in the world of the Matrix, 1999, in that he is a misfit in his day job as a software writer and a "criminal" in his clandestine career as some kind of hacker. Late for work the day after he meets fellow-hacker Trinity, Neo is told by his boss, "You have a problem with authority.... You believe that you are special ... that somehow the rules don't apply to you," and is ordered to show up on time or "find another job." Agent Smith later tells Neo that he is a "criminal ... guilty of virtually every computer crime we have a law for." And Neo feels ontologically displaced in this false reality of 1999 as well: He is seeking Morpheus because he suspects that the world isn't right and that Morpheus may know what is wrong about it; Trinity tells him this is "why you hardly sleep ... why you live alone and why, night after night, you sit at your computer. You're looking for him."

In seeking Morpheus Neo seeks a father-surrogate who can tell him what is wrong with the world. Simultaneously, Morpheus is seeking Neo, whom he believes is the "one" (an anagram of "Neo") who is destined to free humanity from the Matrix. Kimball also points out that "it is overdetermined ... that Morpheus is, above all, a symbolic father" (193), as both Neo and one of Morpheus' crew, Tank, refer to Morpheus as their "father." At this precise moment in the film Neo seeks Morpheus again—after Morpheus has been captured by Agents and is being held prisoner in the Matrix—to save him. Agents are programs that can take over the virtual bodies of any human beings in the Matrix, and are in this sense "pretenders," and Neo triumphs over them by first freeing Morpheus and finally by defeating Agent Smith in super-powered martial arts combat. While it could be argued that Quaid is also seeking a surrogate father in pursuing Kuato, father of the rebellion on Mars, it is Quaid who is the "pretender" in *Total Recall* and his alter-ego, Hauser, who is Cohagen's "true son." Yet Quaid thwarts Cohagen's attempt to replace his persona with Hauser's at the film's conclusion; thus, this film presents an inversion in which the protagonist is the pretender who triumphs over the true son.

In thwarting Cohagen and his henchmen, Quaid is aided by tremendous strength and excellent hand-to-hand combat skills, his exceptional gifts. Neo's exceptional gifts are far more extraordinary: As "the one," he is able to bend and break the rules of the Matrix, the laws of physics that govern this illusory world of 1999; thus, not only does he acquire super-human martial arts talents, but he is also able to defy gravity, to exhibit super-human speed, and, finally, to rise from the dead. Much more emphatically than Quaid, Neo also has no fear of death. The Oracle tells Neo, "You're going to have to make a choice.... One of you [Neo or Morpheus] is going to die. Which one is up to you." And after Morpheus is captured, when Tank is about to "pull the plug" on Morpheus' body in 2199 to prevent him from divulging the human city of Zion's computer codes to Agent Smith, Neo chooses to "go in" to the Matrix (1999) again to sacrifice himself for Morpheus; as no human has ever survived combat with an Agent, Tank tells him, "What you are talking about is suicide."

Moreover, Neo's 1999 and Quaid's Earth—the known worlds—both suffer deficiencies. On their first meeting Morpheus tells Neo, "You've felt it your entire life, that there's something wrong with the world," and what is wrong with it is that it isn't real and it isn't free. Neo's 1999, the Matrix, is a "neural interactive simulation" of the world as it once existed, designed to be the illusion that keeps humanity "enslaved" as organic "batteries" providing heat and energy to the artificial intelligences who rule the world in 2199. On Quaid's Earth the "Northern Block" is at war with the "Southern Block," which has "numerical superiority" but is kept at bay by the North's technological superiority. Unfortunately, this technological superiority depends on the supply of "tribinium" from Mars, which is beset by "terrorists" and on the brink of revolution. The news Quaid watches on Earth is all Northern Block propaganda, security is so tight that people must pass through an x-ray scanner to board the subway, and Richter's pursuit of Quaid suggests that an inordinate amount of automatic weapons fire in public—and the collateral death of numerous innocent civilians—is not uncommon. But it is Mars that lacks freedom: Cohagen is basically a corrupt dictator who "can do anything ... as long as the tribinium keeps flowing"; and Mars' absence of air, a commodity Cohagen also controls, is symbolic of its lack of freedom. Kuato's dying request is that Quaid "start the [alien] reactor [that manufactures atmosphere]. Free Mars."

Much as Neo is dissatisfied with the subliminal artificiality of his 1999, so too is Quaid dissatisfied with his ersatz life on Earth as a "lowly construction worker." He complains to Lori, "I want to do something with my life, to be somebody." It is more Neo, however, who embraces the hero's two-fold role to make the world spiritually significant and to make humankind comprehensible to itself, for in fulfilling his destiny to free humanity from the Matrix he will make humanity aware of the true reality of 2199 and thus make it comprehend its enslavement and delusion in 1999. Neo's last words are, "I came here [back inside the Matrix] to show these people [humanity] ... the world without you [the A.I. and its Agents] without rules ... without borders and boundaries ... a world where anything is possible."

Yet Neo and Quaid share the very same conditional qualities of the hero in much the same way. Both are warriors who change the status quo; both are lovers whose triumph is symbolized by a woman; and both are world redeemers who save, not their own worlds, but the "other" world, although neither satisfies the conditional quality of the world-redeemer in that neither learns that he and the father are one. Neo is a warrior trained via Morpheus' simulations in every form of martial arts combat; he changes the status quo in defeating Agent Smith and offering humanity the possibility of escape from the Matrix. He is a lover who is brought back to life, after Agent Smith initially defeats him in the Matrix, through the agency of Trinity's kiss (in 2199) at the film's climax. And the end of the film implies that he will save the world of 2199 by freeing humanity from delusion and enslavement. Quaid is a warrior who possesses the combat skills of his alter-ego Hauser, and he changes the status quo by starting the alien reactor that supplies Mars with a breathable atmosphere, thus undermining one of Cohagen's levers of authority. He is a lover who is reunited with Melina on Mars, saves her from being brainwashed via a memory implant, and is rewarded with a kiss after he "frees" Mars by providing it with air.

The Departure Stage

Both Quaid and Neo receive a call to adventure that (like Marty's in *Back to the Future*) involves a literal telephone call, but Neo's call to adventure—which he refuses several times—is far more elaborate than Quaid's. Going to ReKall in the first place is the blunder that reveals the unsuspected world to Quaid, as it is the attempt to implant a memory in his brain that "blows" his "cover" by hitting a "memory cap" and revealing that he really is a secret agent who has "actually been to Mars," if this is a dream, and it is the implant procedure that causes the schizoid embolism, if this is a delusion. After subsequently escaping from Harry, Lori, and Richter, Quaid seeks refuge in a shabby room at The Ritz, where he receives a phone call from one of his "buddies in the Agency back on Mars" who tells him, "If you want to live, don't hang up." But this mysterious figure, who leaves Quaid a suitcase filled with a variety of useful objects, is merely the third of Quaid's heralds of the unknown world. The first is Melina, with whom Quaid shares the film's initial dream sequence set on Mars; and the second is Cohagen, the evil mastermind whom Quaid sees being interviewed on TV after he seems to awaken.

Neo's first call (appropriately, via computer) is the text message he receives from Trinity that tells him to "Wake up, Neo. The matrix has you. Follow the white rabbit." Neo first refuses the call, in rejecting the invitation to go with Choi and Dujour to a club, but he changes his mind when he notices the white rabbit tattoo on Dujour's shoulder. At the club he meets Trinity, his first Herald of the world of 2199, who says, "All I can tell you is that you're in danger." At work the next day, after his boss tells him, "The time has come for you to make a choice," Neo receives a FedEx package that contains a ringing cell phone. On the line is Morpheus, Neo's second herald, who offers him the "choice" of escaping his office building via some absurdly dangerous scaffolding or of being taken into custody by Agent Smith. In rejecting the escape via scaffolding as being too "crazy," Neo refuses the call to adventure again and is captured and interrogated by Smith, the third herald. After his interrogation Neo awakens as if from a nightmare and receives a second phone call from Morpheus, who instructs him to meet Trinity at the Arrow Street Bridge. Neo rejects the call to adventure a third time in balking at having Trinity convey him to Morpheus, but finally he relents; and when Morpheus tells him that his "last chance" to escape imprisonment in the Matrix is to take the red pill, a still-skeptical Neo finally acquiesces and accepts the call to adventure by taking the pill.

After accepting the call the hero receives supernatural aid from an old man or crone, who provides a talisman in a setting suggesting a womb-like sense of peace, or from a guide, teacher, wizard, ferryman, hermit, or smith who offers aid in a context of danger or temptation. Morpheus' red pill is Neo's talisman, and Morpheus is also Neo's guide and teacher, as is Trinity, who guides Neo to Morpheus, who in turn leads Neo to yet another guide, the Oracle, whom Morpheus claims can help Neo "to find the faith." The Oracle reconfirms Morpheus' status as guide in telling Neo that "without him we are lost." And Morpheus is also Neo's teacher in being the martial-arts sparring partner who trains him to tap into his potential to "bend" and "break" the rules of the Matrix. Neo's other teacher is Tank, who operates the "combat training" simulations that initially teach Neo a wide range of fighting techniques. Tank is also the ferryman, in 2199, who operates the equipment that inserts others into and extracts them from the Matrix. And Neo finally calls Tank "Mr. Wizard."

Quaid's buddy from the Agency, who is probably working for Cohagen, provides him with his talisman: the suitcase that contains a computerized message from Hauser, Martian money, fake IDs, a device to remove the "bug" in his head through which Richter is tracking him, a holographic projector, candy bars, and possibly the disguise Quaid uses to get to Mars undetected. Through the video message in the suitcase's computer, which urges him to "get your ass to Mars," Quaid's alter-ego Hauser is Quaid's guide to (as well as on) Mars, where Quaid finds another message left him by Hauser that directs him to Melina at The Last Resort. Quaid has ferrymen both on Earth and on Mars: Dr. Lull and Ernie, technicians at ReKall, instigate Quaid's adventure, regardless of whether it is a dream or a delusion, by attempting to implant his ego-trip vacation package; the ferryman on Mars is Benny, the traitorous mutant cab driver. And, although he appears much later, the film's wizard and hermit is Kuato, a psychic mutant in hiding who uses telepathy to help Quaid "remember" details about Mars' alien artifacts that ultimately aid him in starting the reactor.

The hero next crosses the threshold to an unknown world that leads to a sphere of rebirth and that may be defended by protective guardians or destructive watchmen. Whether his experience is a dream or a delusion, Quaid's threshold crossing is his taking a spaceship to Mars while disguised as a huge woman, and Mars becomes a "sphere of rebirth" when it receives a breathable atmosphere at the film's conclusion. Ironically, Quaid's protective guardian is Cohagen, who calls off Richter's pursuit of Quaid at one point and who, throughout Quaid's adventure, is orchestrating events in order to get Quaid to Mars alive so that Quaid can lead him to Kuato and eventually undergo "re-implantation" to become Hauser again. Lori is Quaid's initial destructive watchman: After first trying to kill him in their apartment once Quaid returns from ReKall, she acknowledges, "I was written in[to your memory implant] as your wife so that I could watch you and make sure the erasure [of Hauser's persona and memories] took." Other destructive watchmen include Harry, who says he "was there to keep you out of trouble," and the three other ostensible co-workers who had earlier attempted to kill Quaid as he returns from ReKall to his apartment. But Quaid's principle destructive watchman is Richter, who tries to gun Quaid down on the subway on Earth, tracks Quaid via the "bug" in his head to a cement factory, ignores Cohagen's orders that he cease pursuing Quaid, tries to kill Quaid again as he goes through Martian Immigration disguised as a woman, and attempts to take Quaid's life one last time in the Pyramid mines near the film's climax.

Neo crosses the threshold to the unknown world when he takes the red pill, an act that is soon followed by his metaphorical rebirth from the pod that contains him in 2199—a symbolic rebirth that foreshadows the promised rebirth of humanity from the Matrix through Neo's agency. Neo's protective guardians are, not only Trinity and Morpheus, but also Tank, who kills the traitorous Cypher just as Cypher is about to take Neo's life by disconnecting the jack from the back of his head while he is still within the Matrix. Neo's destructive watchmen are Agent Smith—who tells Neo at his interrogation, "We've had our eye on you for some time now"—and the other Agents, whom Morpheus informs Neo "are the gatekeepers. They guard all the doors. They hold all the keys."

The departure stage's final episode is to be swallowed in the belly of the whale. As he discovers that he is already plugged into the A.I.'s machine in the "real world" of 2199, Neo is already in the belly of the whale from the beginning of *The Matrix*. The myriad others in their pods, nearly all of humanity, are the film's lost souls. On recovering consciousness in 2199 Neo asks, "Am I dead," and Morpheus responds, "Far from it." Neo's awakening in 2199 involves a metaphorical underground journey, as well as a symbolic rebirth, in that his initial instructions are to "follow the white rabbit" and take a trip "down the rabbit hole." "The desert of the real world" that Morpheus then shows him is the hellish 2199 into which Neo has figuratively descended. While he has been in a state of mutilation, in his pod in 2199, since his birth, Neo is also mutilated in 1999 when his mouth horrifically disappears during his interrogation by Agent Smith and a surveillance device that looks like a mechanical bug burrows into his navel. And Neo is literally killed in his climactic battle with Agent Smith in 1999, as he simultaneously flatlines in 2199, but he is restored to life by Trinity's kiss in 2199, which brings him back to life in 1999 also.

Total Recall involves literal underground journeys. On Earth, after Quaid evades them in his apartment building, Richter and his men chase Quaid down into the subway. Moreover, much of the inhabited area of Mars seems to be underground, including specifically Venusville, and all of it is under "cheap domes" that allow in the radiation that has transformed many of the people on Mars—the planet's lost souls—into mutants. En route with Melina to Kuato's underground Martian headquarters, Quaid passes through a series of catacombs where "the first settlers are buried"—the *memento mori* of this underground hell. And the climax of the film occurs in the Pyramid Mines, the underground location in which Quaid starts the reactor. Quaid, with Melina, is then hideously mutilated by exposure to vacuum when they are expelled out of the mines onto the planet's near-airless surface, before the reactor transforms the ice in the planet's interior into the breathable atmosphere that saves them.

The Initiation Stage

The monomyth's initiation stage begins with the road of trials, a series of tests in which the hero is assisted by the talismans, advice, or agents of those who had provided aid, and during which he may also assimilate or be assimilated by his shadow or unsuspected self. Quaid is aided in his tests—evading Richter both on Earth and Mars, getting to Mars, not taking Edgemar's red pill, gaining Kuato's trust in order to have his memory of Martian artifacts restored, and starting the reactor—by nearly everything in the suitcase provided by his buddy in the Agency. On finding the holographic projector, Quaid at first fires at a projection of himself in the rat-infested cement factory; this visually emphasizes that Quaid is in conflict with himself, that he, as Hauser, is his own shadow: While they inhabit the same body, Quaid is loyal to the Martian rebels and Kuato while Hauser is Martian tyrant Cohagen's "bosom buddy"; as Harry tells Quaid while trying to kill him on Earth, "You got *yourself* mixed up with somebody else." Lori then informs Quaid that the Agency "erased your memory and implanted a new one." And Hauser on the suitcase's video message tells him, "You're not really you; you're me." However, the rest of the message is merely the cover story Cohagen and Hauser want Quaid to believe so that he can infiltrate Kuato's rebellion. By thus deceiving him into being a pawn, Hauser initially assimilates Quaid even though it is Quaid who inhabits Hauser's body. And Hauser wants his body back; but Quaid ultimately assimilates Hauser, literally, by refusing to relinquish their body when he escapes from the "memory re-implantation" machinery on Mars and thus succeeds in retaining the Quaid persona.

Neo's task, as Cypher puts it, "is to save the world." To do this he must free his mind in order to "bend" and "break" the rules of the Matrix so that he can hold his own against Agent Smith and the Matrix's other "sentient programs." Neo is aided by Morpheus' advice and mentoring, of course, by the false prophecy given him by the Oracle, and also by Morpheus' agents Trinity—the companion throughout his adventures who resurrects him with a kiss—and Tank, who puts Neo through the martial-arts training programs and finally saves him from Cypher's treachery. Agent Smith is the shadow self whom Neo assimilates. Like Neo, Smith "can't stand" inhabiting the Matrix's world of 1999; but sentient program Smith wants to "get free" of the Matrix by destroying Zion and the human insurgency, while the human Neo wants to "get free" by saving Zion— by rescuing Morpheus before he is forced to divulge Zion's codes to Smith—so that the human rebellion against the A.I.s will survive. In saving Morpheus, Neo moves as fast as an Agent does; and in their final confrontation, Neo and Agent Smith fight with equal abilities. Finally, once Trinity's kiss brings Neo back to life after Smith kills him, Neo literally leaps into Smith's body and shatters it from within to emerge unscathed. Thus, Neo ironically defeats his shadow self by being swallowed by it, and in the film's last shot he dons Agent-like sunglasses and breaks the rules of the Matrix by defying gravity and flying off.

The hero might next encounter a goddess, a temptress, or both. Trinity is Neo's goddess; the mystical location of their mystical marriage is the liminal space between the world of 2199 and the world of the matrix (1999), which Trinity's life-giving kiss bridges; and Trinity might be considered the Lady of the House of Sleep, not only in that she is Neo's bliss, but also in that her surrogate father is Morpheus, the mythological god of sleep. *The Matrix*'s Universal Mother is the cookie-baking Oracle, who combines opposites through being a genuine prophet—she predicts both that Morpheus will find "the one" and that the man Trinity loves "would be the one"—who, nonetheless, lies to Neo, in telling him he is not "the one," because she tells him what he needs to know to choose to save Morpheus, rather than the truth. (The closest thing to a temptress in *The Matrix* is the Woman in Red, a distracting feature in one of Neo's training programs.)

Total Recall features a much more emphatic temptress in Lori, the ersatz wife the Agency provides for Quaid. Lori initially does everything she can to dissuade Quaid from even showing any interest in Mars. Then, after first trying to kill him once he returns from ReKall, she reveals she is not his wife and tries to seduce him to buy time for Richter (her actual husband) to arrive at her and Quaid's apartment. She then turns up, again seductively, with Edgemar on Mars to assist Edgemar in his attempt to convince Quaid to swallow the red pill. (As she twice kicks Quaid in the groin, one might argue that Lori also exhibits a touch of the bad mother who threatens castration.) And *Total Recall* also provides a much more emphatic goddess as the Lady of the House of Sleep in Melina, the woman in the film's (and Quaid's) opening dream sequence of whom Lori claims to be jealous because Quaid dreams of her "every night." Melina is literally Quaid's ideal woman in that, as girl 41A, she is the composite of all the qualities he desires in a woman, which he categorically specifies to ReKall's Dr. Lull. (As she is a hooker/revolutionary who is, as Quaid specifies, both "sleazy and demure," one might argue that Melina also exhibits a touch of the Universal Mother who combines opposites.)

The hero might also experience atonement with the father or a father-figure through whom the hero enters the world; yet this episode can be a negative encounter that might dramatize inter-generational violence; thus, the father can be or appears to be a tyrant or ogre, and father and son are atoned only after the hero sees beyond this negative manifestation of the father. Quaid's/Hauser's father-figure is Cohagen, and it is through Cohagen that Quaid enters the world in that the Quaid persona's very existence is merely a part of Cohagen's scheme to enable Hauser to infiltrate Kuato's rebellion. Quaid and Cohagen finally meet only after Quaid and Melina are captured and Kuato is killed, and there is no reconciliation: Cohagen remains the tyrant who wants to replace the Quaid persona with Hauser, his surrogate son. Morpheus is the father-figure through whom Neo passes into the "real" world of 2199 after taking the red pill. In returning to the matrix to save Morpheus, even though he believes it will cost him his life, Neo chooses to sacrifice himself for the man both he and Tank refer to as a "father," even though no reconciliation is necessary as Neo and Morpheus are never at odds.

The initiation stage's penultimate episode is apotheosis, but this episode is commonly ignored or severely muted in science fiction films that reiterate the monomyth, especially if they have little to do with enlightenment or transcendence thematically. Thus, there is no moment of apotheosis in *Total Recall*. However, as Neo must accept himself as "the one," *The Matrix* does entail a moment of transcendence during Neo's final battle with Agent Smith in which Neo finally is "beginning to believe" he is "the one." After he is resurrected by Trinity's kiss, Neo revives in the Matrix as a being who seems to exercise god-like control over it—and who appears to be beyond the reach of change, free from all fear, and united with time and eternity. While the Matrix in itself is a unification of opposites, in that it is a conflation of illusion and reality, Neo's apotheosis' unification of opposites occurs when he briefly merges with Agent Smith, his shadow, before obliterating him.

Receiving the boon, which ideally leads to the regeneration of the hero's society, is the initiation stage's final episode. Neo's boon is his final awareness that he is "the one," implicitly a revelation, and it entails his new-found ability to exercise god-like power within the Matrix and, through this power, to regenerate human society by ultimately freeing it from the Matrix. Quaid's boon is the terraforming of Mars effected by his starting the reactor that generates atmosphere. This not only saves his own and Melina's lives, but it also saves the lives of the inhabitants of Venusville, who are dying of asphyxiation because Cohagen has callously cut off their air supply. Thus, in providing it with air, Quaid finally "frees" Mars and supplies the means for the regeneration of the society of Martian mutants in Venusville that he has adopted as his own society in the course of his adventure.

The Return Stage

In gifting Mars with a breathable atmosphere, which turns its sky blue, Quaid almost magically completes the return stage of the adventure in moments by transforming Mars into an Earth-like environment. In another sense, however, he also refuses to return and chooses instead, when Melina tells him to "Kiss me before you wake up," to remain at least for a moment longer in the dream he has probably been in since the beginning of the film. Yet this refusal to return is in itself a return in that it brings us back to the film's initial dream sequence, in which Quaid and Melina are about to asphyxiate on Mars' surface when Quaid appears to awaken. Such a refusal to return (or to give the boon to humanity) is the first potential episode of the return stage, many of whose incidents are mutually exclusive.

While Quaid also "returns" to an Earth-like Mars with a talisman of his quest, Melina, Neo's adventure entails more elements of the return stage than does Quaid's. Yet Neo's return to the Matrix occurs out of sequence, as it happens before his apotheosis. And the most difficult threshold crossing at this point in the film is not Neo's final return to the Matrix, but the immediately preceding threshold crossing from the Matrix to 2199, which is impeded by Cypher's treachery: Cypher, who has conspired with Agent Smith to be reinserted back into the Matrix, kills Dozer and incapacitates Tank, prevents Morpheus' crew from returning to 2199, and then kills two more of them before Tank recovers, takes Cypher out, and returns Neo and Trinity to 2199. The danger in finally returning to the Matrix, with Trinity, to rescue Morpheus, in addition to the Agents, is the squad of police guarding the building in which Morpheus is held captive. The heavy ordinance with which Neo and Trinity return to the Matrix is the insulation they bring with them to deal with the danger of returning. And Neo becomes master of both the known (1999, the Matrix) and the unknown (2199) worlds by gaining the freedom to cross the threshold freely as well as by accepting his transcendence. While he is still in the Matrix, Neo's body awakens to kiss Trinity in 2199 without the agency of the telephone exit system the characters have been using to enter and exit the Matrix throughout the film. Finally, Neo also attains the freedom to live in accepting his transcendence: Accepting that he is "the one" also entails his awareness that he is the vehicle of cosmic change; thus, his final challenge to the A.I.s is that he will "show these people [humanity] ... the world without you ... without rules ... without borders or boundaries ... a world where anything is possible."

8

Celebrating a Formula:
The First Ten *Star Trek* Films

More so than in the *Star Wars* films, in which the monomyth is more completely recapitulated in the initial trilogy as a whole than in any single film individually, each of the first ten *Star Trek* movies follows the monomyth's essential quest pattern—a call to adventure, a threshold crossing to an unknown world in which trials must be endured, the acquisition of a boon, and a re-crossing of the threshold back to the known world—in its entirety. Yet all of these films, as do many individual *Star Wars* films, also incorporate many additional elements of the monomyth as well to reproduce this elaborate plot structure more fully and imaginatively. Somewhat as in *The Terminator*, in which the adventure of the hero is shared by Sarah Connor and Kyle Reese, in the first ten *Star Trek* films the monomythic hero, although still male, is likewise more often than not a composite character—a collective hero combining attributes and experiences of several protagonists who crew the various incarnations of the *Enterprise*—and is usually not the single most prominent protagonist (either Kirk or Picard, alone) although this is the case in a few instances. Thus—not surprisingly, given their iconic stature in the franchise—in a sense the recurring monomythic hero in the *Star Trek* films is the *Enterprise* crew as an ensemble and, by extension, the ship itself. The monomyth's appearance in each of the first ten *Star Trek* films is worthy of study not only in itself but also precisely because these films share this characteristic with the *Star Wars* films: Both film series are products of the two far larger, multi-media SF entertainment franchises—all things *Star Trek* and *Star Wars*—that are most obviously in competition with one another as unprecedentedly successful and engaging contemporary popular cultural phenomena; thus, both may owe much of the impact they have had on the popular psyche to their similar uses of this archetypal material.

Only in *Star Trek II: The Wrath of Khan* and *Star Trek IV: The Voyage Home*, the two of the first ten Star Trek films in which the monomyth is most prominent, does Kirk alone assume the attributes and the adventure of the hero. Kirk and Picard share the hero role in *Star Trek: Generations*, the only film in which both appear. And only in *Star Trek: Insurrection* is Picard a solo mono-mythic hero. Kirk shares crucial aspects of the hero role with Decker and Spock in *Star Trek: The Motion Picture* and with Spock and (to a lesser extent) McCoy in *Star Trek III: The Search for Spock, Star Trek V: The Final Frontier*, and *Star Trek VI: The Undiscovered Country*. Picard shares the hero role with Data (in many ways *The Next Generation* iteration of Spock) in both *Star Trek: First Contact* and *Star Trek: Nemesis*. As Kirk, Spock, and McCoy share the mono-mythic hero role in three of the first ten *Star Trek* films—making this configu-ration of the hero role the most common configuration to appear in these first ten films—it is worth noting that Tyrrell has argued that in the 1966–69 *Star Trek* TV series these three characters "form a triumvirate containing all the nec-essary ingredients for a heroic personality, except that they are distributed in three persons" (712–13) and that Reid-Jeffrey concludes that "the episodes (and perhaps the movies) can be viewed as a consistent body of myth" (41). (See Fig-ures 6 and 7.)

Qualities of the Hero

Spock is the sole character whose nativity, and literal rebirth, is ever an issue in these ten films. In *Final Frontier* his Vulcan half-brother Sybok forces Spock to witness the scene of his birth, an occasion on which their father Sarek disparages the newborn Spock for being "so human." While his being half-human and half–Vulcan constitutes a "special birth," one for which Sybok believes Spock should feel shame, his rebirth and subsequent accelerated aging to maturity on the Genesis planet in *Search for Spock* (a result of the Genesis planet's effect on Spock's corpse, which is deposited there at the conclusion of *Wrath of Khan*) is both far more "special" and also far more crucial to *Search for Spock*'s plot. As he is only half–Vulcan, Spock in his youth is an exile on his own planet. Even though he tells Sybok in *Final Frontier*, "I am not the outcast boy you left behind so many years ago. Since that time I have found myself, and my place" as a Starfleet officer, by joining Starfleet he had distanced himself even further from his Vulcan heritage and further alienated his father, who had hoped he would attend the Vulcan Science Academy. In *Search for Spock* the newly reborn Spock is literally in exile from Vulcan (as well as from his "katra" or spirit) on the Gen-esis planet, which Starfleet has placed under quarantine. While separation from

	Motion Picture	Wrath of Khan	Search for Spock	Voyage Home	Final Frontier	Undiscovered Country	Generations	First Contact	Insurrection	Nemesis
Monomythic Hero(es)	Decker, Kirk, & Spock	Kirk	Kirk, Spock, McCoy	Kirk	Kirk, Spock, McCoy	Kirk, Spock, McCoy	Kirk & Picard	Picard & Data	Picard	Picard & Data
Special Birth			Spock		Spock					
Mother a Queen										
Exile or Orphan	Kirk has no ship	Kirk has no ship	Kirk & Spock	Kirk & crew	Spock as a youth	Kirk & McCoy	Kirk is retired	Picard disobeys orders	Picard disobeys orders	(Shinzon: Picard's clone)
Seeking his Father	(V'ger seeks creator)	Kirk (inverted)	Spock & Sarek reunited		(Sybok seeks "god")					(Shinzon seeks Picard)
Triumph over Pretenders	Kirk over Decker	Kirk over Spock	Kirk over Styles	Kirk made captain						
Exceptional Gifts	Kirk as captain	Kirk as captain	Kirk as captain	Kirk as captain	Kirk as captain	Kirk as captain	Kirk as captain	Picard's Borg history	Picard as captain	Picard as captain
No Fear of Death	Kirk, crew, Decker	Kirk & Spock	(David Marcus)		Kirk, Spock, McCoy		Kirk & Picard	Picard	Picard	Picard & Data
World's Deficiencies			bureaucracy	bureaucracy & ecology		war & ecology		war & bureaucracy	bureaucracy & ecology	
Spiritual Significance	(V'ger)				Kirk (inverted)		Kirk	Picard: Vulcan contact	Picard: Prime Directive	
Make Humanity Comprehensible	Decker seizes his destiny	Kirk understands himself	Spock understands himself	Spock understands himself	Spock understands himself		Kirk makes a difference	Data installs emotion chip		Data as exemplar of humanity
Hero as Warrior	Kirk & Decker	Kirk defeats Khan	Kirk defeats Kruge	Kirk saves Earth	Kirk outwits "god"	Kirk outwits Chang	Kirk & Picard	Picard defeats Borg	Picard saves Ba'ku	Picard defeats Shinzon
Hero as Lover	Decker to Ilia			Kirk to Gillian Taylor		Kirk to Martia			Picard to Anij, (Troi & Riker)	(Troi & Riker)
Hero as Ruler										
Hero as World-Redeemer	partial: Decker	Kirk, inverted	Kirk, inverted	partial: Kirk		partial: Kirk	partial: Kirk & Picard	partial: Picard	partial: Picard	Picard, inverted
Hero as Saint or Mystic	Decker									

Figure 6: The Qualities of the Hero in the First Ten *Star Trek* Films.

his katra leaves Spock's reborn body without consciousness, his separation from Vulcan is uniquely excruciating because, due to his accelerated aging, he experiences "pon farr"—a powerful mating drive that requires Vulcans either to mate or to die—on a planet with no indigenous Vulcans. (Lt. Saavik, fortuitously the only Vulcan female around, appears to save young Spock from death, but whatever mating experience they share occurs primarily off camera.)

While there is no hint of anyone's virgin mother being assumed into heaven or crowned a queen, circumstances also cast both Kirk and Picard into several

	Motion Picture	Wrath of Khan	Search for Spock	Voyage Home	Final Frontier	Undiscovered Country	Generations	First Contact	Insurrection	Nemesis
the Call to Adventure	Spock & Kirk	Kirk	Kirk & McCoy	Kirk & crew	Kirk & crew	Kirk	Kirk, Picard, crews	Picard & crew	Picard & crew	Picard & crew
the Call Refused by	(Scotty, temporarily)		Kirk (as a ruse)				Kirk, temporarily	Picard, inverted		
Supernatural Aid Provided by	Negura, Decker, Spock, & Ilia	Spock, Saavik, McCoy, Chekov	Scotty, Chekov, Uhura, & Sulu	Scotty, Spock, Gillian, President	Scotty, Chekov	Spock, Chekov, & Valeris	Guinan, Demora Sulu, & Geordi	Geordi LaForge & Dr. Crusher	Anij, Dr. Crusher, Data, & Worf	Geordi, Riker, Troi, & Crusher
Crossing the Threshold	to/into V'ger	to Regula I	to Genesis planet	back to 20th century	to Sha Ka Ree	leaving space dock	into the Nexus	back to 21st century	to Ba'ku	to Romulan system
in "Belly of the Whale"	wormhole, V'ger	Regula I, Mutara Nebula	the Genesis planet	whales on *Bounty*	Nimbus III, Sha Ka Ree	Rura Penthe mines			caves on Ba'ku	(Shinzon in mines)
Road of Trials	V'ger/Decker, Spock	Khan shadows Kirk	McCoy shadows Spock	Kirk's court martial	Sybok shadows Spock	Kirk's Klingon trial	Picard saves Veridian	Borg Queen/Data	preserve Prime Directive	Shinzon shadows Picard
Meeting with the Goddess	Decker with Ilia	Kirk & Carol Marcus	Spock with Saavik	Kirk & Gillian Taylor			Picard with Guinan	Picard with Lily Sloane	Picard with Anij	(Tel'aura as "bad mother")
Woman as Temptress					Uhura (& to Scotty)	Martia to Kirk		Borg Queen to Data		(Donatra to Shinzon)
Atonement with the Father	Decker/Kirk, inverted	David/Kirk, inverted	Spock with Sarek	Spock with Sarek	Spock/Sarek, negative					Shinzon/Picard, negative
Apotheosis	Decker, (V'ger)		Spock & katra	Kirk valorized			Nexus = nirvana	Cochrane valorized		Data valorized
Receiving the Boon	Earth saved, data	lives of crew saved	Genesis not a weapon	Earth saved again	(Sybok is undeceived)	peace with Klingons	Veridian saved	Earth saved twice	Ba'ku is saved	Earth saved again
Hero Refuses to Return	Decker	Spock	(the *Enterprise*)		(Sybok)	crew & Kirk disobey	captains reject boon		Picard disobeys orders	Data
Magic Flight	ship & crew	ship & crew	Kirk & crew	ship & crew	Kirk	Kirk & McCoy	Kirk & Picard	Picard	Picard & crew	Picard & crew
Rescue from Outside					McCoy, Spock, & Kirk	Kirk & McCoy				*Enterprise* & crew
Re-crossing Threshold	V'ger as talisman	dilation insulation talisman	Spock/*Bounty*: talismans	dilation insulation talisman			time dilation, talisman	time dilation	time dilation, talisman	B-4 as talisman
Master of both Worlds	Decker & Kirk	Kirk acquires ship	Kirk acquires ship	Kirk acquires ship			Picard	Picard disobeys orders	Picard disobeys orders	
Freedom to Live		Kirk		Kirk	Kirk	Kirk	Kirk & Picard	Picard	Picard	Picard

Figure 7: The Stages of the Adventure in the First Ten *Star Trek* Films.

modes of exile in numerous films. As an administrator "flying a damn computer console" at the beginnings of both *Motion Picture* and *Wrath of Khan*, Admiral Kirk is initially in exile in both films from "commanding a starship ... [his] first, best destiny." He forcibly wrests command of the *Enterprise* from its new captain, Decker, early in the first film, on the grounds that he is better equipped to deal with the energy cloud threatening Earth than is the less-experienced subordinate officer; and he finally follows McCoy's advice to "get back your command" in the second film when Spock insists on relinquishing it to him, as "senior officer on board," after *Enterprise*'s crew of inexperienced cadets in Spock's charge is "ordered to investigate" the perplexing message sent by Carol Marcus from *Space Lab Regula I*. In *Search for Spock* Kirk and crew simply steal the ship in order to reunite Spock's katra with his re-born body.

In *Voyage Home* Kirk begins his Captain's Log entry by noting, "We're in the third month of our Vulcan exile," a reference to the fact that he and his crew have been stranded on Vulcan while repairing their commandeered Klingon bird of prey (which McCoy re-christens *Bounty* in reference to their mutinous behavior in having stolen and subsequently destroyed *Enterprise* in *Search for Spock*) and deciding whether or not to return to Earth, where "Admiral Kirk has been charged with nine violations of Starfleet regulations" and will be required to stand trial by court-martial Thus, Kirk is again in exile from *Enterprise*, as well as from Earth (physically) and Starfleet command (legally), when *Voyage Home* begins; and he and his crew are subsequently exiled from the twenty-third century, too, when they travel to and are temporarily stranded in 1986 because *Bounty's* dilithium crystals are "giving out, decrystalizing" due to the energy drain of time travel. In *Undiscovered Country* Kirk and McCoy are effectively exiled from the Federation and its justice system when they are tried for murder on the Klingon homeworld and sentenced to imprisonment on the Klingon penal planetoid Rura Penthe. And in *Generations*, the last film in which he appears, a retired Kirk is again without a command (exiled again from his "first, best destiny") and "finding retirement a little lonely."

Much like Kirk's direct violation of orders in *Search for Spock*, and producing a similar mode of self-imposed exile from Starfleet command, in *First Contact* Picard disobeys orders to patrol the Neutral Zone, choosing instead to return to Earth and save it from the Borg; and in *Insurrection* he discards his Starfleet uniform and disobeys Admiral Dougherty's orders to leave Ba'ku—a sparsely inhabited planet that Starfleet has been persuaded by new allies, the Son'a, to exploit (in violation of the Prime Directive) because metaphasic particles emitted by its rings confer youth, health, and immortality. In *Nemesis* it is Picard's clone, Shinzon, who is both an orphan (parentless because he is a clone) and an exile: He had spent his childhood as a slave in the Reman dilithium mines, where "the only thing the Romulan guards hated more than the Remans was me"; while in the mines, "where he didn't see the sun or the stars," he had been exiled from his (and Picard's) boyhood dream of "looking up at the stars, dreaming of what was up there"; and he tells Picard, "I want to know what it is to be human" because he feels "not quite human" due to his lifelong exile from humanity.

Searches for fathers and triumphs over pretenders occur only in the first five *Star Trek* films, which feature the "classic" crew, and *Nemesis*, which features the *Next Generation* crew, and even then only through a variety of reversals and inversions. It is not any of *Enterprise's* crew, but V'ger, the mechanical antagonist in *Motion Picture*, that is searching for its "creator"—to find "answers" to the question "Why am I here?" from "a father, a brother, a god." Sybok, another antagonist, is also seeking "god," a duplicitous alien who finally appears in the guise of an angry God-the-Father—a pretender over whom Kirk, Spock, and McCoy triumph—at *Final Frontier's* climax. And Picard's clone Shinzon, the antagonist in *Nemesis*, seeks Picard, his symbolic father, because he will die without a transfusion of Picard's genetically compatible DNA. While neither seeks the other, Kirk unexpectedly finds his and Carol Marcus' son, David, from whom he is estranged, in *Wrath of Khan*. And, although incapable of seeking him, the re-born Spock is finally reunited with his father Sarek (as well as with his katra) at the conclusion of *Search for Spock*. Moreover, in regaining command of *Enterprise* in each of the first three films, Kirk triumphs as its true captain (and thus as more of a father-figure than a "son") over characters whom the audience is invited to see as illegitimate usurpers: Decker, a sympathetic officer from whom Kirk wrests command through a meeting with Admiral Negura in *Motion Picture*; Spock, who insists on turning the ship over to Kirk when it is unexpectedly ordered to undertake a real mission rather than a "training cruise" in *Wrath of Khan*; and *Excelsior's* Captain Styles, a priggish officer whom Kirk and Scotty must outwit to steal *Enterprise*, which is to be "decommissioned," in *Search for Spock*. The ironic result of his court-martial at the conclusion of *Voyage Home* is that Kirk is demoted from admiral to captain and, as a happy consequence, given command of a new *Enterprise* (NCC-1701-A), a post he retains for the next two films.

Kirk is, of course, the quintessential leader whose "first, best destiny" is to captain a starship and who characteristically exhibits Odyssean ingenuity in outwitting opponents and evading defeat and death. For example, we learn at the beginning of *Wrath of Khan* that he is "the only Starfleet cadet who ever beat the no-win scenario"—the "Kobayashi Maru" exercise that inevitably ends in every cadet's simulated death—which he had successfully survived through the "unique" solution of "reprogramming the simulation ... cheating," and then "got a commendation for original thinking." At the conclusion of the film Kirk (in *Enterprise*) defeats Khan (in *Reliant*) "only because I knew something about these ships that he didn't" (how to lower a Starfleet ship's shields remotely) and because Kirk, as an experienced starship captain, is more adept at three-dimensional thinking. His exceptional gift is precisely his genius for captaining *Enterprise*, and the Federation Council President "sentences" Kirk to "be given the duties for which you have repeatedly demonstrated unswerving ability, the command of a starship" for this reason at the conclusion of *Voyage Home*. Picard, of course, is an equally capable if less flamboyant captain, but in *First Contact* his more specific exceptional gift is the experience of having previously been assimilated by the Borg, which enables him to detect their presence telepathically as well as to anticipate their behavior and to know their weaknesses.

After Saavik experiences simulated death in the "Kobayashi Maru" exercise and complains that the test affords no other outcome, in *Wrath of Khan*, Kirk tells her, "How we face death is as important as how we face life." Although she later observes that he has never really faced the "no-win scenario," Kirk does face death without fear on numerous occasions (even though he also faces it without defeat, Saavik's point, on every occasion but one—when he is killed during the final confrontation with Dr. Tolian Soran in *Generations*). After witnessing the destruction of space station *Epsilon IX* at the beginning of *Motion Picture*, all aboard *Enterprise* clearly recognize that their assignment to "intercept" the V'ger energy cloud is a suicide mission. Moreover, once within the cloud, Kirk orders Scotty to activate the *Enterprise*'s self-destruct sequence, hoping that this suicidal act will destroy V'ger as well. Decker, who shares the hero role with Kirk and Spock in this film, instead keys the final NASA code sequence to V'ger manually (to complete V'ger's mission and enable it to communicate with its "creator," humanity, and thus save all life forms on Earth from extermination) even though he knows that in doing so he is sacrificing his existence as a human being. And at the climax of *Wrath of Khan* Spock sacrifices his life to save the lives of the others aboard *Enterprise*—because "the needs of the many outweigh the needs of the few ... or the one"—when he exposes himself to lethal radiation in repairing its warp drive so that the ship can escape the already-defeated Khan's vengeful detonation of the Genesis Device within the Mutara Nebula.

At the beginning of *Final Frontier* Kirk attempts to climb Yosemite's El Capitan without safety gear—foolhardily risking his life, which he almost loses, but is saved from a fatal fall by Spock—merely because he "enjoy[s] it." He subsequently tells Sybok, "I'm afraid of nothing"—and proves it later by questioning the identity of the alien masquerading as "god" on Sha Ka Ree (even though McCoy warns him, "You don't ask the Almighty for his I.D") only to be blasted by energy bolts for his expression of doubt. Spock and McCoy, who share the hero role with Kirk in this film, then exhibit similar doubts and are likewise blasted by energy bolts. After Sybok is killed, Kirk is left to face this angry "god" alone when he has Spock and McCoy beamed to the *Enterprise*—even though he had told them earlier, "I've always known I'll die alone." And in agreeing to leave the Nexus with Picard in order to save the inhabitants of the Veridian star system in *Generations*, Kirk relinquishes the virtual immortality everyone experiences within the Nexus because "the odds are against us and the situation is grim.... Sounds like fun." He then dies (although not alone, contrary to his premonition) happy that he has again "made a difference" in helping to prevent Soran from destroying the star.

Of course, Picard—who had earlier told Soran, "It's our mortality that defines us.... It's part of the truth of our existence"—also sacrifices immortality to duty in likewise leaving the Nexus to save the Veridian system. After *Enterprise*'s self-destruct sequence is again initiated and everyone else is evacuated at the climax of the next film, *First Contact*, Picard remains aboard the ship to rescue Data from the Borg Queen. Similarly, at the climax of *Insurrection* Picard initiates the self-destruct sequence on Son'a leader Ra'afo's metaphasic collector even though he believes he cannot escape in time to avoid being killed. And he attempts to use the *Enterprise*'s self-destruct capability again in *Nemesis* to destroy *Scimitar*, Shinzon's battleship, after ramming it, but "auto-destruct is off-line" as a consequence of the collision. Picard then transports himself aboard *Scimitar* to confront Shinzon and blow up his ship before its lethal thalaron radiation can be deployed against *Enterprise*'s crew. But Data, who shares the hero role with Picard in this film, then demonstrates that he doesn't fear death either in sacrificing himself to save Picard by beaming aboard *Scimitar* and using the "emergency transport unit" prototype Geordi had given him earlier, which can transport only one person, to beam Picard back to *Enterprise* just before *Scimitar* explodes.

While the threats confronted by *Enterprise*'s crews in the twenty-third and twenty-fourth centuries, particularly in the earliest films, are often external to Earth and not usually indicative of any intrinsic deficiency on that world or in the Federation generally—as both are consistently portrayed as being near-perfect utopias in which a united, self-actualized humanity has eradicated poverty, disease, and avarice—later films address the deficiencies of the twentieth and twenty-first centuries either by visiting those eras or by allegorically projecting their shortcomings into the future. However, it seems that poverty, disease, and avarice are easier to eliminate than are the evils of bureaucracy, for even in the twenty-third century it is Federation and Starfleet bureaucracy that Kirk and crew must circumvent in violating orders, commandeering *Enterprise*, and embarking on their insubordinate quest to unite Spock's body and katra in *Search for Spock*; McCoy dryly observes that "the bureaucratic mentality is the only constant in the universe" at the conclusion of *Voyage Home*. And bureaucratic shortsightedness and corruption is an even greater problem for Picard in the twenty-fourth century. Starfleet mistakenly decides to sideline Picard and *Enterprise* from its decisive confrontation with the Borg in *First Contact* because it considers him to be a security risk due to his having been "captured and assimilated by the Borg" previously, even though it is Picard's familiarity with the Borg that enables him to save Earth within minutes once he disobeys orders and returns to Earth space to confront them. Moreover, in *Insurrection* Picard must disobey Admiral Dougherty's command to leave Ba'ku in order to prevent the

Federation and Starfleet, seduced by the lure of potential immortality, from violating the Prime Directive by relocating Ba'ku's population and rendering the planet uninhabitable in collecting its metaphasic particles.

There is also an implicit ecological theme in *Insurrection*, as Dougherty's and Ra'afo's intended crimes against Ba'ku include destroying its ecosystem (the collateral damage from collecting the metaphasic particles) as well as relocating its inhabitants and thus destroying their way of life. This is a projection into the future of the twentieth century's failure to adequately protect its ecology from human exploitation, and such ecological shortsightedness is explicitly identified as being a deficiency of Earth history in *Voyage Home*. Because it cannot communicate with Earth's whales, which are extinct in the twenty-third century, an alien probe is, perhaps inadvertently, destroying Earth's ecology by "vaporizing our oceans.... We cannot survive unless a way can be found to respond to the probe." Therefore, Kirk and crew time travel to the twentieth century to capture some whales and convey them back to the twenty-third century so that they can communicate with the probe and thus end its destructive rampage. During this mission *Enterprise*'s crew discusses, and finally witnesses, twentieth century humanity hunting whales to extinction. Spock observes that "to hunt a species to extinction is not logical," Kirk deduces that "when man was killing these creatures he was destroying his own future," and the Federation Council President later praises Kirk for saving Earth "from its own shortsightedness." Thus, the general ecological lesson that species diversity is a treasure of unknowable value to which humanity must be worthy stewards is particularized in the impending extinction of whales in the late twentieth century.

In 1991's *Undiscovered Country*, which also features this recurring ecological theme in that the Klingon ecology faces imminent collapse, "the undiscovered country" is "peace." In presenting the Federation's evolving relationship with the Klingon Empire—and the threat of war that resistance to this change provokes—as an allegorical echo of the contemporaneous dissolution of the cold war following the collapse of Soviet Russia's "evil empire," this film projects into its twenty-third-century setting a glaring deficiency of the twentieth century, recurring warfare resulting in the deaths of scores of millions, just as 1966–69's "classic" *Star Trek* TV series often allegorically projected the contemporaneous reality of the Viet Nam War into the twenty-third century. The Federation is the United States and its western allies; Kirk is a frustrated, die-hard cold-warrior ordered by politicians to make peace with the enemy; the Klingons—whose ecology faces imminent destruction due to their struggle to keep pace militarily and technologically with the Federation, and whose empire will go bankrupt in fifty years as a consequence—are the Russians; and the cold war itself is the "seventy years of unremitting hostility" between the Federation and the Klingons that this film's events conclude. Similarly, the evil legacy of war is the deficiency the *Next Generation* crew witnesses in returning to the twenty-first century to save humanity from the Borg in *First Contact*, as they discover in 2063 a fragmented and vulnerable humanity that would be easy prey for the Borg because its social, political, and physical infrastructures have been destroyed by a nuclear war (in which 600,000,000 had died) that had occurred ten years earlier.

In time traveling to 2063 and circumventing the Borg's attempt to prevent space pioneer Zefram Cochrane from successfully testing his warp drive, the *Next Generation* crew makes this benighted twenty-first-century world spiritually significant by assuring that "first contact" with the Vulcans occurs; for this first contact, the consequence of a passing Vulcan ship detecting Cochrane's "warp drive signature," is the singular event that will unify and revitalize humanity by opening the galaxy to it—thus giving it purpose and propelling it from the dystopian chaos that follows 2053's "World War III" towards the near-utopia of the twenty-third and twenty-fourth centuries. The *Next Generation* crew also makes the world spiritually significant in the twenty-fourth century, in *Insurrection*, by upholding the Prime Directive, for Picard points out that in being a party to the exploitation of Ba'ku "we are betraying the principles on which the Federation was founded. It's an attack upon its very soul." However, the hero's role in making the world spiritually significant is seen only through reversal and inversion in earlier films featuring the "classic" crew. In *Motion Picture* Decker makes the universe spiritually significant, not to humanity, but to its antagonist, V'ger, in enabling it to contact and merge with its "creator," humanity as personified by Decker, and in thus giving it "the ability to create its own sense of purpose out of our own human weaknesses and the drive that compels us to overcome them." This function of the hero is completely inverted in *Star Trek V*, in which Kirk reveals that the "god" Sybok seeks is false. Yet Kirk finally does discover personal spiritual significance in *Generations*: Early in the film a retired Kirk regrets that he can no longer "make a difference," yet at the film's conclusion Kirk dies happily because he knows he has "made a difference" one last time in helping save the Veridian system.

Decker comprehends and seizes his destiny in merging with the Ilia-probe at the climax of *Motion Picture*. And McCoy accuses Kirk of "hiding from" himself by denying that he is unhappy without a starship to command at the beginning of *Wrath of Khan*, but by the film's conclusion Kirk has overcome his bad faith. However, Spock is the character who most pointedly comes to comprehend himself, and particularly his human qualities, in those films featuring the "classic" crew; and the *Next Generation* iteration of Spock, Data, through his explicit attempts to be more human, most pointedly comes to comprehend himself and humanity—and thereby enables others to comprehend their humanity—in the later films. Reborn and reunited with his katra in *Search for Spock*, Spock is completing his reeducation as *Voyage Home* begins; yet he is so divorced from the human aspects of his dual heritage that he is unable to answer the question "How do you feel?" that his human mother, Amanda, has inserted into his reeducation program. At the film's conclusion Spock sends his mother the message, "I feel fine," indicating that he has connected with his humanity during his twentieth-century adventure; thus can he assure Sybok, "I have found myself, and my place. I know who I am," in *Final Frontier*. In *Generations* Data installs an "emotion chip" in his "positronic" brain to understand "humor" and "to become more human, grow beyond my original programming." He must then learn "to live with" his emotions, a difficult but truly human challenge, after the emotion chip fuses with his "neural net," and by the end of the film Geordi observes that Data has "been behaving like a human." At the conclusion of *Nemesis*, after Data sacrifices himself to save his captain, Picard eulogizes the android by declaring that his attempts to become more human have prompted the rest of *Enterprise*'s crew to better comprehend their own humanity: "In his quest to be more like us, he helped us to see what it is to be human.... His wonder, his curiosity about every facet of human nature, allowed all of us to see the best parts of ourselves."

It belabors the obvious to note that, as Starfleet officers, both Kirk and Picard are professional warriors and that both change the status quo repeatedly. Kirk and Decker, another Starfleet officer, save Earth in *Motion Picture*. Kirk also demonstrates that he is a master strategist by defeating Khan in *Wrath of Khan*, defeats Klingon Captain Kruge in *Search for Spock*, saves Earth again in *Voyage Home*, outmaneuvers both Klingon Captain Klaa and "god" in *Final Frontier*, outwits General Chang to prevent a war with the Klingons in *Undiscovered Country*, and saves *Enterprise* prior to helping Picard save the Veridian system in *Generations*. McCoy mockingly offers to "call Valhalla and reserve a room for" Kirk, when his death becomes a topic of conversation early in *Final Frontier*; and Klaa later reflects, "If I could defeat Kirk, I would be the greatest warrior in the galaxy." In *Undiscovered Country* Chang greets Kirk, albeit insincerely, with "sincere admiration ... from one warrior to another" and later tells him, "In space, all warriors are cold warriors." In addition to defeating Soran to save the Veridian system in *Generations*, Picard also preserves the course of history while defeating the Borg twice to save Earth in *First Contact*, saves Ba'ku while preserving the Prime Directive in *Insurrection*, and defeats Shinzon to save Earth again in *Nemesis*. Even though he tells Shinzon early in the film, "I think of myself as an explorer" rather than as a warrior, he ultimately notes that he "feels like a thousand other commanders on a thousand other battlefields" in finally acting to thwart Shinzon's plot to use thalaron radiation to wipe out Earth's population.

Although notorious womanizer Kirk flirts with twentieth-century whale biologist Dr. Gillian Taylor in *Voyage Home* and with the duplicitous, shape-changing alien prisoner Martia on Rura Penthe in *Undiscovered Country*, and although Picard indulges in a more serious romance with Ba'ku inhabitant Anij in *Insurrection* (while Riker and Troi rekindle their romance in *Insurrection* and subsequently marry in *Nemesis*), the best example of the hero as lover in the first ten *Star Trek* films is Decker in *Motion Picture*. Accomplishing the difficult task of defeating Shinzon's Viceroy in hand-to-hand combat aboard *Enterprise* literally leads Riker to his bridal bed in *Nemesis* by enabling him to arrive with Troi, finally, on Betazed to conclude their marriage ceremony. Yet Decker accomplishes the more impressive and heretofore impossible task of preventing V'ger from destroying all life on Earth and then, as an immediate consequence, merges with V'ger in the form of the Ilia-probe—a perfect mechanical duplicate of the Deltan crewmember killed earlier by V'ger, Ilia, with whom Decker had previously had a Platonic affair and is clearly still in love. Even though this merging with a probe that merely resembles the lover he has never sexually possessed is only a symbolic mating in a metaphorical "bridal bed," it represents the physical union that had previously been denied Decker because sex with Deltans is fatal to humans. Thus, the impossible task of saving Earth leads Decker to the equally impossible task of consummating his love, however figuratively.

None of the monomythic heroes in the *Star Trek* films are rulers who return from the unknown as lawgivers; and while Decker is a world-redeemer once while Kirk and Picard save a variety of worlds repeatedly, the condition that any learn that he and the father are one is met only through inversion. Kirk learns that he is a lot more like his son (not his father) than either of them suspects; and Picard is even more similar to Shinzon, his clone, but this similar inversion is complicated further by the fact that Shinzon is at best merely Picard's symbolic son. From the first scene in which he appears in *Wrath of Khan*, Kirk's son David is hostile towards his father, and he physically attacks Kirk when they first meet within Regula. Yet Carol Marcus tells Kirk, "He's a lot like you in many ways"; and Kirk, who muses that his son "would be happy to help" Khan kill him, later thinks of David as "my son, my life that could have been, but wasn't." On learning in *Search for Spock* that David had used "unstable proto-matter," a substance shunned by reputable scientists, in constructing the Genesis Device, Saavik tells him, "Like your father, you changed the rules." David sacrifices himself to save Saavik and the reborn Spock from their Klingon captors on the Genesis planet at this film's climax, and Kirk so mourns this loss that he resists the Federation's rapprochement with the Klingons in *Undiscovered Country* because he holds them responsible for David's death.

A blood sample proves that Shinzon is genetically identical to Picard, the evidence that prompts Dr. Crusher to conclude that he is Picard's clone. This, their striking physical similarities (most obviously, that both shave their heads), and Shinzon's youthfulness establish him as the childless Picard's symbolic son (not his father); and Shinzon repeatedly claims that the two are "one." Moreover, Picard is finally able to defeat Shinzon, whom he is ultimately forced to kill, by exploiting their similarity in counting on Shinzon to exhibit the same "over-confidence" that had been a younger Picard's salient characteristic. While Decker does not meet the conditional quality of the world-redeemer—seeking the father—even through inversion, he does satisfy the condition for being a saint or mystic, which is to enter an inexpressible realm beyond forms. His merging with V'ger provides the logic-bound machine with the necessary "human quality, our capacity to leap beyond logic," that enables the composite being, "a new life form," to "evolve" into a "higher form of consciousness" that can access "higher dimensions," and Decker/Ilia/V'ger finally dissipates from this universe in a spectacular pyrotechnical display that Spock speculates is its entrance into the inexpressible realm beyond form of some unknown higher dimension.

The Departure Stage

The hero receives a call to adventure in the form of a blunder that reveals an unknown world or the appearance of a herald of or from that world—usually a beast, some shadowy, hooded or veiled, mysterious figure, or someone dark, loathly, terrifying, or evil—who may literally call the hero to live or to die. This occurs in all ten films; in all but *Insurrection* the "call" is literal and explicit, in addition to being signaled by a blunder and/or herald; and in three of them (*Motion Picture*, *Search for Spock*, and *Undiscovered Country*) the call is in some way, although always temporarily, refused. *Motion Picture* begins with a blunder that reveals the unknown to Starfleet when several Klingon vessels rashly fire on V'ger and are summarily disintegrated; V'ger then blunders in "mistaking [*Epsilon IX's*] scans as a hostile act" and destroying the space station soon after its personnel receive the Klingon distress call and alert Starfleet that V'ger is headed for Earth. A spectacular blunder in the form of a transporter malfunction subsequently kills two crew members, including new Vulcan science officer Sonak, as they attempt to beam aboard *Enterprise*; this is relevant to the impending encounter with V'ger in that it creates a vacancy that will be filled by Spock, who shares the hero role in this film with Kirk and Decker. Spock receives a more literal call to adventure when he telepathically senses V'ger as a "consciousness ... calling from space" that interrupts him as he is about to begin the rite of Kolinahr on Vulcan; he believes that "the intruder may hold ... answers" to his quest for "exacting, perfect order," the Kolinahr ritual's goal of eradicating emotion. And Kirk receives an even more explicit call in the form of "orders to intercept, investigate, and take whatever action is necessary" against V'ger. Yet this call is temporarily refused by Scotty, who repeatedly complains that the refitted *Enterprise* "needs more work, a shakedown ... the crew haven't had near enough transition time with the new equipment, and the engines haven't even been tested at warp power," but who finally promises that "she'll launch on time, sir, and she'll be ready" when he learns that Kirk has been reappointed captain.

Two blunders, a herald, and a similarly literal "call" occur early in *Wrath of Kahn*. Seeking a lifeless planet on which to test the Genesis Device, *Reliant's* crew mistakes Ceti Alpha V for Ceti Alpha VI, a blunder that gives Khan—the hooded, dark, evil herald character who greets Captain Terrell and Chekov on the planet—his opportunity to capture their ship and lure Kirk into an ambush by tricking Carol Marcus (on *Space Station Regula I*) into believing that Starfleet may have ordered *Reliant* to seize the Genesis Device. This ruse does call Kirk to action—when *Enterprise* is "ordered to investigate" Marcus' consequent complaint—but Kirk then fails to follow regulations that require him to raise shields when approaching a ship that does not respond to hails (Khan's commandeered *Reliant*), a second blunder that allows Khan to launch an attack that cripples *Enterprise* and kills some crewmembers. Kirk receives yet another literal call to adventure in *Search for Spock* when Sarek charges him with "find[ing] a way" to "bring [Spock and McCoy] to Mt. Seleya on Vulcan. Only there can both find peace." Kirk seems to refuse this call when he appears to accept Starfleet's decision not to mount such a rescue mission, but he then tells Sulu and Chekov, "The word is 'no.' I am therefore going anyway." And McCoy, who shares the hero role with Kirk and Spock in this film, encounters a herald when, while under the influence of Spock's katra, he attempts to recruit an alien who talks like Yoda (in a scene that parodies *Star Wars: Episode IV*'s Cantina scene) to transport him to the Genesis planet. The herald in *Voyage Home* is the alien probe, the film's first image, whose destructive rampage prompts Kirk and crew to journey to the twentieth century in search of whales; the blunder is humanity having previously hunted whales to extinction; and the literal call to adventure is the distress signal advising all ships "to avoid the planet Earth at all costs" that Kirk and crew receive while returning to Earth aboard *Bounty*.

Sybok, who first appears as a cloaked and hooded wanderer, is the herald in *Final Frontier*; his scheme to lure a starship to Nimbus III by holding three diplomats hostage bears fruit when *Enterprise*'s crew is recalled from shore leave and ordered to "get those hostages back safely"—a recall that is simultaneously yet another literal call to adventure as well as a blunder, in that it plays into Sybok's hands. As it prompts the Klingons to negotiate with the Federation, the industrial accident that blows up the Klingon moon Praxis is a blunder that once again literally calls Kirk to adventure when he reluctantly receives orders to be the "first olive branch" and escort Klingon Chancellor Gorkon safely to the peace conference on Khitomer in *Undiscovered Country*. Kirk does his best to refuse the call by objecting to the very idea of negotiating with the Klingons, arguing that "this is a terrifying idea.... They're animals. Don't trust them.... Let them die."

Dr. Soran and, to a lesser extent, *Enterprise-D* bartender Guinan, both of whom are aliens, are the heralds who introduce the unknown world of the Nexus in *Generations*: Both are among the many survivors beamed aboard *Enterprise-B* when the Nexus destroys their El-Aurian transports in the twenty-third century, and Soran is also one of the few survivors of a brutal attack on the Amargosa Observatory who are rescued by *Enterprise-D* in the twenty-fourth century. While Soran has spent centuries scheming to return to the Nexus—and has recently been manipulating gravity, by destroying stars, to alter its path so that he can intercept it—Guinan, who has also experienced it, warns Picard that the joy of being in the Nexus is so addictive that he will never want to return if he enters it. As both *Enterprise-B* and *Enterprise-D* respond, respectively, to the El-Aurian transports' and the Amargosa Observatory's "distress call[s]," both crews receive literal calls to adventure. And while Picard inadvertently enters the Nexus in trying to save the Veridian system, whose sun he and Data deduce is Soran's next target, the fact that *Enterprise-B* has left space dock on its "maiden voyage" without being properly equipped is the blunder that reveals the Nexus to Kirk, who is retired and on board merely as an honored guest when he is swept into the Nexus while attempting, characteristically, to save the ship, which has no tractor beams or photon torpedoes, by manually adjusting its deflector relays.

First Contact begins with Picard's nightmare of being Locutus of Borg—his identity when he had once been assimilated, in several *Next Generation* TV episodes—and Picard as Locutus is the herald of the unknown world, the twenty-first century. Picard then receives orders from Admiral Hayes to patrol the Neutral Zone rather than engage the Borg—even though "the Borg ... have begun an invasion of the Federation.... One [cube] is on a direct course for Earth"—precisely because Picard "was once captured and assimilated by the Borg" and is therefore considered a security risk. But when a subsequent transmission reveals that Earth's defense is going badly, Picard violates orders and has *Enterprise* set course for Earth at maximum warp; due to his intimate knowledge of the Borg, Picard's directions to the fleet defending Earth quickly result in the Borg cube's destruction. Starfleet's initial decision to sideline Picard is the blunder that reveals the unknown world of the twenty-first century in that it allows the Borg to survive long enough to send a "sphere"—which *Enterprise* pursues—back in time to conquer Earth in the past, resulting in a totally assimilated twenty-fourth-century Earth that only *Enterprise*'s crew realizes is anomalous (because the sphere's "temporal wake must have somehow protected us from the changes in the time line"). Although Hayes' order, when combined with the subsequent transmission, is also the call to adventure, Picard heeds the call, ironically, by refusing to obey the order—an interesting inversion of refusing the call.

In *Insurrection* the call is Admiral Dougherty's request for Data's schematics because the android has run amok on Ba'ku, this film's unknown world; *Enterprise* then goes there to investigate and, if necessary, to disable and capture Data—who is a variation on the herald as beast because he is not human. The blunder that also reveals this unknown world to *Enterprise*'s crew, and that had prompted Data's rebellious behavior, is the Federation's decision to ally with the Son'a and conspire to violate the Prime Directive by relocating Ba'ku's population and harvesting its metaphasic particles. The call is again literal and explicit in *Nemesis*, in which Admiral Janeway orders Picard and *Enterprise* to undertake a "diplomatic mission" to Romulus because its new Praetor, Shinzon, has requested a Federation envoy. But this call (much like the one in *Final Frontier*) is also a blunder in that Shinzon's request is not a peace gesture, as the Federation believes, but the first step in his plot to destroy all life on Earth. And this film's herald is Shinzon—who initially appears as a shadowy figure in near darkness (as he was raised by Remans, who inhabit only the dark side of their planet) and whose ship, *Scimitar*, often employs a "perfectly undetectable cloaking device" (i.e., is often cloaked or "hooded").

After accepting the call the hero receives supernatural aid from an old man or crone, who provides a talisman in a setting suggesting a womblike sense of peace, or from a guide, teacher, wizard, ferryman, hermit, or smith who offers aid in a context of danger or temptation. *Enterprise* itself is the talismanic object in all ten films. Admiral Negura is the old man who returns command of *Enterprise* to Kirk in *Motion Picture*; Spock relinquishes command to Kirk in *Wrath of Khan*; and the Federation Council President gives Kirk command of the rebuilt *Enterprise-A* in the peaceful aftermath of the adventure at the conclusion of *Voyage Home*. With few exceptions, crewmembers serve as the guides, teachers, wizards, ferrymen, hermits, and smiths providing aid in a context of danger. Due to Kirk's "unfamiliarity with the ship's new design," which leads to some ill-advised command decisions, deposed Captain Deckard determines early in *Motion Picture* that he must "nursemaid [Kirk] through these difficulties" and teach him about *Enterprise*'s reconfigured systems. Whale biologist Gillian Taylor serves as the classic crew's guide to twentieth century San Francisco and environs in *Voyage Home*; Guinan becomes Picard's guide within the Nexus in *Generations*; and in *Insurrection* Anij is Picard's guide on Ba'ku—an isolated planet whose 600 inhabitants are effectively hermits living in seclusion from the rest of the galaxy—while Data, Worf, and Dr. Crusher assist Picard in preventing Federation personnel and the Son'a from forcibly relocating Ba'ku's population and then rendering the planet uninhabitable in extracting the metaphasic particles from its rings.

When he replaces the Vulcan Science Officer killed in the transporter accident, Spock assumes his usual post as the classic crew's scientific wizard in *Motion Picture*—in which he also picks up V'ger's thought transmissions, attempts to mind-meld with it, and finally figures out how to communicate with it. As Chief Engineer, Scotty is the classic crew's resident smith, yet his legendary expertise often elevates him to the status of wizard as well. In *Search for Spock* he acknowledges that he maintains his "reputation as miracle worker" by "always multiply[ing] ... repair estimates by a factor of four" and, soon after he is reluctantly reassigned because Starfleet "needs [his] wisdom on the new *Excelsior*," he jumps ship to join his old crewmates in stealing *Enterprise*, is the only one aboard who can open space dock's "space doors" to facilitate the theft, and had already sabotaged *Excelsior*'s trans-warp drive to thwart any pursuit. In *Voyage Home*, in which McCoy refers to him as a "miracle worker," Scotty shows a twentieth-century engineer how to make "transparent aluminum" in return for enough plexiglas to house the captured whales. Yet, while Scotty gets the transporters to operate well enough to beam up Spock and McCoy from Sha Ka Ree in *Final Frontier*, Sybok possesses the mysterious ability to make others relive traumatic events and then to relieve them of their "pain"; thus, while he is an even more impressive wizard, he uses his ability to work "miracles" to co-opt most of *Enterprise*'s crew, not to provide aid.

The ship's transporter operator, navigator, or helmsman would be the crewperson most comparable to a ferryman. Scotty often operates as well as repairs the transporter, and Chekov is often the helmsman. Ilia is the new navigator in *Motion Picture*; Lt. Saavik is the new navigator in *Wrath of Khan*, *Search for Spock*, and *Voyage Home*; the traitorous Lt. Valeris, a member of the conspiracy to assassinate Gorkon, is the new helmsman in *Undiscovered Country*, in which Spock transports Kirk and McCoy from Rura Penthe; and Ensign Demora Sulu is the "new helmsman" in *Generations*. A retired McCoy—who objects to having been "drafted" back to duty aboard *Enterprise* in *Motion Picture* and then crankily complains about everything, from the computerization of the new medical facilities to being frightened out of his "wits" when the ship is caught in a wormhole—is the classic crew's blustery, curmudgeonly hermit (if only figuratively), and the post of ship's doctor also makes him and *Next Generation* crew's

Dr. Crusher a species of smith. Yet the *Next Generation* crew's preeminent smith is Chief Engineer Geordi LaForge, who installs an emotion chip in Data in *Generations*, reconfigures *Enterprise*'s "warp field to match the chronometric readings of the Borg field" in *First Contact* (in order to "recreate the vortex" that had brought them to the twenty-first century and thus return them to the twenty-fourth century), and gives Data the emergency transport unit prototype that ultimately saves Picard in *Nemesis*, in which Troi and Riker also provide crucial aid, respectively, by first telepathically locating and then defeating in hand-to-hand combat Shinzon's Viceroy.

The hero next crosses the threshold to an unknown world that leads to a sphere of rebirth and that may be defended by a protective guardian and/or a destructive watchman. Although it may seem that this happens more often, in nearly every film the *Enterprise* goes to warp speed on screen only twice—at the beginning and the end of the adventure—and this is usually a crossing and re-crossing of the threshold. In *Motion Picture* the *Enterprise* crosses Jupiter's orbit under impulse power but then, "in order to intercept the intruder [V'ger] at the earliest possible time ... must ... risk engaging warp drive while still within the solar system." This leads to a "sphere of rebirth" (defended by V'ger) in that Decker's climactic merging with the Ilia-probe is "the beginning of a new life form" that Spock describes as "a birth, possibly the next step in our evolution," while McCoy muses, "It's been a long time since I helped deliver a baby." The threshold crossing leading to a sphere of rebirth in *Wrath of Khan* occurs when *Enterprise* goes to *Regula I* at warp speed to investigate Carol Marcus' claim that Starfleet has ordered her to "give up Genesis," which is designed to create "life from lifelessness" but "would destroy such life in favor of its new matrix" if deployed on a life-bearing planet—and which Roth notes "is a science fiction metaphor for the death-rebirth cycle" (163): At the film's climax Khan, the destructive watchman, triggers the rebirth of the Mutara Nebula as the Genesis planet; thus, in eulogizing the deceased Spock later, Kirk notes that "this death takes place in the shadow of new life, the sunrise of a new world ... life from death."

In *Search for Spock* the *Enterprise* first crosses a literal threshold in breeching space dock's space doors before crossing its customary, figurative threshold in going to warp speed en route to the Mutara Sector and its Genesis planet, literally an unknown and "forbidden" world, where Saavik and David discover a reborn Spock. Kirk is aided in abducting *Enterprise* by Uhura, Chekov, and Sulu, as well as by Scotty—all of whom, with McCoy, become protective guardians of Spock's katra—and, while *Excelsior*'s Captain Styles is an ineffective watchman who is ordered to pursue them but can't because Scotty has sabotaged *Excelsior*'s trans-warp drive, Kruge is the destructive watchman whose Klingon Bird of

Prey cripples the *Enterprise* as it completes the threshold crossing in entering the Mutara Sector. *Voyage Home*'s threshold crossing occurs when *Bounty* goes to "warp 10" in order to slingshot around the sun and travel back in time to the twentieth century—a comically unknown world to the crew and one that Kirk warns "is *terra incognita*; many of their customs will doubtless take us by surprise." The twentieth century is also a sphere of rebirth in that the whales found there, one of which is pregnant, enable the rebirth of that species on Earth in the twenty-third century. In *Final Frontier* the *Enterprise* evades destructive watchman Klaa's attack at Nimbus III by going to warp speed en route to Sha Ka Ree, which is reputed to be "the place from which creation sprang"; however, to reach Sha Ka Ree it must also cross another, literal threshold, "the Great Barrier," beyond which lies "the unknown." *Enterprise* crosses yet another literal threshold in *Undiscovered Country* when it again traverses space dock's space doors to begin its mission to pick up Chancellor Gorkon; at the "rendezvous point" a destructive watchman in the form of a cloaked Bird of Prey hidden beneath *Enterprise* fires two torpedoes, which appear to have come from *Enterprise*, at Gorkon's ship to destroy the Chancellor's peace initiative by killing him and framing *Enterprise*'s crew for his murder.

Enterprise-D goes to warp speed to get to the Veridian system in time to prevent Soran, one destructive watchman, from destroying its sun in *Generations*; ironically, Geordi is the other destructive watchman, for Soran has rigged Geordi's visor to transmit what he sees to Soran's allies on a Klingon Bird of Prey so that they can learn *Enterprise-D*'s "shield modulation frequency" and destroy the ship. Yet this film's threshold is not so much the jump to warp speed as it is the "energy ribbon" traversing the Veridian system that Guinan tells Picard is "a doorway to ... the Nexus," this film's unknown world; and dual threshold crossings occur when Picard and Soran are swept up by the ribbon on Veridian III after Soran destroys its sun, in the twenty-fourth century, and when Kirk is swept into the ribbon in the twenty-third century while trying to save *Enterprise-B*. Moreover, the Nexus is a sphere of rebirth in several ways: Kirk is alive within it even though "history" records that he had died attempting to save *Enterprise-B*; Kirk's dog Butler (who has "been dead seven years"), Picard's deceased nephew Rene, and Guinan (who is killed when *Enterprise-D*'s saucer section is destroyed in the detonation of Veridian) are all alive within the Nexus, too; and both Picard and Kirk finally uses the Nexus as a time-travel mechanism by leaving it and returning to Veridian III at a point in time before Veridian is destroyed in order to prevent its destruction and the consequent deaths of Guinan, the others aboard the saucer section, and the 250,000,000 inhabitants of Veridian IV.

In *First Contact*, another time-travel adventure, the *Enterprise* crosses the threshold to the unknown world in following the Borg sphere back to the twenty-first century, where the crew thwarts the Borg's attempts to prevent humanity's first contact with the Vulcans through sabotaging Zefram Cochrane's first use of warp drive; the destructive watchmen are Borg from the sphere who board *Enterprise* and nearly succeed in assimilating it; and the twenty-first century is a sphere of rebirth in that this historical first contact with the Vulcans in 2063 initiates a new era of peace and prosperity for a fragmented, war-ravaged humanity by unifying it behind the exhilarating adventure of exploring the galaxy. En route to Ba'ku, the unknown world of *Insurrection* and a sphere of rebirth in that its few inhabitants have only gotten younger in the 309 years they have lived there, *Enterprise* crosses one threshold in penetrating a dense nebula in the anomaly filled "Briar Patch" region of space, and Picard and Worf subsequently cross another in penetrating the planet's atmosphere in a shuttlecraft that is attacked by Data, who is simultaneously both the planet's protective guardian and a destructive watchman in his efforts to prevent the shuttlecraft from landing. Picard observes that "we are truly sailing into the unknown" as *Enterprise* goes to "warp 8" en route to Romulus and his prospective meeting with Shinzon in *Nemesis*; Shinzon's warbird *Scimitar*, which meets *Enterprise* above the planet and houses the thalaron radiation weapon with which Shinzon plans to destroy all life on Earth, is the destructive watchman; and the Romulan system is a sphere of rebirth for Data, who is destroyed there in saving Picard's life and yet finally appears to be reborn, symbolically, in the form of B-4—his less-advanced prototype and physical double (recovered earlier on Kolarus III and subsequently reassembled) into whom Data had downloaded his memory engrams and who concludes the film by singing "Blue Skies," the same tune Data had sung earlier at Riker's and Troi's wedding.

In the departure stage's final episode the hero is swallowed in the belly of the whale. Obvious variations on this pivotal episode, which are often surprisingly convoluted and elaborate, occur in each of these films except *Generations* and *First Contact*. In *Motion Picture* the *Enterprise* is swallowed by a "wormhole" (a figurative underground journey) almost immediately after engaging its warp drive; it subsequently penetrates deeper and deeper into V'ger's energy cloud until it is seized by a "tractor beam" and drawn through an "aperture" (another threshold) that closes behind it, leaving it "trapped" and "looking down their throats," symbolically swallowed again. After Spock then leaves the ship to pass through another "orifice" (yet another threshold) into "the next chamber of the alien's interior"—and informs Kirk, "We are inside a living machine"—*Enterprise* is finally drawn by tractor beam, again, into V'ger's innermost chamber, where the crew disembarks to witness the "birth" of a "new life form" when Decker literally dies in merging with the Ilia-probe, which is itself the reborn replica of the deceased Ilia.

Wrath of Khan—the single film in which the monomyth is most promi-nent—features the film series' most extensive variety of both literal and figurative underground journeys and is also most explicit in portraying them as symbolic descents into hell that represent death and rebirth, this film's central and unremitting motif. The opening sequence seems to depict a "training mission" that appears to end with *Enterprise* "dead in space" and the deaths of Spock and his "trainee crew"; yet everyone then rises from this ersatz death as Kirk enters the fake bridge to reveal that this has been a simulation, the infamous "no-win scenario" Kobayashi Maru exercise. Kirk jokingly asks Spock, "Aren't you dead?" And when he later meets the crew again aboard *Enterprise* he observes, "We've been through death and life together." It is Kirk's birthday, and McCoy tells him, "Other people have birthdays. Why are we treating yours like a funeral?" Indeed, Kirk subsequently complains that he feels "old, worn out" when he is trapped in the interior of Regula; but Carol Marcus then offers to show him "something that'll make you feel young, as when the world was new," Stage II of the Genesis project, which has created a lush paradise within a huge cave in the "lifeless underground" of Regula's barren core; and Kirk's last words at the film's conclusion are "Young, I feel young."

The film's literal underground journey is this descent "deep inside Regula ... underground," where Carol and David Marcus had transported themselves and their equipment to escape being captured by Khan and to which they are later followed by Kirk, McCoy, Saavik, Chekov, and Terrell. Khan and his fol-lowers, whom Kirk had already resurrected from several centuries of cryogenic freeze fifteen years earlier, are figuratively resurrected again from the nearly life-less desert their world had become when Khan, who claims they have been "buried alive" on Ceti Alpha V, tricks *Reliant*'s crew into beaming them "up." And when Terrell and then Chekov—both of whom have been zombified by Khan's will-draining slugs—manage to resist Khan's command to kill Kirk in this underworld, Khan gloats, "I shall leave you as you left me: marooned for all eternity in the center of a dead planet, buried alive, buried alive!" However, echoing Khan's own symbolic resurrection from Ceti Alpha V, Kirk employs a ruse to signal Spock to beam him and the others "up." (Reinforcing the death-and-rebirth motif that permeates the entire film, Chekov then seems to die when the slug emerges from his ear, but he later turns up alive and recovered.) While (in a noteworthy inversion) Regula's transformed interior is an underground Eden rather than a symbolic hell, Khan—whose "pride" is his undoing and who swears he will "chase [Kirk] around perditions flames before I give him up"—is nonetheless the film's symbolic devil: He initially presides over the hellish Ceti Alpha V; and at the conclusion of the battle between *Enterprise* and Khan's *Reliant* in the Mutara Nebula, the film's other symbolic hell, the defeated Khan declares, "From hell's heart I stab at thee!" as he triggers the Genesis Device in the heart of the nebula.

At the climax of *Wrath of Khan* Spock sacrifices his life in repairing its warp drive so that *Enterprise* can escape the "Genesis wave"; his body is "buried" in space on a trajectory that takes it to the Genesis planet; and the film's last image is his tube-like coffin resting on the new planet's verdant surface. In *Search for Spock* Federation Science Vessel *Grissom*'s crew finds that "Spock's tube" is emitting "animal life form" readings, even though "there shouldn't be any" on Genesis, while Kirk deduces that Spock had transferred his katra to McCoy prior to his death. David and Saavik beam down to Genesis and discover "evolved ... microbes on the tube's surface" but—in a Biblical allusion to the discovery of Christ's empty tomb, and thus to his resurrection—only Spock's robe, no body, is found in the tube. They then find a rapidly aging child, and Saavik concludes, "The Genesis effect has in some way regenerated Captain Spock." *Enterprise*'s crew eventually joins them on Genesis, where Klingons kill David; Spock's body matures into its adult state, a painful metamorphosis that may be considered a symbolic mutilation; the planet destroys itself in a series of fiery volcanic eruptions (which identify it as the film's symbolic hell) as Kirk fights Kruge (its devil), who plunges to his death into molten lava; and Spock, with the others, is resurrected from the dying planet when all are beamed aboard Kruge's bird of prey—as Kirk had eliminated the remaining Klingons by luring them to *Enterprise* just as it completes its self-destruct sequence—and Spock is finally reunited with his katra on Vulcan. Scheduled to be "decommissioned" at the film's beginning because "her day is over," and destroyed at *Search for Spock*'s climax, *Enterprise*, too, is resurrected as the newly rebuilt *Enterprise-A* at the conclusion of *Voyage Home*, which also features a comic inversion of being swallowed in the belly of the whale when Scotty beams two whales aboard *Bounty*.

Final Frontier begins on Nimbus III, a hot, arid planet that is one of the symbolic hells into which *Enterprise*'s crew descends. The other is Sha Ka Ree, which is ironically reputed to be an "Eden" but turns out to be at least as arid and desolate as Nimbus III; its resident alien—who, in a Biblical allusion to Lucifer, wants to be worshipped as "god"—is its devil. Kirk, Spock, and McCoy—who share the hero role in this film—are first swallowed in the belly of the whale when Sybok throws them into *Enterprise*'s brig after co-opting the rest of the crew, except Scotty, with his telepathic abilities. On Sha Ka Ree—where Kirk and Spock are mutilated by "god's" energy bolts—Kirk, Spock, and McCoy are symbolically swallowed again, with Sybok, in rib-like spires of rock that spring from the desert floor to form a dark, cave-like prison—thus combining the visual imagery of being inside the carcass of a great beast with that of an underground journey—that is hellishly illuminated by garish red light after

Enterprise fires a photon torpedo at "god." In *Undiscovered Country* Kirk and McCoy endure a literal underground journey that is also a symbolic descent into hell when they are imprisoned, in what is intended to be a *de facto* death sentence, in the dilithium mines on Rura Penthe, "the aliens' graveyard," which duplicitous, shape-shifting fellow-prisoner Martia aptly calls a "hell-hole." To evade the attacking Son'a in *Insurrection*, Picard leads some *Enterprise* crew and all of Ba'ku's inhabitants to refuge in a series of mountain caves, where he and Anij are trapped by a cave-in. Yet in *Nemesis* it is not Picard but his clone, Shinzon, who had spent ten years underground in the symbolic hell of the Reman dilithium mines—where he had been sent "to die," and where "in those terrible depths lived only the damned"—and it is not Data but his double, B-4, who is literally dismembered when initially found on Kolarus III.

The Initiation Stage

The first incident in the monomyth's initiation stage is the road of trials. Each film involves tests and trials (some of them repetitive) that challenge the various members of *Enterprise*'s crew, of course, and in all but *Voyage Home*, *Generations*, and *Insurrection* a hero overcomes an antagonist who is clearly his shadow. These films' most explicit tests and trials include Decker sacrificing himself to prevent V'ger from destroying all life on Earth in *Motion Picture*; the "Kobayashi Maru" exercise that begins *Wrath of Khan*, a "test" that Kirk was "the only Starfleet cadet ever [to] beat"; the necessity to violate orders and regulations, and steal *Enterprise*, in order to reunite Spock's body and katra in *Search for Spock*; the challenge of going to and recovering whales from the twentieth century, as well as Kirk's trial by court-marshal for "nine violations of Starfleet regulations," in *Voyage Home*; Kirk, Spock, and McCoy unmasking "god" as well as, with Scotty, resisting Sybok's seductive offer to relieve them of their "pain" in *Final Frontier*; Spock unraveling the mysteries of who had fired torpedoes at Gorkon's ship and boarded it to kill Gorkon, as well as Kirk and McCoy standing trial for the murder before the Klingon High Council and then escaping Rura Penthe in time to prevent more assassinations, in *Undiscovered Country*; Picard and Kirk preventing Soran from destroying Veridian in *Generations*; defeating the Borg in both the twenty-fourth and twenty-first centuries in *First Contact*; the necessity for Picard to violate orders and rebel against Starfleet Command in order to uphold the Prime Directive, as well save Ba'ku, in *Insurrection*; and Picard and Data preventing Shinzon from destroying all life on Earth in *Nemesis*, which also features the clearest example of a hero being aided by a helper's talisman when Data uses the "emergency transport unit"

Geordi had given him to beam Picard back to *Enterprise* before sacrificing himself in destroying Shinzon's *Scimitar*.

As V'ger, through seeking its "creator," is attempting to evolve beyond the state of "no emotion, only pure logic" to which Spock aspires through the Vulcan rite of Kolinahr, they are depicted as shadows from the very beginning of *Motion Picture*; in addition to attempting a mind-meld with it after being symbolically swallowed in passing through its "orifice," Spock later acknowledges, "I weep for V'ger as I would for a brother as I was when I came aboard—empty, incomplete, searching; logic and knowledge are not enough." And Kahn is Kirk's shadow in *Wrath of Khan*: Kirk begins this film, too, exiled (as an administrator) from "commanding a starship ... [his] first, best destiny," yet Khan claims that Kirk had previously "exiled" him to Ceti Alpha V; he later tells Kirk, "I shall leave you as you left me ... marooned ... in the center of a dead planet, buried alive" on Regula I; each escapes his figurative interment by employing a ruse to be beamed aboard a starship; and each acquires command of a starship prior to their final confrontation and Khan's defeat in the Mutara Nebula. While Kruge—whom Kirk likewise outwits in space, and then outfights on the Genesis planet—is to some extent Kirk's shadow in *Search for Spock*, Spock and McCoy are this film's more crucial shadows. McCoy's histrionic and emotional secular humanism is constantly juxtaposed to Spock's reserved and emotionless scientific rationalism throughout the classic TV series as well as in each of the first six films. And McCoy both assimilates and is assimilated by Spock when he becomes the unwilling recipient of Spock's katra at the climax of *Wrath of Khan;* he must then bear Spock's katra throughout *Search for Spock*, and as a consequence often appears to be possessed by Spock, until he returns it at that film's conclusion.

And Spock's shadow in *Final Frontier* is Sybok, his half-brother: Sybok is a "heretic" who "was banished from Vulcan, never to return," for categorically renouncing the Vulcan logic Spock embraces; yet Spock is also an exile—a "cast out boy" in his youth, due to his mixed genetic heritage, who is still often in self-imposed exile from Vulcan due to his Starfleet career. Both General Chang and Martia are shadows to Kirk in *Undiscovered Country*. Chang and Kirk both oppose any prospective rapprochement between the Klingons and the Federation, yet Kirk also opposes and thwarts the conspiracy to prevent it that Chang has organized; and Chang greets Kirk as "one warrior to another" and finally confronts him "warrior to warrior" above Khitomer before *Enterprise* and *Excelsior* destroy his Bird of Prey. Martia, a fellow prisoner who betrays Kirk and McCoy to the Klingons during their mutual attempt to escape from Rura Penthe, is a shape-shifter who assumes Kirk's appearance, fights him in that form, and is consequently mistaken for Kirk and killed by the warden just before Kirk and McCoy are beamed aboard *Enterprise*.

The Borg Queen, a woman who has almost entirely transformed herself into a machine, and Data, an android who aspires to be human, are shadows in *First Contact*; Data finally destroys her by disintegrating what remains of her humanity, her head and spinal column, after resisting her offer to cover him with human skin. And B-4 is Data's shadow in *Nemesis*: B-4, Data's "prototype," differs from Data physically only in having a redundant memory port, yet he also has a significantly less-advanced positronic brain and fails to understand Data's "human" ambition "to be better than he was"; thus, B-4 is easily ensnared in Shinzon's scheme to use him to destroy *Enterprise*, but Data thwarts this scheme by posing as B-4 and then freeing Picard. However, the most obvious shadows in the first ten films are Picard and Shinzon, his clone. In *Nemesis* Shinzon observes, "I feel exactly what you feel, don't I, Jean-Luc? ... Just the two of us, or should I say, 'Just the one of us?' ... You are me ... had you lived my life, you'd be doing exactly as I am." Yet Picard insists that he is "incapable" of such behavior—even though he replies, "I'm a mirror for you as well" when Shinzon asserts that he is Picard's "mirror." As they are shadows, Picard is correct both times: Each is willing to die to "complete our mission," but Picard's mission is to protect Earth while Shinzon's is to destroy all life on it; however, by recognizing that Shinzon possesses the same "overconfidence" he himself had exhibited as a young man, Picard is able to defeat him, for Picard thus realizes that Shinzon "thinks he knows exactly what I am going to do" and is, therefore, able to surprise him by doing the unexpected, ramming *Scimitar* with *Enterprise*, before killing him in hand-to-hand combat.

The hero might also encounter a goddess, a temptress, or both. After telling Scotty, "They gave her back to me," Kirk's expression on first seeing "her" in space dock in *Motion Picture* reveals that to him, of course, the true goddess is and always will be *Enterprise*; he also acknowledges this to Picard in *Generations*. Yet females (if not, in every case, human women) do appear as versions of the goddess or temptress, however perfunctorily on occasion, in each film. In *Motion Picture* Ilia, a Deltan who has taken a Diana-like vow of chastity vis-à-vis humans, is the goddess to Decker, who had had an apparently Platonic romance with her while stationed on Delta IV. On first boarding *Enterprise* Ilia assures a flustered Sulu, "I'm sworn to celibacy.... That makes me as safe as any human female," and reiterates to Decker, "I would never take advantage of a sexually immature species." As sex with her is apparently dangerous to humans—and is, in any case, "forbidden"—Ilia possesses attributes of the bad mother; yet to Decker—who insists, "I want this!"—Ilia is clearly the Lady of the House of Sleep, not only in that the opportunity to merge with her is the reply to his desires and literally the goal of his quest, but also because she has by then already died and been replaced by the Ilia-probe. Decker consummates their Platonic romance through the mystical marriage of merging with her mechanical duplicate in a special location, the core of the V'ger energy cloud, at the film's climax.

Kirk encounters the goddess in *Wrath of Khan*: Dr. Marcus, the mother of his son and originator of the Genesis Project, which creates life, shows him a barren cave she has transformed into a glistening paradise during his underground journey to the core of Regula, where Khan has left him "buried alive," and Roth argues that this "metamorphosis of grave into womb ... recalls the mythic hero's encounter with a fertility goddess who helps reclaim him from the underworld" (164). In *Search for Spock* an adolescent, reborn Spock appears to have at least a mystical marriage—and possibly a more carnal one—with Saavik, here the goddess who helps him survive pon farr at the special location of the dangerously unstable Genesis planet. His human mother Amanda is the goddess who wants Spock to get in touch with his "feelings" at the beginning of *Voyage Home*; later, in the twentieth century, Kirk playfully romances another goddess when he has dinner with Dr. Gillian Taylor, whose deep ecological concern for the plight of whales suggests that she is symbolically, and specifically, another nature goddess. Uhura plays a comic temptress twice in *Final Frontier*: She repeatedly flirts with Scotty, especially while under Sybok's influence—which she declares "has ... put us in touch with feelings we've always been afraid to express.... Scotty, Scotty, there's so much I want to tell you," but an injured Scotty implores her "to wait until I'm a wee bit stronger. I don't think I could take it in my present condition ... or yours"—and later seduces Sybok's followers on Nimbus III into abandoning their posts by performing a ludicrous hoochi-koochi dance atop a sand dune while attired only in a skirt of fronds.

Martia, a more dangerous temptress in *Undiscovered Country*, seals with a kiss her pact to assist Kirk (and McCoy, who is scandalized) in escaping Rura Penthe, yet this apparent partnership is merely a ploy to entrap Kirk in an escape-attempt ambush that will justify his summary execution. The closest approximation of a goddess-figure in *Generations* in Guinan, who is a Lady of the House of Sleep in that she both explains the dream-like nature of the Nexus to Picard and later turns up in the Nexus after dying when Soran destroys Veridian. Cochrane's friend Lily Sloane, who is beamed aboard *Enterprise* when injured and then takes Picard prisoner in *First Contact*, is a goddess who deflects Picard (whom she calls "Ahab") from his counterproductive, personal vendetta against the Borg in forcing him to recognize that initiating its self-destruct sequence is the only way to rid *Enterprise* of the Borg infesting it; Picard plants a kiss on her cheek as they part. And the Borg Queen, who recalls that she had previously wanted to make Picard (as Locutus of Borg) her "counterpart ... a human being with a mind of his own who could bridge the gulf between humanity and the Borg," is a temptress who grafts "organic skin onto [Data's] endoskeletal structure" and then "stimulates" him in attempting to seduce him into divulging *Enterprise*'s encryption codes; Data acknowledges that he was "tempted by her offer ... for 0.68 seconds." Picard's most serious cinematic romance occurs in *Insurrection*, in which he indulges in a mystical marriage on Ba'ku with Anij—who exhibits attributes of a goddess in being apparently immortal and able to slow time. The bad mother in *Nemesis* is Romulan Senator Tel'aura, who murders everyone in the Romulan Senate chamber with a small thalaron radiation generator in the film's first scene; this film's temptress is Commander Donatra, whose attempt to seduce Shinzon is rebuffed when he dismisses her as "not a woman, you are a Romulan" and warns her, "If you ever touch me again, I'll kill you."

Atonement with fathers and/or father figures occurs in *Motion Picture*, *Wrath of Khan*, and *Voyage Home*, while three negative encounters occur in *Final Frontier*. As the superior officer who has wrested command of *Enterprise* from him, Kirk is a father figure as tyrant/ogre to Deckard in *Motion Picture*; yet, as both share the hero role (with Spock) in this film, their atonement at its climax—when Decker acknowledges that Kirk has compensated him for usurping his command in permitting him to merge with the Ilia-probe—is a partial inversion in which both "son" and "father" are heroes. *Wrath of Khan* completely inverts the hero's role in that Kirk is both the film's sole monomythic hero and the father as tyrant/ogre who is atoned with his son: David vilifies Kirk, the father he accuses of having abandoned him, when they first meet at the core of Regula; but at the film's conclusion he faces Kirk and confesses "I was wrong about you, and I'm sorry.... I'm proud, very proud to be your son."

At *Search for Spock*'s conclusion Sarek shares the role of initiating priest through whom the hero passes into the world when he implores a Vulcan priestess to perform the risky fal-tor-pan ceremony of re-fusion that will reunite Spock's katra with his resurrected body. At the conclusion of *Voyage Home* the two are atoned when Sarek faces Spock, acknowledges "You are my son," and confesses that he may have been "incorrect" in having "opposed [Spock's] enlistment in Starfleet," which had caused the rift between them. And *Final Frontier* reveals the extent to which Sarek had been an ogre-father when Spock recalls how Sarek had tainted his original opportunity to serve as Spock's initiating priest, at his birth, in having disparaged him for being "so human." Sarek's reconciliation with Spock in *Voyage Home* occurs immediately after Kirk is atoned with the Federation Council President, a particularly authoritative father figure who embodies Starfleet and the Federation in essentially exonerating Kirk for the nine violations of Starfleet regulations to which he has pleaded guilty. *Final Frontier* also contains two additional negative encounters: McCoy recalls having taken the father he could not cure off life-support at his own request, "to preserve his dignity," only to learn "not long after [that] they found a cure"; and a false "god"-the-father—who assumes Sybok's likeness and is foreshadowed in this film's negative characterization of Sarek, Sybok's (and Spock's) father—later smites Kirk and Spock with energy bolts on Sha Ka Ree. Finally, Picard killing his symbolic son Shinzon at the climax of *Nemesis* is an inverted negative atonement.

The penultimate incident in the initiation stage is the hero's apotheosis. While significant conjunctions of opposites occur at the conclusions of each of the first four films—and while apotheosis is at least suggested by the association of the Nexus with nirvana in *Generations* and, more mundanely and ironically, by the elevation of a hero in *Voyage Home* and *First Contact*—the closest approximation of a literal apotheosis in these films occurs at the end of *Motion Picture*, when Decker transcends his humanity and unites time and eternity (in evolving into a higher form of consciousness that enters a higher dimension) by merging with the Ilia-probe. This is not only a symbolic and spectacularly visual union of male and female but also a union of self and other (in that the probe is and embodies a machine) as well as a unification of birth and death that entails loss of ego (in that Decker must sacrifice his humanity and identity to participate in this "birth" of a "new life form").

Life and death also merge at the climax of *Wrath of Khan* when Khan's suicidal attempt to destroy *Enterprise* in the expanding Genesis wave not only costs him his life but also transforms the Mutara Nebula into the vital, life-bestowing Genesis planet; echoing this death-into-life transformation, Spock simultaneously sacrifices himself to enable the rest of the crew to escape the Genesis wave and live. As he has no katra, the re-born Spock's consciousness is already annihilated for most of *Search for Spock* until the fal-tor-pan rite unites his flesh and spirit, which entails yet another merging of opposites in requiring the melding of *Star Trek*'s preeminent foils Spock and McCoy. At the beginning of *Voyage Home* Spock indicates that he is still out of touch with his human emotions when he does not understand the question "How do you feel?" Yet in saying "I feel fine" at the film's conclusion he signals that he has unified his human and alien qualities (self and other) in successfully integrating his emotions with Vulcan logic, yet another merging of opposites that echoes the previous film's melding of Spock and McCoy. Kirk and Picard experience something like an apotheosis in entering the nirvana-like Nexus in *Generations*: Guinan says that being within it "was like being inside joy," while Soran asserts that "time has no meaning" in the Nexus and that his prospective rendezvous with it is "an appointment with eternity." And, like Kirk's exoneration for having saved Earth at the end of *Voyage Home*—which, however, results in an ironic inversion, his demotion to captain—another completely demystified and ironic, albeit more emphatic, suggestion of apotheosis occurs at the climax of *First Contact* when

Cochrane attains warp speed—which, much to his dismay, assures that history will remember and venerate him as a great hero.

Receiving the boon, which ideally results in the regeneration of the hero's society, is the final incident in the initiation stage and is implied by the hero's apotheosis, for the boon in its highest form is transcendent revelation or enlightenment, the perfect illumination that apotheosis encompasses as well as symbolizes; however, the hero usually seeks such lesser gifts as immortality, power, or wealth. While the boon is literally the regeneration of the other world's society (in the twenty-first century) in *First Contact*, and is most often a symbolic regeneration of the hero's society in the form of the salvation of humanity or Earth (in *Motion Picture*, *Voyage Home*, *First Contact*, and *Nemesis*) or of life on another planet (Veridian IV and Ba'ku, respectively, in *Generations* and *Insurrection*)—which is also a variation on immortality in that it implies the continuation and potential immortality of the species—the boon in several films involves significant revelations, more explicit intimations of immortality, or the salvation of life on a smaller scale as well. In addition to halting the prospective extermination of "every living thing on Earth," another boon gained through Decker's apotheosis in *Motion Picture* is knowledge, for V'ger also transmits to humanity all the data it has gathered in its three centuries' exploration of the universe; moreover, Spock finally has the revelation that "logic and knowledge are not enough" and consequently abandons his attempt to attain Kolinahr. Life and peace are the similar boons in *Wrath of Khan* and *Search for Spock*—as in the former all but Spock survive Khan's use of the Genesis device as a weapon, while in the latter, despite Kruge's efforts, it is not transformed into a weapon after all—as well as in *Undiscovered Country*, in which war with the Klingons is averted. Sybok seeks "ultimate knowledge" in *Final Frontier*, but his revelation is only the knowledge that that the "god" he had sought is false and that he is the victim of his own "arrogance" and "vanity," while Kirk finally has the revelation that Spock and the rest of the *Enterprise* crew are his "brothers ... family." Immortality is specifically a boon in *Generations*, as those in the Nexus enjoy an eternal as well as a blissful existence, and in *Insurrection*, in that the preservation of Ba'ku will permit the continued apparent immortality of its inhabitants; but immortality is rejected by Kirk in *Generations* and by Picard in both films.

The Return Stage

In the return stage the hero could refuse to return or to give the boon to humanity, his return could be a magic flight opposed or furthered by magic means, his attempt to return could end in failure, or he could be rescued from outside the unknown world; in crossing the return threshold the hero might convey new wisdom to the known world, reject the unknown world to embrace the known world, experience a dilation of time, encounter dangers in returning that require him to insulate himself, or return with a talisman of his quest; finally, on returning, the hero may become the master of the two worlds, which involves acquiring the ability to pass freely between them, or he might achieve the freedom to live, to participate in the known world without anxiety as a conscious vehicle of the cosmic cycle of change. In *Motion Picture* Decker can save Earth and convey new wisdom to it (acquire the boons) only by merging with V'ger and thus refusing to return, much as Spock refuses to return when he sacrifices himself to save *Enterprise* and its crew in *Wrath of Khan*. Similarly, although the boon of peace is attained, *Enterprise*'s crew refuses to return twice in *Undiscovered Country*: So that they can rescue Kirk and McCoy from Rura Penthe (and then thwart further assassination attempts at Camp Khitomer), Spock, Chekov, Scotty, and Uhura initially conspire to ignore Starfleet orders to return *Enterprise* to space dock; and at the film's conclusion Kirk finally ignores the order to "return [*Enterprise*] to space dock to be decommissioned" in instead instructing Chekov to set course for the "second star to the right and straight on 'til morning." In choosing to leave the Nexus and return to the known world to prevent the destruction of Veridian in *Generations*, Picard and Kirk reject the boon of immortality that remaining in the Nexus confers in order to bestow the boon of extended life on those in the system and aboard *Enterprise*. In a similar partial inversion Picard refuses to give the boon of immortality to his own society in *Insurrection*, although Ba'ku's inhabitants retain it, in that destroying Ra'afo's metaphasic collector to preserve Ba'ku denies the possibility of potential immortality to Federation citizens, those in the known world; moreover, Picard had earlier refused to return in ignoring Admiral Dougherty's order that *Enterprise* leave the Ba'ku system. And, much like Spock in *Wrath of Khan*, Data refuses to return at the climax of *Nemesis* when he sacrifices himself to facilitate Picard's return.

Although he does not return from his quest to Sha Ka Ree but dies there, Sybok is an antagonist, not a hero, in *Final Frontier*. In this film, however, McCoy and Spock are rescued from outside the unknown world when Scotty transports them from Sha Ka Ree back to *Enterprise*; Kirk's return from Sha Ka Ree is then opposed by Klaa's attack on *Enterprise*; but Kirk, too, is finally rescued from outside the unknown world when Spock convinces General Korrd to pull rank on Klaa and order that Kirk be beamed from Sha Ka Ree to the Klingon Bird of Prey. Likewise, Kirk and McCoy are rescued from outside the unknown world when Spock transports them from Rura Pente to *Enterprise* after their escape has been both furthered and opposed by Martia's shape-shifting

ability. Rescue from outside the unknown world is similarly, but more convo-
lutedly, combined with several elements of magic flight in *Nemesis*: Shinzar's
warbird *Scimitar* opposes the return by attacking *Enterprise* and damaging its
warp drive; rescue from outside the unknown world then occurs unexpectedly
when two Romulan battleships de-cloak and come to *Enterprise*'s aid; Troi subsequently furthers the return through extraordinary means when she uses Shinzar's Viceroy's telepathic link with her to locate him, and thus also locates the
cloaked *Scimitar* so that *Enterprise* can attack it; but the return is then opposed
by extraordinary means again, when warriors from *Scimitar* board *Enterprise* to
capture Picard so that Shinzon can extract his DNA, only to be furthered by
extraordinary means again, finally, when Data uses the emergency transport
device to beam Picard back to *Enterprise* but fails to return himself.

Most often, however, the return is simply opposed and furthered—or, more
simply still, merely furthered—by extraordinary means. In *Motion Picture* the
Enterprise crew returns from within V'ger's energy cloud, which has by then
reached Earth without their volition (a return via extraordinary means), by dis-
sipating it when Decker finally keys the NASA code to V'ger. Spock sacrifices
himself to enable *Enterprise* to attain warp speed and return from the Mutara
Nebula in *Wrath of Khan*. In *Search for Spock* the return is opposed by extraordinary means when Kruge's crew boards *Enterprise* and Kirk initiates its self-
destruct sequence, but is then furthered by extraordinary means when *Enterprise*'s crew beams aboard Kruge's nearly abandoned Bird of Prey, captures its
lone remaining crewmember, and escapes from the Genesis system as the planet
blows up. In *Voyage Home* Spock must make "the best guess I can" to determine
the slingshot trajectory around the sun that will return *Bounty* successfully to
the twenty-third century, an unlikely outcome that "miracle worker" Scotty
terms "a miracle." In *Generations* the return is most inexplicably a magic flight
in that Kirk and Picard merely exit the Nexus to a point in time of their choosing.
The return only seems to be opposed by extraordinary means in *First Contact*,
when Data appears to have been co-opted by the Borg Queen and to have
betrayed his crewmembers, but is finally furthered by extraordinary means when
Geordi reconfigures *Enterprise*'s "warp field to match the chronometric readings
of the Borg field" to return it to the twenty-fourth century. And Riker beams
Picard onto *Enterprise* moments before Ra'afo's metaphasic collector explodes
in *Insurrection*.

The various heroes in these films often experience a dilation of time in the
unknown world, sometimes encounter dangers in returning to the known world
that necessitate "insulation" in the form of precautions, and frequently return
with a talisman (or several) that is always a sentient being. The ruse Spock and
Kirk employ to rescue Kirk and his companions from the core of Regula I in

Wrath of Khan involves a figurative dilation of time: Knowing that their conversation is being overheard, they refer to hours as days in communicating between *Enterprise* and the planet's interior. Later, Spock transfers his katra to McCoy, a form of psychic insurance, before exposing himself to lethal radiation in restoring *Enterprise's* warp drive. And *Enterprise* finally leaves the Mutara Nebula (to return to Ceti Alpha V and retrieve *Reliant's* crew) with Kirk's former lover Carol and son David, both of whom had previously been rescued from Regula I with Kirk, on board as living talismans. Similarly, Spock's re-born body is the living talisman retrieved from the Genesis planet and returned to Vulcan, to be rejoined with his katra, at the conclusion of *Search for Spock*; and the crew also acquires Kruge's Bird of Prey (later christened *Bounty*), which transports them to Vulcan, after *Enterprise* is destroyed. Much as in Marty McFly's time-travel adventure in *Back to the Future*, a more literal dilation of time occurs in *Voyage Home*, in which the crew spends a day or so in 1986 but returns to the twenty-third century a few minutes before they had departed; *Bounty* is then caught immediately in the alien probe's power drain and plunges into San Francisco Bay with its cargo of whales, George and Gracie—who serve as both the sought-after "insulation" against the danger posed by the probe and, with twentieth-century whale biologist Gillian Taylor, as the living talismans of the quest as well. A similar dilation of time also occurs in both *Generations*—in which Picard leaves the Nexus, where "time has no meaning," with Kirk, the living talisman he recruits there, minutes before Picard and Soran had enter it— and *First Contact*, in which the crew return to the twenty-fourth century at the moment they had left it after having spent several days in 2063. A more minor, albeit the most literal, dilation of time occurs in *Insurrection* when Anij slows time for Picard as they savor their brief romance on Ba'ku. And Data is the sentient talisman retrieved from Ba'ku in *Insurrection*, while B-4 is the sentient talisman retrieved from Kolarus III in *Nemesis*.

Decker symbolically becomes master of both the mundane and the unknown worlds at the climax of *Motion Picture* through accepting a literal transcendence in merging with V'ger; and Kirk simultaneously becomes master of the two worlds by literally gaining the freedom to cross the threshold of space freely when he thus, if only temporarily, retains command of *Enterprise*, as a consequence, because the new captain whose position he had already usurped, Decker, is "missing." Kirk forcefully asserts this freedom again at the beginnings of both *Wrath of Khan* and *Search for Spock*, respectively, by again accepting command of and then stealing *Enterprise*, and he regains it more permanently at the conclusion of *Voyage Home* when he is officially given command of the newly constructed *Enterprise-A*. At the end of *Wrath of Khan* Kirk also indicates that he has overcome his anxiety about aging, and thus attained the freedom to live, in saying "I feel young." And at the end of *Voyage Home* Kirk again attains the freedom to live—both because he can now work in the known world without anxiety, again, having freed Earth from the ravages of the alien probe as well as having regained command of "a starship ... [his] first, best destiny," and also because the Federation Council President's official acknowledgement that he has "saved this planet" reinforces his awareness that he is the vehicle of cosmic change, a role he reprises in the next three films. Signaling his acquisition of the "freedom to live" yet again at the conclusion of *Final Frontier*, Kirk—who had earlier lamented that "men like us don't have families"—exhibits freedom from anxiety by singing around a campfire with Spock and McCoy in the film's last scene after realizing that Spock is his "brother" and the *Enterprise* crew his "family."

Similarly, Picard reinforces the fact that commanding a starship likewise affords him the freedom to cross the threshold of space freely, making him another master of the two worlds, when he muses at the conclusion of *Generations*, after *Enterprise-D* is totally destroyed, "Somehow I doubt that this will be the last ship to carry the name *Enterprise*"—and is, indeed, discovered in command of *Enterprise-E* at the beginning of *First Contact*. As if to further emphasize this freedom, and analogous to Kirk's insubordinate act of stealing *Enterprise*, Picard repeatedly disobeys Starfleet orders regarding the disposition of *Enterprise-E* in both this and the following film. He is also conscious that he is the vehicle of cosmic change in having saved the Veridian system in *Generations*; in having twice saved Earth from assimilation by the Borg, while assuring that Cochrane makes first contact with the Vulcans, in *First Contact*; in having saved Ba'ku and the Prime Directive in *Insurrection*; and in having saved Earth again in *Nemesis*, at the conclusion of which he returns the badly damaged *Enterprise-E* to space dock for repairs and thus suggests that he will continue to possess the freedom to cross the threshold of space freely in the future.

This analysis reveals that in the typical *Star Trek* film the monomythic hero, while occasionally Kirk or Picard, is most often a combination of characters—usually either Kirk, Spock, and McCoy, or Picard and Data. This individual or composite hero almost always experiences some mode of exile; exhibits a genius for command and no fear of death; inhabits a world whose most prominent deficiencies are bureaucratic ineptitude and corruption, a failure to preserve the ecology, or war; acquires a more profound understanding of his humanity; and is a warrior who changes the status quo and is literally a world-redeemer. In the earlier films this hero also often seeks or finds a father or father-figure, although usually this involves some inversion, and frequently triumphs over pretenders. Moreover, this individual or composite hero always receives a literal call to adventure that is only infrequently refused; always receives supernatural aid, usually from other *Enterprise* crewmembers; always undertakes a dramatic threshold crossing to an unknown world that is usually a sphere of rebirth defended by protective guardians and destructive watchmen; almost always experiences a literal or figurative underground journey that is frequently a symbolic descent into hell; always endures tests and trials (sometimes literally) and usually assimilates a shadow self; almost always encounters a goddess-figure; often, but only in the later films, encounters a temptress; sometimes, but most often in the earlier films, experiences an inverted or negative atonement with a father or father-figure; occasionally experiences some approximation of apotheosis but always receives a boon, which is sometimes refused; frequently refuses to return, either by choosing to sacrifice himself or to disobey orders; almost always experiences a magic flight from the unknown world and is less often rescued from outside it; frequently experiences a dilation of time in re-crossing the threshold and returns with a sentient talisman; and usually becomes master of the two worlds and acquires the freedom to live.

9

Star Trek Rebooted:
J. J. Abrams' *Star Trek*

As it is the underlying plot structure of each of the first ten *Star Trek* films (the last of which, *Nemesis*, was released in 2002), it is not that surprising that the monomyth appears yet again—but in a somewhat different way—as the underlying plot structure in 2009's *Star Trek* reboot, J. J. Abrams *Star Trek*. Abrams' variation on the monomyth not only connects *Star Trek* to each of the ten preceding films, aesthetically as well as narratively, but also breaks new ground in ringing a few brand new changes on this ancient, archetypal plot structure. As in each of the first ten *Star Trek* movies, but unlike the *Star Wars* films, *Star Trek* follows the monomyth's essential quest pattern in its entirety while also incorporating many additional elements of the monomyth to reproduce this elaborate plot structure, yet again, fully and imaginatively. Aside from the earlier *Star Trek* movies, all but one of those science fiction films considered in this volume feature the archetypal adventure of a single male hero; this sole exception, *The Terminator*, diverges significantly from the others and from most of the many myths, legends, and fables upon which Campbell bases his study in that its protagonist is a woman, Sarah Connor, who evolves into the heroine through sharing with Kyle Reese, her protector from the future, most of the monomythic hero's characteristics and nearly all of the incidents that comprise his adventure. In the first ten *Star Trek* films the monomythic hero, although still male, is likewise more often than not a composite character—a collective hero combining attributes and experiences of several protagonists who crew the various incarnations of the *Enterprise*—and is usually not the single most prominent protagonist, either Kirk or Picard, alone. Thus—not surprisingly, given their iconic stature in the franchise—in a sense the recurring monomythic hero in these earlier films is the *Enterprise* crew as an ensemble and, by extension, the ship itself. Yet, as *Star Trek*'s primary temporal setting—2233 to 2258—precedes those of the earlier *Star Trek* films and occurs before Kirk and Spock have established their legendary friendships with one another and the rest of the *Enterprise* crew, here *Enterprise* and its remaining personnel are relegated to purely supporting roles, are not a composite hero, and here Kirk and Spock are each presented as a complete monomythic hero in his own right as well as the antagonist as shadow character to the other, a change that effects some particularly interesting variations in the hero's attributes and adventure.

Qualities of the Hero

Spock and Kirk each embody the qualities of the hero so thoroughly as to be presented as double characters, almost—despite their different temperaments, which ultimately make them shadows—in *Star Trek*'s first five scenes. While Spock is the sole character whose nativity—and, far more so, literal rebirth—ever becomes an issue in the earlier films, which all occur in an alternate reality, Kirk's birth in 2233 is a focus of *Star Trek*'s extended, pre-title opening sequence and is special in that it occurs on a Medical Shuttle in deep space during the evacuation of the *USS Kelvin*, which is destroyed by renegade Romulan Nero's mining-ship-from-the-future *Narada* while Kirk's father, George, sacrifices his life during his twelve minutes as *Kelvin*'s acting captain by remaining on board and ramming *Narada* to effect the successful escape of *Kelvin*'s shuttles. Thus, in *Star Trek*'s reality, Kirk is partially orphaned at birth. The film's next scene depicts a "young Kirk" (Jimmy Bennett) as an alienated pre-teen evading police pursuit while joyriding in his step-father's stolen antique convertible, which he drives off a cliff. And three scenes later, in 2255, a young Uhura rejects "farm boy" and "townie" Kirk's offer to buy her a drink (while refusing to divulge her given name) immediately before Kirk (Chris Pine) provokes a bar fight with four other Starfleet cadets; this establishes Kirk as a social misfit—as Captain Pike notes at the scene's conclusion, "the only genius-level repeat offender in the Midwest."

The two intervening scenes occur on Vulcan. The film's third scene introduces a "young Spock" (Jacob Kogan) as a unique social outcast enduring his 35th victimization by three other young Vulcans who taunt and physically abuse him, claim that he is "neither human nor Vulcan and, therefore, [has] no place in this universe," and call his father a "traitor" and his mother "a human whore." Implicitly, Spock's had been a special as well as an alienating birth in that he is the universe's only human–Vulcan hybrid. In the fourth scene a young-adult

Spock (Zachary Quinto) refuses acceptance into the Vulcan Science Academy because the Academy's Admissions Minister deems it "truly remarkable" that he has "achieved so much despite your disadvantage ... your human mother." The only Vulcan ever to "decline" admission to the Academy, Spock is still a social outcast as a young adult, too, which is consistent with his characterization in the earlier films. He further distances himself from his Vulcan heritage in joining Starfleet; and he becomes a literal exile when the *Narada* subsequently destroys Vulcan in 2258, by generating a black-hole/singularity in its core, and becomes another partial orphan when his mother, Amanda, is killed before his eyes in the process. Kirk and Spock meet, earlier in 2258, when Spock accuses Kirk before a Starfleet Academy tribunal of violating Starfleet's "ethical code of conduct" by having "cheated" in reprogramming Spock's "Kobayashi Maru" exercise, confirming that Kirk is still a misfit even as he graduates from Starfleet; thus, he is on "academic probation ... grounded until the Academy Board rules," when *Enterprise*'s green crew musters in response to a distress call from Vulcan that interrupts the Board's proceedings.

Immediately prior to his mother's death Spock had literally and successfully sought his father, Sarek, in having beamed down to Vulcan's surface to rescue the Vulcan High Council, of which Sarek is a member, from the planet's impending destruction. Kirk cannot seek his father, who is dead, but he is challenged to—and subsequently does—seek to be worthy of his father by Captain Pike, who "dares" Kirk (after the bar fight in 2255) "to do better" than George, who had saved 800 lives in his twelve minutes as captain of the *Kelvin*. Ironically, Kirk triumphs over a "pretender" to be the "true son," a starship captain like his father, when he wrests command of *Enterprise* from Spock near the film's conclusion. The elderly "Spock Prime" (Leonard Nimoy), who is marooned on Delta Vega in the Vulcan system, informs Kirk that he, not Spock, is the rightful captain of the *Enterprise* and advises Kirk to return to the ship and claim his true role by demonstrating that Spock is unfit to command because he is "emotionally compromised" by the destructiuon of Vulcan and, as First Officer, to replace him. Conversely, in the film's final scenes Spock assumes his rightful place from Kirk when Kirk subsequently appoints Spock as *Enterprise*'s First Officer, a post Kirk had previously filled.

In the earlier films Kirk, already promoted to the rank of Admiral, initially, is the quintessential leader whose "first, best destiny," in Spock's opinion, is to captain a starship and who characteristically possesses Odyssean ingenuity for outwitting opponents and evading defeat and death. He reveals this potential early in *Star Trek* by exhibiting a variety of special gifts: In 2255 Pike praises Kirk's "instinct to leap without looking that was your father's nature, too ... and in my opinion ... something Starfleet lost.... Your aptitude tests are off the charts

... genius level." While Spock's aptitude is in many ways superior to Kirk's, his preeminent special gift is his ability to subordinate emotion to logic; the last *Enterprise* crewmember to "leap without looking," Spock is for this reason Kirk's shadow rather than his double. Kirk literally leaps without looking several times in the course of the film (as does Spock, but less often and uncharacteristically), and in a sense he outwits Spock, not only by goading Spock into revealing late in *Star Trek* that he is "emotionally compromised" by Vulcan's destruction and his mother's death, despite his Vulcan dedication to logic, but also in being the only cadet ever to beat Spock's Kobayashi Maru exercise's no-win scenario.

Spock accuses Kirk of having "failed to divine the purpose of the test ... to experience fear in the face of certain death," but Kirk's acknowledgement that he does not "believe in the no-win scenario" also indicates that he has no fear of death; and his riposte—that Spock, as a Vulcan-human hybrid theoretically devoid of emotion, cannot experience the fear his test is intended to provoke, either—suggests that Spock, too, has no fear of death. Both exhibit this quality simultaneously at the film's conclusion when they both "leap without looking" in undertaking together the suicide mission of beaming aboard the *Narada* to locate the singularity-generating device and rescue Captain Pike. Kirk's world is deficient in that, in Pike's opinion, Starfleet has lost this ability to "leap without looking"; and the pervasive Vulcan prejudice against humanity is Spock's world's deficiency. Neither make the world spiritually significant nor humanity more comprehensible to itself, but Kirk comes to comprehends his destiny and—as is often the case in the earlier films—Spock comes to comprehend both his destiny and his humanity more fully by *Star Trek*'s conclusion, when Spock Prime finally advises Spock to remain in Starfleet and "in this case, do yourself a favor; put aside logic; do what feels right."

While it belabors the obvious to note that, as Starfleet officers, both Kirk and Spock are professional warriors, by saving Earth in *Star Trek* they preserve the status quo rather than change it. However, on a smaller scale, Kirk does change the status quo on *Enterprise* in supplanting Spock as Captain, and as a Vulcan Spock changes the status quo in Starfleet by simply enlisting. Even though in this film Spock also indulges in a romance with Uhura while Kirk beds a green-skinned cadet, her roommate, both are essentially the hero as world-redeemer, and the conditional quality of the world-redeemer is to discover that he and the father are one. Spock learns that his alternate-future self, Spock Prime, will become Vulcan Ambassador to Earth, like his father Sarek. And Kirk becomes a heroic starship Captain in an emergency situation, like his father George, and outdoes George (who, in saving the 800 aboard the *Kelvin*, likewise leaps before he looks and is also not afraid of death) in then saving Earth's entire population; at the film's conclusion Kirk is officially promoted to "Captain" and given command of *Enterprise* as the "relief" for also-promoted father-figure Admiral Pike, who tells Kirk, "Your father would be proud of you."

The Departure Stage

The hero receives a call to adventure, which he might refuse to heed, in the form of a blunder that reveals an unknown world or the appearance of a herald of or from that world. The universe beyond Iowa is Kirk's unknown world, and Kirk's herald is Pike, the starship captain who also provides Kirk's first call to adventure in trying to convince him to enlist in Starfleet in 2255. At first Kirk rudely dismisses Pike's invitation, but the next day he shows up at Starfleet's Iowa shipyards to enlist. Spock permanently refuses a very different call in declining admittance to the Vulcan Science Academy to join Starfleet instead. In 2258 both receive a more literal and explicit call to adventure in the form of the distress call from Vulcan that musters *Enterprise*'s crew. But this call is not addressed to Kirk, who is on "academic suspension" (a form of refusing the call, again, but involuntarily) and is initially not permitted to board *Enterprise*. However, he does board with the rest of the crew through a ruse perpetrated by McCoy. Vulcan and its star system is the specific unknown world to which the call summons Kirk, but his homeworld Vulcan is also an unknown world to Spock by the time he beams down to it to rescue the Vulcan High Council, as it is by then in the throes of geological upheaval and minutes from complete destruction. The blunder that precipitates this explicit "distress call" is Spock Prime's failure to use the singularity-generating device in time to save Romulus from destruction by a supernova in 2387, the event that sends the *Narada* back in time to 2233 and that inspires Nero to seek revenge, first by forcing Spock Prime (and Spock as well, as it turns out) to witness the destruction of Vulcan, and then by attempting to destroy every other Federation planet so that Romulus will be unfettered in the alternate reality he would thus fashion.

After accepting the call, the hero receives aid from an old man or crone, who provides a talisman in a setting suggesting a womblike sense of peace, or from a guide, teacher, wizard, ferryman, hermit, or smith who offers aid in a context of danger or temptation. Spock Prime, now over 150 years old, is the old man from whom Kirk receives much-needed information about his own alternate-reality destiny and the importance of his taking command of *Enterprise*, on how to provoke Spock in order to do so, and on how to beam aboard a vessel traveling in warp space to do that. Previously marooned on Delta Vega by Nero, as Kirk is marooned there by Spock, Spock Prime is also the hermit, as well as the guide and teacher, who further assists Kirk in the context of the dangerous mission in which he is involved by introducing him to Scotty, who subsequently aids Kirk as Spock Prime's agent, in effect, if not as a human talisman.

With the help of Spock Prime's knowledge of Scotty's future scientific achievements, Scotty assists Kirk—and, eventually, both Kirk and Spock—as the film's wizard and as one of its several ferrymen. Referred to as a "miracle worker" in both *Search for Spock* and *Voyage Home*, Scotty is here wizard and ferryman, simultaneously, in beaming both himself and Kirk from Delta Vega to *Enterprise* as it travels in warp space, a feat believed in 2258 to be impossible; in subsequently beaming Kirk and Spock from *Enterprise*'s orbit around Saturn to *Narada*'s Earth orbit, which is also believed to be impossible, but which Scotty acknowledges is easier; in beaming "three people from two targets onto one pad" in transporting Kirk and Pike from the *Narada* back to *Enterprise* while simultaneously beaming Spock to *Enterprise* from the singularity-generating device's spacecraft just as it impacts *Narada*, which is destroyed by the resulting black hole; and in then suggesting that *Enterprise* eject and detonate its warp core to escape the black hole's gravity well. Pike, as *Enterprise* captain, and Sulu, as helmsman, are the initial ferrymen who transport Kirk and Spock to the Vulcan system; Chekov is the ferryman who beams Kirk and Sulu back to *Enterprise* as they subsequently plunge from *Narada*'s mining platform to Vulcan's surface; and Sulu is the ferryman as helmsman who successfully warps *Enterprise* to an orbit within Saturn's ring system, where *Narada* cannot detect it. McCoy is the smith who gets Kirk aboard *Enterprise*, despite his being on "academic probation," by injecting him with an exotic viral vaccine to induce the variety of comical symptoms that enable Kirk to pass as McCoy's patient.

The hero next crosses the threshold to an unknown world that may be defended by a protective guardian and/or a destructive watchman. In nearly every *Star Trek* film, as in this one, *Enterprise* goes to warp speed on screen only twice—at the beginning and the end of the adventure—and this is usually a crossing and re-crossing of the threshold. Here, *Enterprise* warps from the Solar System to the Vulcan system, with Kirk and Spock aboard, in response to the Vulcan distress call. McCoy is the protective guardian who injects Kirk with the viral vaccine to get him on board. And Nero in the *Narada* is a destructive watchman lying in ambush in the Vulcan system (as he prepares to destroy the planet), for *Enterprise* arrives there amidst the wreckage of six other Federation starships that had responded earlier to the same distress call.

In the departure stage's final episode the hero is swallowed in the belly of the whale. While there is no explicit suggestion of symbolic rebirth in *Star Trek*, Spock visits a symbolic hell—the fiery surface of an erupting Vulcan to which he beams to save the Vulcan High Council, whose chambers and statuary suggest a temple guarded by gargoyles—and in the process is almost consumed by the black hole that destroys the planet, a symbolic threat of being swallowed. Moreover, when Spock maroons Kirk on Delta Vega for "mutiny," Kirk experiences three underground journeys and is literally in peril of being eaten: his pod lands in a deep impact crater; he climbs out only to be pursued by two gigantic ice-planet creatures intent on consuming him; and he is saved by Spock Prime, who first takes him to an ice cavern and then to the Federation's underground installation on Delta Vega. Kirk and Spock are again at risk of being symbolically swallowed at the film's climax, when the singularity that destroys the *Narada* nearly consumes *Enterprise* as well. And Kirk is comically mutilated by the symptoms McCoy's viral vaccine gives him, which include grossly swollen hands.

The Initiation Stage

The first incident in the monomyth's initiation stage is the road of trials, a series of tests in which the hero is assisted by the advice or agents of those who had offered supernatural aid; in this episode the hero may also assimilate his shadow. Spock is first seen being tested in an immersive Vulcan educational environment in the film's third scene, and he must subsequently endure the trials of his homeworld's destruction, his mother's death, and being deposed as *Enterprise* captain by Kirk, a test from which he successfully emerges as Kirk's supporter and friend. This is a test for Kirk as well, who must on Spock Prime's advice board *Enterprise* with Scotty's assistance to taunt Spock into revealing that he is emotionally compromised. Kirk had literally been tested earlier in 2258, when he famously passes Spock's Kobayashi Maru exercise, and his consequent indictment for cheating before Starfleet Academy's tribunal appears to be a literal trial.

Kirk not only triumphs over a pretender as the true son, but he also simultaneously assimilates his shadow self in goading Spock into attacking him by claiming Spock "never loved" his mother—thus supplanting Spock as *Enterprise* captain when Sarek then insists that Spock step down. While their dissimilar temperaments prevent them from being doubles, Spock is more like Kirk in *Star Trek* than in any previous film or TV episode. Not only are both fearless natural leaders initially presented as misfits of special birth who refuse a call, and not only are both primarily world redeemers who discover similarity to their fathers, but Spock also uncharacteristically exhibits Kirk's trait of leaping before he looks twice: earlier, when he insists on being beamed to Vulcan as the singularity consumes it, and soon after Kirk supplants him, when both beam to *Narada*'s bridge from *Enterprise*'s Saturn orbit to save Earth. This film's most original innovation regarding the monomyth is its presentation of dual heroes who each overcomes the other as his shadow, as well as in its presentation of dual heroes who are both the "true son" (Kirk) and the "pretender" (Spock) over whom he triumphs. This innovation invites one to see the monomyth as an interior psychic drama in which all the characters are really facets of the hero personality and in which the adventure is an internal psychological struggle; this is completely consistent with Campbell's interpretation that the hero's literal geographical journey is symbolic of everyone's inward journey of the psyche.

The hero might also encounter a goddess, a temptress, or both; and the goddess may assume the guise of the unattainable bad mother, the bliss-bestowing Lady of the House of Sleep, or the Universal Mother, who is the combination of opposites. While these often-muted incidents are even more understated in this *Star Trek* film than in most of the preceding films, Spock's mother Amanda, as a human married to a Vulcan, is the Universal Mother who combines opposites. The hero may also experience atonement with the father or a father figure, who might be the agent through whom the hero passes into the world. Kirk's father George is just such an agent in that he sacrifices his life so that Kirk can be born during *Kelvin's* evacuation, and Captain Pike subsequently appears as a father-figure to Kirk in 2255. Kirk and Spock, but specifically Kirk, rescue Pike, a starship captain like George, from *Narada* at the film's climax, as Spock had earlier rescued his father Sarek from the destruction of Vulcan. Sarek is characterized as being estranged from Spock due to his enlistment in Starfleet, in *Voyage Home*, and because Spock is "so human," in *Final Frontier*; while a similar reconciliation also occurs at *Voyage Home's* conclusion, the two reconcile for the first time in *Star Trek*, when Sarek tells Spock, after advising him to surrender command of *Enterprise* to Kirk, "You will always be a child of two worlds. I am grateful for this ... and for you.... I married [your mother] because I loved her." This reconciliation is echoed at the film's conclusion when Spock Prime advises Spock both to remain in Starfleet and to "put aside logic"; Spock is his own father-figure, here, due to Spock Prime's advanced age and because he, like Sarek, is Vulcan Ambassador to Earth.

The penultimate episode in the initiation stage is the hero's apotheosis. As in the earlier films, this incident, too, is muted in *Star Trek*, in which Kirk merely receives a Starfleet "commendation," promotion to Captain, and official command of *Enterprise* at the film's conclusion. Receiving the boon is the final episode in the initiation stage and is implied by the hero's apotheosis, for the boon in its highest form is transcendent revelation; however, the hero usually seeks such lesser gifts as immortality, power, or wealth. As in *Motion Picture*, *Voyage Home*, *First Contact*, and *Nemesis*, the boon in *Star Trek* is Earth's salvation, which implies the immortality of humanity and human society. Kirk's crucial revelation is his realization relatively early in the film that the "lightening storm in space" described by Chekov in 2258 is the same lightening storm in space that had occurred at his birth in 2233, that *Narada* must again be involved, and that *Enterprise* must be heading into a trap in the Vulcan system. This film's final revelation, however, is reserved for Spock: after Earth is saved Spock Prime tells Spock that what awaits him is "the revelation of all you [Spock and Kirk] could accomplish together, of a friendship that would define you both in ways you cannot yet realize," which is in a sense another conjunction of opposites.

The Return Stage

In the Return Stage the hero could refuse to return or to give the boon to humanity, his return could be a magic flight opposed or furthered by magic means, his attempt to return could end in failure, or he could be rescued from outside the unknown world; in crossing the return threshold the hero might convey new wisdom to the known world, reject the unknown world to embrace the known world, experience a dilation of time, encounter dangers in returning that require him to insulate himself, or return with a talisman of his quest; finally, on returning, the hero may become the master of the two worlds, which involves acquiring the ability to pass freely between them, or he might achieve the freedom to live, to participate in the known world without anxiety as a conscious vehicle of the cosmic cycle of change. It is Spock's refusal to return to Earth, his determination to rendezvous with the Federation fleet instead, that makes it necessary for Kirk to supplant him as *Enterprise* commander. As is often the case in the earlier films, here the return (to Earth) is furthered by unprecedented scientific (i.e., magical) means: Scotty beams himself and Kirk to *Enterprise* while it is in warp space, warps *Enterprise* to an orbit within Saturn's rings so that its presence in the solar system will be masked by "magnetic distortion," and then beams Kirk and Spock from *Enterprise*'s Saturn orbit to *Narada* in Earth orbit. Moreover, Spock then uses his Vulcan mind-meld on a *Narada* crewman to learn the locations of "the black-hole device ... and Captain Pike," and immediately uses the singularity-generating ship—which miraculously identifies and responds to him, through "facial recognition," as "Ambassador Spock" (i.e., Spock Prime)—to destroy the drill boring to Earth's core at San Francisco Bay and then to destroy *Narada*. Finally, *Enterprise* escapes the resulting black hole by ejecting and detonating its warp core.

Crossing the return threshold occurs when *Enterprise*, with Kirk and Spock aboard, warps to the near–Saturn orbit from which Kirk and Spock beam to *Narada* in Earth orbit. Spock Prime had experienced a dilation of time when the moments of subjective time it takes him to follow *Narada* through the black hole in 2387 occupy 25 years of real time, so that *Narada* reappears in 2233 but Spock's ship reappears in 2258. And Kirk and Spock return to Earth, as is often the case in earlier films, with a sentient being, in this instance Scotty, as talisman of the quest. Finally, in becoming *Enterprise*'s Captain and First Officer, respectively, both Kirk and Spock become masters of the known and unknown worlds by attaining the freedom to cross the threshold of outer space freely. *Star Trek* is a distillation and a compendium of all the myriad ways in which the monomyth is replicated in all ten of the previous *Star Trek* films and, as such, recapitulates

Monomythic Hero	Kirk	Spock
Special Birth	on a medical shuttle in deep space during *Kelvin*'s evacuation	born the universe's only human-Vulcan hybrid
Mother a Queen		
Exile or Orphan	his father dies at his birth; a social misfit in his youth; on academic probation in Starfleet	a Vulcan social outcast who joins Starfleet; his mother is killed & he is exiled in Vulcan's destruction
Seeking his Father	challenged by Pike to seek to be worthy of his father	beams down to save his father during Vulcan's destruction
Triumph Over Pretenders	wrests command of *Enterprise* from Spock by proving him to be "emotionally compromised"	Kirk finally appoints Spock as *Enterprise*'s First Officer, a post formally held by Kirk
Exceptional Gifts	a "genius" with the instinct to "leap without looking," he beats Spock's "Kobayashi Maru" test	the Vulcan ability to subordinate emotion to logic, as well as keen scientific intellect
No Fear of Death	often leaps before he looks; suicide mission to board *Narada*	can overcome fear as a Vulcan; suicide mission to board *Narada*
World's Deficiencies	Pike feels that Starfleet has lost that "leap before you look" trait	pervasive Vulcan prejudice against humanity that victimizes Spock
Spiritual Significance		
Make Humanity Comprehensible	comes to comprehend and accept his own destiny	comes to comprehend more fully his own destiny and his humanity
Hero as Warrior	a Starfleet officer who saves Earth with Spock	a Starfleet officer who saves Earth with Kirk
Hero as Lover	(dalliance with Uhura's green-skinned roommate)	(incipient romance with Uhura)
Hero as Ruler		
Hero as World Redeemer	like father in having the instinct to "leap without looking" and in becoming a heroic starship captain in an emergency situation	Spock learns that Spock Prime is, in the future, Vulcan Ambassador to Earth, like his father Sarek is in the present
Hero as Saint or Mystic		

Figure 8: The Qualities of the Hero in *Star Trek*

the monomyth more comprehensively (if not, in some cases, so redundantly) than any earlier individual film. (See Figures 8 and 9.)

As in each of the earlier films, in depicting a science-fiction quest that recapitulates in varying degrees of fine detail and fidelity nearly all of the seventeen episodes encompassed by the monomyth's essential departure-initiation-return structure, *Star Trek* also collectively symbolize, as does the monomyth itself, "transcendence"—which Joseph Henderson defines as "man's striving to attain … the full realization of the potential of his individual Self" (149–50, passim)—

	Kirk	Spock
The Call to Adventure	Pike invites Kirk to join Starfleet; the distress "call" from Vulcan	Spock Prime fails to save Romulus; the distress call from Vulcan
The Call Refused by	dismisses Pike's invitation, at first; later, on "academic suspension"	(had declined admittance to Vulcan Science Academy)
Supernatural Aid Provided by	Bones, as smith, gets him aboard *Enterprise*; Spock Prime—as old man, guide, teacher, hermit—provides info; Scotty as ferryman and wizard; Pike, Sulu, and Chekov as ferrymen	Scotty as ferryman and wizard; Pike and Sulu as ferrymen
Crossing the Threshold	*Enterprise* warps to Vulcan system; Bones as protective guardian; Nero in *Narada* as destructive watchman	Enterprise warps to Vulcan system; Nero in *Narada* as destructive watchman
in "The Belly of the Whale"	Delta Vega: pod impact crater, Spock Prime's cave, Federation installation; threat of being eaten by beasts; black hole consuming *Narada*; vaccine	Vulcan erupting, as hell; Vulcan High Council chambers' statuary; black hole consuming Vulcan; black hole consuming *Narada*
Road of Trials	"Kobayashi Maru" test; Starfleet tribunal; must supplant Spock	Vulcan education system; mother killed, Vulcan destroyed; deposed by Kirk
Meeting With the Goddess		muted: mother, Amanda, as Universal Mother who combines opposites
Woman as Temptress		
Atonement with Father	father, George, as initiating priest; Pike, a father-figure, is rescued	Sarek reconciles with Spock; Spock Prime, a father-figure, echoes this
Apotheosis	muted: commended, promoted to Captain, given *Enterprise* command	
Receiving the Boon	recognizes "lightening storm in space" is an ambush; Earth is saved	Earth is saved; anticipates the revelation of his friendship with Kirk
Hero Refuses to Return		Spock refuses to return *Enterprise* to solar system and Earth
Magic Flight	Scotty's help; warp core detonated	Scotty's help; warp core detonated
Rescue From Outside		
Recrossing Threshold	*Enterprise* warps back to solar system in Saturn orbit; Scotty as talisman	Spock Prime's time dilation; *Enterprise* warps back to solar system/Saturn
Master of Both Worlds	becomes *Enterprise* captain	becomes *Enterprise* First Officer
Freedom to Live		

Figure 9: The Stages of the Adventure in *Star Trek*

in imagery especially appropriate to the late twentieth and early twenty-first centuries. Jung notes that "The universal hero myth ... always refers to a powerful man or god-man who vanquishes evil ... and ... liberates his people from destruction and death" (80). Commenting on and extending the work of both Jung and Campbell, Joseph Henderson argues that "at the most archaic level" of the symbolism of transcendence this hero reappears as "the shaman ... whose ... power resides in his supposed ability to leave his body and fly about the universe as a bird" (151). While Joseph Henderson also observes that "one of the commonest dream symbols for this type of release through transcendence is the theme of the lonely journey or pilgrimage"—that is, of the quest—he argues further that "not only the flight of birds or the journey into the wilderness represents this symbolism, but any strong movement exemplifying release" represents it as well; and he specifically identifies "space rockets" as contemporary "symbols of release or liberation ... for they are the physical embodiment of the same transcendent principle, freeing us at least temporarily from gravity" (151, 152, 157). Thus, it is symbolically appropriate that space flight is the essential, common element in this series of films that repeatedly recapitulates the monomyth and is initiated by a film in which one hero, Decker, explicitly transcends his humanity. Yet to be freed from the constraints of time and, even more so, from the physical universe itself are far more fantastic releases or liberations than to be freed from either destruction and death or the constraint of gravity; and these two still-more-fabulous symbols of transcendence each occur in both the classic *Star Trek* and the *Next Generation* films—when Decker transcends this universe as well as his humanity in evolving into a "higher form of consciousness" that can access "higher dimensions" in *Motion Picture*, when Kirk and Picard enter the nirvana-like Nexus as well as travel forward (Kirk) and backward (Picard) in time when they exit it in *Generations*, and when *Bounty* and *Enterprise-E* travel back and forth through time in *Voyage Home* and *First Contact*, respectively—as well as in *Star Trek*, which is a time-travel and an alternate-reality film as well as a space-travel film.

Notes

Introduction

1. Spinrad's "Emperor of Everything," which discusses the monomyth in the first three *Dune* novels and in *The Stars My Destination* at greater length, notes that this plot structure appears in *The Book of the New Sun* as well. In addition, Spinrad asserts that such science fiction novels as "*Neuromancer* ... most of Gordon Dickson's Dorsai cycle ... *The Three Stigmata of Palmer Eldrich, Lord of Light, Nova, The Einstein Intersection*, Philip Jose Farmer's *Riverworld* books, [and] *Stranger in a Strange Land* ... are brothers between the covers, at least in plot summary terms, to the Ur-action-adventure formula" explicated in "Campbell's *The Hero with a Thousand Faces*" (151). Yet most of these other science fiction novels, while they do correspond to the more general "Ur-action-adventure formula" that Spinrad discusses in very broad terms, do not exhibit nearly as close a correspondence to the numerous specific details of Campbell's analysis of the monomyth as do those novels and films mentioned in this paragraph. Palumbo discusses the monomyth in the *Flowers for Algernon, The Stars My Destination*, Herbert's *Dune* series, and Wolfe's *The Book of the New Sun* and *The Urth of the New Sun* in, respectively, "The Monomyth in Daniel Keyes' *Flowers for Algernon*," "The Monomyth in Alfred Bester's *The Stars My Destination*," "The Monomyth as Fractal Pattern in Frank Herbert's *Dune* Novels," and "The Monomyth in Gene Wolfe's *The Book of the New Sun*."

2. All references to Campbell in this volume are to *The Hero with a Thousand Faces* unless otherwise indicated.

3. Campbell laments the fact that the modern ceremonies that have replaced these primitive rites of passage—and contemporary culture generally—are inadequate to the task of reconciling the individual to his new stations of life; see 104–05.

4. In chaos-theory terminology, for those readers familiar with it, this "nuclear unit" of the monomyth is also its "strange attractor."

Chapter 4

1. A ghola is a potentially exact duplicate of a deceased individual that is grown from the cadaver's cells in a Tleilaxu axlotl tank. (The resemblance to the original is not necessarily exact because a ghola can be altered through genetic manipulation or surgical procedures.) A ghola differs from a clone only in that a clone is grown from cells taken from a living organism. Thus, gholas are always physical replicas of the dead, while a clone may be a replica of someone who may still be alive. While physical duplicates of

their originals, gholas and clones do not initially possess the original's personality or memories; however, a ghola or clone can subsequently recover the original's persona and memories. Idaho–2, created as a gift for Paul, is the first Duncan Idaho ghola and appears in *Messiah* and *Children*. Idaho–4, the last of the vast number of Idaho gholas created for Leto II, appears in *God Emperor*. (An Idaho–3 is Idaho–4's immediate predecessor in Leto II's service and also appears briefly in *God Emperor*.) Idaho–5, the last of a dozen Idaho gholas created for the Bene Gesserit, appears in *Heretics* and *Chapterhouse*.

2. Whereas in the novel, as is the case implicitly in the miniseries, the Guild Navigators make space travel possible by using the spice to produce a limited form of prescience that enables them to see the future of their destination, so that they can see where they are going even though they are travelling faster than the speed of light, in Lynch's film the Guild Navigators use the spice to "fold space" so that they can "travel without moving."

3. In Herbert's *Dune* series, Idaho–2 is only the first of hundreds of Idaho gholas created by the Tleilaxu over the 4,500 years that follow *Children of Dune*. Most are created for Leto II during his 3,000-year reign, but at least a dozen are created for the Bene Gesserit 1,500 years after that.

Bibliography and Filmography

Aldiss, Brian. *Space Opera*. London: Futura, 1974.

Back to the Future. Robert Zemeckis, Dir. Universal, 1985.

Back to the Future Part II. Robert Zemeckis, Dir. Universal, 1989.

Back to the Future Part III. Robert Zemeckis, Dir. Universal, 1990.

Begley, Sharon. "Religion and the Brain." *Newsweek* (7 May 2001), 50–57.

Bester, Alfred. *The Stars My Destination*. Introd. Neil Gaiman. Alex Eisenstein and Phyllis Eisenstein, eds. New York: Bantam, 1956; Vintage, 1996.

"The Birth of the Light Sabre." Featurette on the *Star Wars Trilogy Bonus Materials* DVD. Lucasfilm, 2004.

Briggs, John, and F. David Peat. *Turbulent Mirror*. New York: Harper and Row, 1989; Perennial Library, 1990.

Campbell, Joseph. *The Hero with a Thousand Faces*. 2d ed. Bollingen Series XVIII. Princeton, NJ: Princeton University Press, 1968. 1st ed. published in 1949.

_____. *The Hero's Journey: The World of Joseph Campbell*. New York: Harper and Row, 1990.

"The Characters of *Star Wars*." Featurette on the *Star Wars Trilogy Bonus Materials* DVD. Lucasfilm, 2004.

Collins, Robert G. "*Star Wars*: The Pastiche of Myth and the Yearning for a Past Future." *The Journal of Popular Culture* 11:1 (Summer 1977), 1–10.

Dick, Philip K. "We Can Remember It for You Wholesale." *The Road to Science Fiction #3: From Heinlein to Here*. James Gunn, ed. New York: New American Library, 1979.

Dreamscape. Joseph Ruben, Dir. Chevy Chase Films, 1984.

Dune. David Lynch, Dir. De Laurentiis, 1984.

"Empire of Dreams: The Story of the *Star Wars* Trilogy." *Star Wars Trilogy Bonus Materials* DVD. Lucasfilm, 2004.

Escape From New York. John Carpenter, Dir. Avco Embassy Pictures, 1981.

"The Force Is With Them: The Legacy of *Star Wars*." Featurette on the *Star Wars Trilogy Bonus Materials* DVD. Lucasfilm, 2004.

Frank Herbert's Children of Dune. Greg Yaitanes, Dir. Sci Fi Pictures/New Amsterdam Entertainment/Blixa Film Production GmbH/Hallmark Entertainment Distribution, 2003.

Frank Herbert's Dune. John Harrison, Dir. SciFi Channel/New Amsterdam Entertainment/Victor Television Productions/Betafilm GmbH, 2000.

Galipeau, Steven A. *The Journey of Luke Skywalker: An Analysis of Modern Myth and Symbol*. Chicago and La Salle, IL: Open Court, 2001.

Gleick, James. *Chaos: Making a New Science*. New York: Penguin, 1987.

Gordon, Andrew. "*Star Wars*: A Myth for Our Time." *Literature and Film Quarterly* 6 (1978): 314–26.

Hayles, N. Katherine. *Chaos Bound: Orderly Disorder in Contemporary Literature and Science*. Ithaca, NY: Cornell University Press, 1990.

Henderson, Joseph L. "Ancient Myths and Modern Man." *Man and His Symbols.* Carl G. Jung et al., eds. Garden City, NY: Doubleday, 1964.

Henderson, Mary. *Star Wars: The Magic of Myth.* New York: Bantam, 1997.

Herbert, Frank. *Chapterhouse Dune.* New York: G. P. Putnam Sons, 1985; Ace, 1987.

_____. *Children of Dune.* New York: Berkeley, 1981.

_____. *Dune.* New York: Chilton, 1965; Berkley, 1977; Ace, 1987.

_____. *Dune Messiah.* New York: Berkley, 1975.

_____. *God Emperor of Dune.* New York: G. P. Putnam's Sons, 1981; Berkley, 1983; Ace, 1987.

_____. *Heretics of Dune.* New York: G. P. Putnam's Sons, 1984; Berkley, 1986.

Jung, Carl G. "Approaching the Unconscious." *Man and His Symbols.* Carl G. Jung et al., eds. Garden City, NY: Doubleday, 1964.

Kelly, Kevin, and Paula Parisi. "*Star Wars*: What's Next for George Lucas." *Wired* (February 1997): 160–66, 210–17.

Keyes, Daniel. *Flowers for Algernon.* New York: Harcourt Brace and World, 1996; Bantam, 1975.

Kimball, Samuel A. "Not Begetting the Future: Technological Autochthony, Sexual Reproduction, and the Mythic Structure of *The Matrix.*" *Journal of Popular Culture* 35.2 (2001): 175–203.

Laplante, Phil. *Fractal Mania.* New York: Windcrest/McGraw Hill, 1994.

The Last Starfighter. Nick Castle, Dir. Lorimar/Universal, 1984.

Logan's Run. Michael Anderson, Dir. MGM, 1976. Based on William E. Nolan's novel.

Mackay, Daniel. "*Star Wars*: The Magic of the Anti-myth." *Foundation* 28:76 (1999), 63–75.

The Matrix. Andy and Larry Wachowski, Dirs. Warner Bros./Village Roadshow Pictures/Groucho II Film Partnership/Silver Pictures, 1999.

Palumbo, Donald E. *Chaos Theory, Asimov's Foundations and Robots, and Herbert's Dune: The Fractal Aesthetic of Epic Science Fiction.* Westport, CT: Greenwood, 2002.

_____. "The Monomyth as Fractal Pattern in Frank Herbert's *Dune* Novels." *Science-Fiction Studies* 25:76 (1998): 433–58.

_____. "The Monomyth in Alfred Bester's *The Stars My Destination.*" *The Journal of Popular Culture* 38:2 (2004): 333–368.

_____. "The Monomyth in *Back to the Future*: Science Fiction Film Comedy as Adolescent Wish Fulfillment Fantasy." *Journal of the Fantastic in the Arts* 17:1 (Spring 2006): 60–76.

_____. "The Monomyth in Daniel Keyes' *Flowers for Algernon.*" *Journal of the Fantastic in the Arts* 14:4 (2004): 427–446.

_____. "The Monomyth in Gene Wolfe's *The Book of the New Sun.*" *Extrapolation* 42:2 (Summer 2005): 189–234.

_____. "The Monomyth in James Cameron's *The Terminator*: Sarah as Monomythic Heroine." *The Journal of Popular Culture* 41.3 (2008): 413–27.

_____. "The Monomyth in *Star Trek* (2009): Kirk & Spock Together Again for the First Time." *The Journal of Popular Culture* 46:1 (2013): 143–172.

_____. "The Monomyth in *Star Trek* Films." *The Influence of* Star Trek *on Television, Film, and Culture.* Critical Explorations in Science Fiction and Fantasy #4. Lincoln Geraghty, ed. Jefferson, NC: McFarland, 2007.

_____. "The Monomyth in Time Travel Films." *The Celebration of the Fantastic: Selected Papers from the Tenth Anniversary International Conference on the Fantastic in the Arts.* Donald E. Morse, Marshall B. Tymn, and Csilla Bertha, Eds. Contributions to the Study of Science Fiction and Fantasy, Number 49. Westport, CT: Greenwood, 1992.

Rabkin, Eric S. *The Fantastic in Literature.* Princeton, NJ: Princeton University Press, 1976.

Reid-Jeffrey, Donna. "*Star Trek*: The Last Frontier in Modern American Myth." *Folklore and Mythology Studies* 6 (1982): 34–41.

Return of the Jedi: Official Collectors' Edition. Newton, CT: Paradise, 1983.

Roth, Lane. "Death and Rebirth in *Star Trek II: The Wrath of Khan*." *Extrapolation* 28:2 (1987): 159–66.

Sherman, Marilyn R. "*Star Wars*: New Worlds and Ancient Myths." *Kentucky FolkloreReview* 25 (1979): 6–10.

Spinrad, Norman. "Emperor of Everything." *Science Fiction in the Real World*. Carbondale and Edwardsville: Southern Illinois University Press, 1990.

Star Trek. J. J. Abrams, Dir. Paramount Pictures/Spyglass Entertainment, 2009.

Star Trek: First Contact. Jonathan Frakes, Dir. Rick Berman, 1996.

Star Trek V: The Final Frontier. William Shatner, Dir. Paramount, 1989.

Star Trek IV: The Voyage Home. Leonard Nimoy, Dir. Paramount, 1986.

Star Trek Generations. David Carson, Dir. Rick Berman, 1994.

Star Trek: Insurrection. Jonathan Frakes, Dir. Rick Berman Productions, 1998.

Star Trek: Nemesis. Stuart Baird, Dir. Rick Berman Productions, 2002.

Star Trek: The Motion Picture. Robert Wise, Dir. Paramount, 1979.

Star Trek VI: The Undiscovered Country. Nicholas Meyer, Dir. Paramount, 1991.

Star Trek III: The Search for Spock. Leonard Nimoy, Dir. Paramount, 1984.

Star Trek II: The Wrath of Khan. Nicholas Meyer, Dir. Paramount, 1982.

"*Star Wars*: The Year's Best Movie." *Time* (30 May 1977), 56.

Star Wars Episode V: The Empire Strikes Back. Irvin Kershner, Dir. 20th Century–Fox,1980.

Star Wars Episode IV: A New Hope. George Lucas, Dir. 20th Century–Fox, 1977.

Star Wars Episode I: The Phantom Menace. George Lucas, Dir. 20th Century–Fox,1999.

Star Wars Episode VI: Return of the Jedi. Richard Marquand, Dir. 20th Century–Fox, 1983.

The Terminator. James Cameron, Dir. Hemdale/Pacific Western, 1984.

Terminator II: Judgment Day. James Cameron, Dir. Pacific Western/Canal Plus/ Lightstorm, 1991.

Tiffin, Jessica. "Digitally Remythicised: *Star Wars*, Modern Popular Mythology, andMadame and Eve." *Journal of Literary Studies* 15:1–2 (1999): 66–88.

Time After Time. Nicholas Meyer, Dir. Warner Bros., 1979.

The Time Machine. George Pal, Dir. MGM, 1960. Based on H. G. Wells' novel.

Total Recall. Paul Verhoven, Dir. Carolco International, 1990.

Tron. Steven Lisberger, Dir. Walt Disney Pictures, 1982.

Tyrrell, William Blake. "*Star Trek* as Myth and Television as Mythmaker." *Journal of Popular Culture* 10:4 (1977): 712–13.

Wolfe, Gene. *The Citadel of the Autarch*. Volume Four of *The Book of the New Sun*. New York: Pocket, 1982.

_____. *The Claw of the Conciliator*. Volume Two of *The Book of the New Sun*. New York: Pocket, 1981.

_____. *The Shadow of the Torturer*. Volume One of *The Book of the New Sun*. New York: Pocket, 1980.

_____. *The Sword of the Lictor*. Volume Three of *The Book of the New Sun*. New York: Pocket, 1981.

Index